MARC SLONIM

From Chekhov to the Revolution

RUSSIAN LITERATURE
1900 -1917

The Galaxy Book edition
reproduces, with corrections,
the first ten chapters of
Modern Russian Literature

D1378056

New York   OXFORD UNIVERSITY PRESS

PRINTED IN THE UNITED STATES OF AMERICA

Contents

Foreword

THIS BOOK reproduces the first ten chapters of my *Modern Russian Literature: from Chekhov to the Present,* published in 1953 and presently out of print. Its aim is to offer a comprehensive picture of Russian literature from the end of the nineteenth century, when the era of Great Classics came to a close, through Chekhov, Gorky, Bunin, Kuprin, and Andreyev, down to the modernist movement in the arts and the symbolist school of our century which includes a score of remarkable poets headed by Blok. This whole period between 1890 and 1917 has been called the Silver Age, or the last bloom of Imperial Russia, and its achievements are both significant and exciting; their study, moreover, is indispensable for the proper understanding of Russian artistic and cultural evolution in the post-revolutionary years.

In this survey of novelists and poets, as in my other works, such as *The Epic of Russian Literature: from its Origins through Tolstoy* (Oxford University Press, New York, 1950), I have endeavored to combine the analysis of individual writers and the aesthetic currents they represent with the outline of their socio-political, psychological, and cultural background; I devoted more attention than is customary in American and English studies of Russian letters to poetry, to criticism, and to the philosophical, religious, and social debates that reflect the very essence of national spirit and intellectual life.

MARC SLONIM

Sarah Lawrence College
Bronxville, New York
Fall 1962

1

The Populist Movement

I   The cultural and social history of
Russia in the nineteenth century is divided into two main parts: the first,
rooted in the times of Peter the Great and his heirs, runs from the eighteenth century and the Napoleonic wars until the Crimean campaign of
1854–6; poetry and prose, arts and science had their early blossoming in
this pre-reform epoch of St. Petersburg autocracy and serfdom.

The emancipation of the Russian serfs in 1861 and the subsequent
reforms in the administrative, judicial, military, and educational branches
of the government marked the rise of a new world. Modern Russia began
in this era, and all the problems, drives, and aspirations that shaped its
course for decades to come stemmed from the great change the Empire
had undergone in the 'sixties. The tremendous impact of this transitional
period is analogous to that of the years immediately following the American
civil war.

During the reign of Alexander II (1855–81) new political and social,
artistic and intellectual patterns were established; the technical and economic expansion of the 'sixties and 'seventies opened the way for the
development of capitalism; and a new generation of builders and revolutionaries displayed their energy and enthusiasm in many different fields.

At every level of society there was a cultural quickening. The eagerness for learning and for action, the desire for self-improvement, the increased pace of Westernization, the new trends in science and literature —
all seemed to justify the most optimistic outlook.

The remnants of feudal slavocracy, however, were far from uprooted,
and the living standards of the masses were incredibly low; the peasants
were burdened by taxes and payments for their land-allotments — the
price of their emancipation — and were treated as third-class citizens;

3

caste distinctions were strictly maintained; the government remained autocratic, political freedom was still forbidden, and coercion, abuse of office, and authoritarianism characterized Russian administration. The dreams of educated society went unrealized when the Czar and his ministers refused to crown the reforms with a liberal constitution. In the mid-sixties it became obvious that the brave hopes of the intelligentsia were without foundation, and the frustrated and discontented intellectuals minced no words in their criticism of the regime. The government, impressed by the growth of the opposition, alternated concessions with repressive measures. Bureaucracy, red tape, police reprisals, and arrests of popular writers all served to exasperate the younger element, which became turbulent and aggressive. In 1866 Karakozov, a university student, attempted to shoot the Emperor and was duly executed. This attempt, so indicative of the rising revolutionary tide, also served to intensify the forces of reaction.

Between 1866 and 1872 socialist ideas made considerable headway, especially among university students and the Raznochintsi (intellectuals from the clergy, peasantry, and the middle class). All the leading critics and sociologists of the period — Herzen, Chernyshevsky, Pisarev, Lavrov, Bakunin — and a number of minor journalists espoused the cause of socialism; others were only friendly to socialist doctrine. After 1861 many Russian men and women went to foreign universities. In Paris and Geneva, in Heidelberg and Bonn, they met *émigrés* who had fled from Siberia or had simply gone abroad to escape the clutches of the Imperial Police. These associations led to the formation all over Europe of hundreds of intellectual circles where young Russians listened avidly to lectures on social conditions and discussed the future of their country. A number of them organized printing plants and smuggled books and tracts into Russia. Those returning home concealed quantities of subversive literature in false-bottomed trunks or other ingenious hiding places. Socialist propaganda soon assumed vast proportions and by the beginning of the 'seventies two prominent *émigrés,* Lavrov and Bakunin, were heading the most important factions of the new movement.

Peter Lavrov (1823–1900) was forty-five when, in 1868, under the pen name of Mirtov, he began to publish his *Historical Letters,* as a serial in a monthly magazine. The following year, when they were published in book form, the *Letters* were ordered suppressed, but the police could not find a single copy in bookstores: they all had been sold. The author, who was a colonel and a Professor of Philosophy at the Artillery School in St. Petersburg, was arrested and banished to Siberia. Shortly afterward he escaped and went to Paris, where he remained until his death.

Scientist and revolutionary, Lavrov published numerous books (including the bulky *Essay on History of Thought,* which contained the outline of his doctrine of anthropologism), and directed various radical publications. The success of his *Letters* was the sign of a new era. It marked the passing from Nihilism, with its emphasis on the natural sciences, to Populism, with its main interest in social problems.

According to Lavrov, all cultural progress was made possible by the millions who sweated and toiled, thus gaining for a privileged minority the opportunity for observation, study, and creativeness. His appeal, addressed to the youth of the educated classes, contended that they were indebted to the people for their artistic and intellectual pleasures. The happy few could cultivate the precious flowers of philosophy, literature, and the emotions of refined love because the unhappy majority was compelled to crush rocks, lay roads, dig tunnels, till the land, and mine coal. Their anonymous labor made possible the erection of magnificent temples of learning and beauty, yet access to these was denied to the poverty-stricken and ignorant masses. Whoever realized that this was the price of culture should pay his debt to the people by working for their education and emancipation. A new regime must be established that would put an end to oppression, exploitation, and social injustice, and make culture universal and available to all. Lavrov believed that the social revolution which would create such a regime would be brought about by the working masses, but he insisted on the necessity of first awakening their dormant conscience and acquainting them with their true interests. This was the task assigned to the intellectuals: 'go to the people' and spread the truth among peasants and workers.

In the early 'seventies Lavrov had scorned democratic reforms as of secondary importance: Why trim the twigs, asked his disciples, when the axe of revolution can fell the tree itself? It was not worth while expending time and energy in promulgating constitutionality and liberty in Russia when social revolution could take care of all such issues. Lavrov told his followers not to worry if there were but ten of them today: there would be a hundred tomorrow and a thousand within a month. Social revolution could be achieved through propaganda among the people, because the Russian peasant had 'unconscious socialistic leanings,' as manifested in the *mir* (or rural commune), the *artel* (artisans' co-operative), and in the independent spirit of the religious sects. Here Lavrov's Populism joined hands with Herzen's revolutionary messianism.

Rejecting fatalism or determinism, whether religious or scientific, Lavrov emphasized the creative role of the individual in history, and addressed himself to the moral sense of his contemporaries. Although later he came to share many ideas of economic socialism as formulated by Marx, he never accepted the Marxian interpretation of historical processes. The class struggle, economic conflicts, the clash of the opposing interests of the haves and the have-nots are evidently of great importance, Lavrov declares, but we must also take into consideration other factors of human life and psychology. The future regime is not merely a matter of economic necessity but also one of moral justification. Socialism must be based on ethical grounds and serve the cause of freedom, justice, fraternity, and 'the harmonious development of the individual.' It has to be reached through a revolution, since the ruling classes would never surrender their power without a struggle: this belief in the inevitability of the 'supreme battle' made Lavrov call himself a socialist-revolutionary, and he thus initiated one of the most important political movements in Russia.

The Lavrovists, aroused by their master's individualistic ethical ideas, set themselves the task of enlightening the people by means of mass education. These were the tactics so sharply criticized by the disciples of Bakunin.[1]

Michael Bakunin (1814–76), one of the founders of international anarchism, had taken part in the European revolution of 1848, and had been imprisoned and eventually extradited by the Austrian government. Brought back to Russia, he was chained to the wall of a cell in the Fortress of SS. Peter and Paul, but later gained some mitigation of this treatment by 'confessing' his errors in a long document, obviously intended for the Emperor Nicholas I. Finally deported to Siberia, he made an adventurous escape in 1861, crossed the Pacific and the Atlantic, and returned to Europe, where for fifteen years he agitated, fomented strikes, provoked uprisings, and participated in all sorts of conspiracies.

The rival and enemy of Marx, he established militant workers' groups and revolutionary societies throughout the Continent (particularly in Latin and Slav countries), and practically undermined the First Socialist International. Adored by his followers and hated by his opponents, this formidable man, who firmly believed in the imminence of world revolution and displayed irresistible energy in preparing for it, was the first Russian revolutionary to play a leading role in the European labor movement. Even more than Lavrov, he despised the petty game of politics and denied the importance of democratic institutions for the total emancipation of the working classes. He endorsed Proudhon's statement that universal suffrage is counter-revolution, and saw but two opposing forces: the State, which he identified with coercion, injustice, exploitation, and falsehood (in which he included State Religion as the greatest falsehood of all), and Revolution, which to him meant liberty, complete emancipation of the individual, and a socialistic organization of economy based on autonomous self-governing labor unions.

[1] See Marc Slonim, *The Epic of Russian Literature* (New York, 1950), ch. 6, 7.

Despite Herzen's warnings Bakunin clung to the formula he had announced in the 'forties: The lust for destruction is a creative lust; the old world has to be demolished before the building of any new order can begin. Bakunin therefore considered a waste of time any activity that was not strictly revolutionary, while democracy he regarded as an utter sham, as sheer nonsense. To encourage the revolutionary movement in Russia he recommended an immediate appeal to the insurrectionary impulse of the masses and a resort to direct action. 'Go to the people' was his slogan, too, yet he urged his followers not to trust the Lavrovist methods of slow, planned propaganda, but rather to adopt the tactics that would bring out the Russian peasants' inherent desire for rebellion.

The teachings of Lavrov and Bakunin went straight to the hearts of Russian intellectuals. In Western Europe, during the same period (the late 'sixties and early 'seventies), socialistic ideas held an appeal for only a small fraction of cultivated society, but in Russia they became the gospel to a large majority of the intellectuals. Among university students and, in general, among those under thirty, socialism grew to be a sort of unofficial religion. The slogan 'Go to the people' found an enthusiastic response: the people, their sufferings, their future, and their education constituted the focal problem of the period.

Among the upper classes the desire to help the underprivileged was combined not only with compassion but also with a sense of guilt which gnawed at the conscience of the repentant noblemen. Ashamed of their social status and their economic security, they yearned to atone for all their advantages of birth and education and strove to turn their backs on the class to which they belonged. As a matter of fact, most Russian social reformers, from Pestel to Leo Tolstoy, and most revolutionaries, from Bakunin to Lenin, were well born. For most of them, this disposition toward social atonement was coupled with the longing for a 'clean' life. The men and women of the 'seventies pursued sacrifice with an almost masochistic eagerness, and their political activity bore all the stigmata of a psychological complex. They created a myth. Many young radicals, whether followers of Lavrov or of Bakunin, idealized the *muzhik*, that lofty symbol of kindliness, wisdom, and patience; they were convinced that the people were ready to join in their socialistic strivings and to support their revolutionary dreams.

'Service for the people' had the sound of an incantation on the lips of a repentant nobleman; it had a more realistic ring when used by the Raznochintsi, with whom the nobly born idealists were constantly mingling. The differences in backgrounds and psychological motivations did not prevent the two groups from joining forces in what they considered the supreme expression of social consciousness: by 'going to the people' they hoped to bridge the gap between educated society and the working masses, and thus correct the fundamental evil of Russian history.

In this the Populists were striving to realize the dream of the Slavophiles. During the 'thirties and 'forties, however, the image of the people was somewhat theoretical, and it remained part of a vast utopian scheme engendered by the awakening of national consciousness. The Populists cherished utopian illusions about the people which led to tragic results, but as men of action they began to carry out their program. And their 'discovery' of the people, their meeting the *muzhik* face to face, became the most important event in the evolution of the Russian educated classes. For the first time the issue of the relation between the two elements of the nation — the educated elite and the large masses of toilers, the division of which had been sharpened by the reforms of Peter the Great and the subsequent St. Petersburg period of the monarchy — was raised not as an abstract problem but as a concrete proposition. This was the true historical significance of the Populist movement.

II The freedom and happiness of the people, for which the idealists were ready to devote their lives, were passionately discussed in clandestine circles. Thousands of young men and women in various parts of the country spontaneously arrived at the same decisions: they wanted to 'go to the people,' to share their existence of toil and deprivation; they wanted to bring to the peasant and to some extent to the worker the enlightenment of socialistic propaganda. Theoretical speculations soon led to practical conclusions, and thus began a movement which rapidly assumed the nature of a true crusade. The 'mania' overwhelmed even many who were mature and held important positions: magistrates, government officials, army officers, physicians, teachers.

The summer of 1873 marked the great trek led by a few scions of the aristocracy. Prince Peter Kropotkin (1842–1921), whose family claimed more right than the Romanovs to the throne of Russia, worked as a house painter in the suburbs of the northern capital; Sophie Perovskaya, daughter of the military governor of St. Petersburg, went to work at a cheese maker's; Catherine Breshkovskaya, who was later to earn the title of the Grandmother of the Russian Revolution, Lisogub the millionaire, whose tragic fate was described by Leo Tolstoy in *Divine and Human,* and thousands of others went to live with the peasants in their godforsaken villages. But the results of this collective sacrifice seemed meager enough. The efforts of the Populists were scattered, no contacts had been made between the spontaneous crusaders, and the people remained cool and in many instances actually hostile to their preaching.

The Czarist police adopted all sorts of repressive measures against the Populists. By 1875 the futility of this first wave became obvious; since the failure was attributed mainly to administrative reprisals and lack of organization, the Populists decided to unite their forces and to establish a rudimentary political party. Its name, Land and Freedom, was also their favorite slogan. The aim of the various groups that formed the party remained the same: 'Social revolution prepared by propaganda' — but its members, now numbering several thousand active militants, their ranks swelled by numerous sympathizers, had already begun discussing the problems of political democracy as a necessary prerequisite for the success of socialism in Russia.

The new party was decidedly more revolutionary than the pioneering Populists. The Land and Freedom party established not only secret printing plants and various executive agencies, but also special detachments whose specific task it was to organize escapes of political prisoners from Siberia and elsewhere, or to carry out dangerous missions, such as those of 'defense' and counter-espionage. A central committee directed the activity of all these sections, and also organized mass demonstrations in the streets of the capital to bring to the notice of the public the sufferings of the people. In 1875 the central committee gave the signal for a new crusade: Populists again made their way to the villages and to the factories.

Despite new methods and the moral support of public opinion, the second wave also fell short of expectations. Government countermeasures thwarted many excellent plans. During the six years of the Populist movement more than seventeen thousand persons were imprisoned or banished by the authorities, and the leaders of the Land and Freedom party felt the need to revise their tactics. Violent disputes were already endangering the unity of the organization. The Bakuninists urged still more vehemently a shift to direct action and some of them actually organized an uprising in the Ukraine. The newly formed circles of Marxists (*Capital* was published in Russia in 1872) recommended an intensification of propaganda among factory workers (the pioneer labor organizations, such as the Northern and the Southern Unions joined the party), while some Jacobins, such as Peter Tkachev (1844–85), claimed that autocracy, devoid of any real social foundations, was in an indefensible position and that a resolute group of revolutionaries could seize power and then promulgate reforms from above. In general, by 1876 the idealistic propagandists were being supplanted by more aggressive individuals, who were ready to use force in their fight against the authorities.

The government retaliated by ordering court-martial for all 'political criminals,' and by creating the notorious Okhrana, or Security Section, a secret police force with unlimited funds and wide powers. The Okhrana had virtual control over the country. All these measures, however, instead of frightening the Populists, merely embittered them and increased their terroristic tendencies.

As a matter of fact, the events of 1875–9 forced the Populists to admit that autocracy constituted their immediate and primary enemy, and that no social revolution was possible in Russia unless the Czarist regime were overthrown. Thus the struggle for political freedom, which Lavrov was inclined to disregard and which Bakunin rejected with contempt, was imposed upon the Populists by the logic of events. They now spoke of political revolution and democratic freedoms as constituting but one milestone on the road toward socialism.

It is most important to see that democracy as a political regime was accepted by the Populists not as an end but only as a means for attaining a still higher form of social equity. They were ready to fight for democracy in so far as it facilitated the achievement of their socialistic ideals. While in other countries the struggle for political democracy had been led and supported by the third estate, the bourgeoisie, in Russia it was the socialists who had been compelled, really against their will, to wage the political battle. Furthermore, when they finally became convinced of the necessity of taking on what was really the task of the bourgeoisie, they had to resort to force and revolutionary tactics.

In 1879 the clash between the Economist faction and the partisans of a struggle for political reforms came out into the open at the underground convention of Populist leaders. The meeting ended in a schism. The orthodox Populists formed the short-lived group known as the Black Division, with most of its members, such as G. Plekhanov, V. Zassulich, L. Deutsch, and others faithful to the dogma of 'pure' socialism, subsequently joining the Marxists. They contended that people's rights, political liberty, universal suffrage, and so forth, were of no immediate importance, and that the socialists who were fighting for democratic freedom were merely playing into the hand of the bourgeoisie, since the latter would profit from a democratic regime, largely at the expense of the working masses. Their opponents led by Andrei Zheliabov, Alexander Mikhailov, Nicholas Morozov, and others, formed the famous Party of the People's Will, which was destined to give its name to a whole era of Russian history. They affirmed that the leadership of the socialists in the political struggle in Russia was bound to have significant results. So long as socialists, backed by the working masses, directed the fight for freedom, the downfall of autocracy was inevitable, and this would immediately open the way for vast social reforms, chief among which must be a socialist land reform.

The main innovation, however, was in tactics. The Populists decided to initiate 'destructive and terroristic activities' which would suppress the most obnoxious among the ruling clique, defend the party against spies, and punish officials guilty of special violence and abuses. These activities were designed to awaken the revolutionary spirit in the people by undermining their faith in the Imperial power and by offering continued evidence that opposition to the government was possible.

However this phenomenon is interpreted — and some historians claim it reflects the very essence of the 'Russian mentality' — the Party of the People's Will (as well as other Russian revolutionary parties, including the Bolsheviks) was more akin to some sort of priestly order than to a political organization in the Western sense.

Russians brought to their political struggle a religiosity, an all-embracing spirit of total and self-annihilating devotion, an enthusiastic sharing of a doctrine, extremism in action, and often a Byzantine rigidity of thought and ritual unknown to Western tradition. The problem of terrorism represented for the Populists no mere question of political opportunity; it was, first and foremost, a moral issue that caused poignant psychological conflicts. Each terrorist had to pass through a painful crisis before making his final decision. Most of the members of the party felt that their right to kill was won by their readiness to die. To become a terrorist signified a moral and physical sacrifice: they had to overcome all doubts, to conquer fear and pity, to renounce family, love, security, to bend all their will and thought toward a single sinister end; they had to lead the life of hunted animals, persecuted by a powerful enemy and facing untold dangers. Their socialist fervor had a strong religious tinge, but the historians of this most heroic period of the Russian Revolution have failed to stress the fact that these idealistic devotees of terror also possessed a keen practical sense. As a matter of fact, despite their limited means and all the obstacles they had to overcome, they succeeded in forming a vast and complicated organization which included printing plants, workshops for the fabrication of explosives, special meeting places, codes, surveillance agencies, forged-passport bureaus, and so on. In August 1879, the executive committee pronounced sentence of death on Emperor Alexander II, and from that moment all its efforts were directed toward one goal: the 'liquidation' of the Czar.

Between 1879 and 1881 several attempts on his life took place: mines exploded under the wheels of Imperial trains, delayed-action bombs blasted the Imperial dining room in the Winter Palace. At the same time a number of government officials were shot or knifed. Despite the mobilization of all the forces of the state and gigantic police operations that resulted in thousands of arrests and deportations and several executions, the invisible committee continued its fanatical warfare against the regime.

Czar Alexander II, who felt like a hunted beast and who changed his bedroom every night, alternated between reprisals and the preparation of reforms. After the explosion in the Winter Palace he granted dictatorial powers to General Loris-Melikov, who worked out a project of constitutional changes but, at the same time, continued to suppress the socialists with an iron hand. On 1 March 1881, the Emperor, while riding through the streets of St. Petersburg, was killed by bombs thrown by the terrorists.

This supreme deed proved their undoing. Of the thirty-six initial members of the committee, five, including Andrei Zheliabov and Sophie Perovskaya, were hanged despite the appeals for mercy addressed to the new Czar by Leo Tolstoy and Vladimir Solovyov,[2] the philosopher; one was driven insane, twelve died in prison, while the rest (with the exception of three who had escaped abroad) were sentenced to hard labor in Siberia.

III   The assassination of the Emperor proved to be a Pyrrhic victory for the revolutionists. It did not fulfil their expectations: the masses remained unstirred, the regime remained uncompromising. The new sovereign, Alexander III, after briefly hesitating between Loris-Melikov, who was proposing a moderate attitude, and Pobyedonostzev, the leader of the die-hard conservatives, decided to follow the latter's advice and to extirpate the 'subversive elements' with fire and sword. Two months after the death of his father, Alexander III made it known that he would rule over Russia 'with faith in the strength and truth of autocracy.' An oppressive reaction set in throughout the country. The supporters of the regime rallied all their forces and launched a counteroffensive against the socialists and liberals. Their leader, Konstantin Pobyedonostzev (1827–1907), the head of the Holy Synod and therefore of the Church, concealed his cold cynicism and his lust for power under a mask of Christian humility. Erudite and highly intelligent, he held knowledge and intellectuality in contempt. Like Dostoevsky's Grand Inquisitor, for whom he probably served as a model, he was convinced that men are corrupt, rebellious, capable of all evil, and that culture and reason are of no avail. He preferred to back the 'forces of inertia,' and to preserve the status quo through repression and fear.

According to Pobyedonostzev, whose subtle mind had a Jesuitic twist enhanced by Byzantine formalism, the Russians were innately rebels and troublemakers; the peril of revolution was therefore real and great, un-

[2] See ch. 6.

less the combined authority of Church and State could rule both soul and body. To control education, Pobyedonostzev established a network of parochial schools in the villages, with the catechism as the basic study, while Count Dmitri Tolstoy, appointed Minister of Public Instruction because he was a known enemy of science, decided to fight subversive ideas in secondary schools by establishing a fixed curriculum with Latin and Greek predominating, and by severe censorship. His successor, Delianov, made himself notorious by ordering the *gymnasias,* in 1887, not to enroll the 'sons of coachmen, servants, laundresses, petty grocers, cooks' and so on; unless they were exceptionally gifted, the leader of the Russian educational system explained, 'they ought to remain where they belong.' In 1884 the universities were deprived of all academic freedom and scores of professors were dismissed, while special measures were taken to discourage higher education for women.

The internal policy of the government was openly inspired by the support of the landed gentry, who were granted financial assistance, while at the same time special rural police officers, recruited from the nobility and vested with broad administrative powers, were flogging the recalcitrant peasants.

In a monument put up in St. Petersburg the sculptor Prince Paolo Trubetzkoy represented Alexander III as a clumsy giant whose weight so overburdens his steed that it cannot move. After the October Revolution the Bolsheviks decided to preserve this monument as a symbol of the 'reign that had crushed the whole country. The atmosphere of the 'eighties was as stifling and oppressive as the air in the small, low-ceilinged rooms of the Imperial dwelling at Gatchina, where Alexander III and his family led the life of the typical petty bourgeois. Moral prostration and apathy pervaded educated society; Russia seemed to have resigned itself to the rule of a narrow-minded bureaucracy, to conformism, to mediocrity.

At the same time the decade of 1880–90 was decisive in the economic development of the country. The peasants continued to fare badly. Of nine million peasant households, two and a half million did not possess so much as a horse. A great many of the poorer peasants were slaving as farm hands at very low wages, or struggling on their tiny holdings. The agrarian crisis was aggravated by the drop of prices on the world wheat market, and the low level of husbandry turned droughts or poor crops into catastrophes for vast regions. In 1891–2 a famine spread over an area with thirty-five million inhabitants. Hundreds of thousands of peasants perished from starvation and epidemics of typhus and cholera. The hardships in the villages compelled the have-nots to flee to towns, and the industrial labor of the period was drafted almost entirely from the poorest elements of the peasantry. On the other hand, the industrial output of Russia increased steadily, and by 1887 had reached the volume of one and a half billion gold rubles; the railroads underwent vast expansion, and the textile, steel, and coal industries made enormous progress.

While these developments brought about revisions in socialistic and liberal doctrines, they were also not without influence upon the monarchist ideology. The die-hards listened to Prince Vladimir Meshchersky (1839–1914), editor of *The Citizen* and author of various political essays, whose 'Speeches of a Conservative' and 'The Evidence against the Times' (1879) were as widely read in high society as were his novels, wherein he caricatured the revolutionaries (particularly in *Mysteries of Contemporary St. Petersburg, 1876–7*). Those who looked for a more original approach turned to Konstantin Leontiev (1831–91). A landowner who had given up a brilliant diplomatic career for monastic seclusion (after many tribulations he finished his life as Father Kliment in an Orthodox monastery), Leontiev wrote novels, stories, and essays, both political and literary (among the latter are penetrating articles on Tolstoy and Dostoevsky in which he displayed an uncommon artistic sense). Toward the end of the 'seventies he formulated his religious and political opinions in a two-volume collection, *The Orient, Russia, and Slavdom*. He had a consistent philosophy, a blend of aestheticism, religion, and science: 'Mysticism is only for the faithful,' he used to say; 'ethics and politics for men; biology only for the organic world; but physics and aesthetics apply to all men and all things.' His contemporaries underestimated him as a religious thinker, since they were chiefly impressed with his frank approval of reaction and his 'voluptuous cult of flogging.' Leontiev, who loved his ancestral estate as much as Leo Tolstoy did his, and who worshipped whatever reminded him of the 'good old times of serfdom,' sincerely hated anything that might threaten his way of life as a wealthy squire, whether that threat came from the 'disgusting Nihilists,' whom he wanted flogged, women as well as men, or from the 'contemptible bourgeoisie.'

Democracy and freedom he considered consequences of the 'general disintegration engendered by the French Revolution,' which had brought the Third Estate to the fore. Leontiev warned autocracy against the danger of making concessions to the middle class and the bourgeoisie. As for the common folk, he recommended 'fear, as a foundation of wisdom.' In his essay, 'The Principles of Byzantium and Slavdom' (1875), he contended that 'a firm monarchical power, strict to the verge of ferocity, and an authoritarian Church are the only elements capable of maintaining the cultural structure of a nation.' He recommended that Russian society be, as it were, congealed or crystallized, so as to preserve its idiosyncrasies. A great believer in Russia's mission in the Orient and among the

Slavs of the Balkans, Leontiev was inclined toward anti-Western isolationism: 'Instead of dancing,' he wrote, 'we ought to pray; but if we still want to dance, let us dance in our own way.'

Another leader of Slavophiles and nationalists in the 'eighties was Nicholas Danilevsky (1822–95), a historian and naturalist. Firmly opposed to Darwin's theory of evolution, he believed in immutable prototypes of species and also sought such prototypes in history. He discerned ten cultural types: Hindu, Iranian, Hebrew, Greek, Arabian, Latin-Germanic, and so on. Russia and Slavdom were one of the types, but he was dubious whether North America would be able to produce any. His analysis of the historical process included four areas of activity, in which the originality of each type was manifested: religion, culture proper (science, the arts, industry, crafts), politics, and socio-economics. While some peoples concentrated in but one field (Jews in religion, for example), Russia was destined to attain high objectives in all the four fields of human endeavor. The development of Russia and Slavdom as special historical categories presented, in Danilevsky's opinion, a superior degree of fulfilment and integration.

Danilevsky's practical conclusions were paradoxical and anti-liberal. He saw the essence of the Russian people in absolutism, and identified the originality of the Russian cultural type with the immutability of the Empire's political regime. Capitalism suited Europe but was alien and even hostile to the spirit of Russia and Slavdom. The dealings of Russia with the West had, therefore, to be based on cold calculation and opportunism: all international problems ought to be considered by the Russians solely in the light of their own national interests. In keeping with this point of view, Russia could gain nothing from supporting any balance of power in Europe; Russia's chief aim was the union of all the Slavs with Constantinople as their capital. 'The idea of Slavdom must be the supreme idea, above freedom, science, or enlightenment,' he wrote. Dostoevsky, and Solovyov after him, criticized this new brand of Pan-Slavism, which led to national smugness and cultural isolationism. Danilevsky's magnum opus, *Russia and Europe* (published in 1871, with second and third printings in 1888 and 1889), gained a wide audience after the death of its author; it was translated into German after the 1917 Revolution and exerted a strong influence on Oswald Spengler, who adopted many of Danilevsky's ideas on cultural types and the cyclic process of history. Danilevsky's Russian disciples — Konstantin Bestuzhev-Riumin and Nicholas Strakhov, a well-known literary critic — added little to the theories of their master.

The official tendency of the reign of Alexander III was blatantly nationalistic. The Czar loved to be called a 'fundamentally Russian and

Orthodox ruler.' The Russian Style, which was an ugly conglomerate of pseudo-folk art and ornamentation, was proclaimed the Style of the Empire. Militant nationalism was called upon to construct a barrier against subversive Western ideas. Michael Katkov, the watchdog of autocracy and editor of the *Moscow Gazette,* and the St. Petersburg daily, *The New Times,* waged vociferous propaganda for 'Russism' and adopted the slogan 'Russia for the Russians.' In practice this meant boasting of successes in international politics (since the 'eighties Russia had outdistanced England in Asia, had consolidated its positions in the Balkans despite the tension with Austria, had begun a rapprochement with France, and was gaining foreign markets), and a forced Russification of the various peoples and nationalities that formed the Empire. This policy was applied not only to the vast regions of Central Asia, where Kokand, Khiva, Bokhara, and Turkmenia became Russian provinces, but to all other parts of the country. The ban on publishing books in Ukrainian was reinforced. National languages were prohibited in Byelorussia and Lithuania, and ignorant administrators tried to stamp out the spirit of independence in Poland. Non-Orthodox Christians as well as Mohammedans were treated as aliens and conversion to Orthodoxy was imposed upon the native tribes of Siberia and Central Asia.

Jews particularly were affected by this policy of aggressive nationalism: anti-Semitism was part and parcel of the official program. Jews were not allowed to live or travel outside a restricted area — the Jewish Pale, which formed a sort of gigantic ghetto in the southwest of the Empire. They had no right to buy land or settle down as farmers; a *numerus clausus* restricted their enrollment in schools and universities; they were excluded from all state posts and the navy, and were accepted in the army only as conscripted privates. Their rights were curtailed in trade and the professions, and the government advised local authorities to take 'special protective measures against the pernicious activities of the Jews.'

In 1881–2, to create a diversion from revolutionary troubles and to offer an outlet to the discontent of the lower classes, the Czarist administration provoked pogroms against the Jews in Southern Russia. When General Gurko reported this to the Czar, Alexander III answered: 'Speaking frankly, I am pleased when the Yids get beaten.' The Jews became the scapegoats of the regime; 'Freemasons and Jews are fomenting all the trouble in the country,' proclaimed the chauvinist newspapers.

Official imperialism had borrowed part of its terminology from the Slavophiles, whose right wing was gradually incorporated into various monarchistic groups. After the death, in 1881, of Dostoevsky, the last original thinker of Slavophilism, the reactionary doctrine of the three sacred principles of Autocracy, Orthodoxy, and Nationalism was developed, under Alexander III, into a state ideology. It soon became vitiated by all the evils the great leaders of liberal Slavophilism had denounced with disgust: nationalistic vainglory, contempt of Europe, blatant boasting, political provincialism, and cultural isolationism. These are recurrent whenever Russia suffers from fits of nationalism.

After the war against the Turks in 1877–8, when the Empire acted as a champion of the Slavs and Russian soldiers displayed remarkable stamina and courage on the shores of the Danube and in the mountain passes of Shipka, the liberal Slavophiles, led by the venerable Ivan Aksakov, showed signs of a political Indian summer. They had been bitterly disappointed by the Congress of Berlin, at which Bismarck, Germany's Iron Chancellor, and the British diplomats had outwitted Russia, compelling her to grant substantial concessions in the Near East. This outcome of the war for the liberation of Balkan Slavs again threw the Slavophiles into the ranks of the opposition. Without ever becoming an organized body they were fairly influential among the educated nobility, which charged the government with enslaving the Church and treating the people brutally. Subsequently many of the Slavophiles served as links between the government and the mild opposition, and tried to unite the Bureaucratic Left with the Liberal Right. In 1905 most of them joined the party of the Octobrists; in the 'eighties, however, they remained relatively passive.

The Westernizers of the liberal stamp did not fare much better: the Liberal League, their clandestine organization, and the Union of the *Zemstvos*,[3] which had propagandized in favor of constitutional monarchy and whose spokesmen, Malchinsky and Dragomanov, had published their organ *The Free Word* abroad, were dissolved by 1884. Like everyone else, the moderate liberals were infected by the viruses of the times — apathy, indecision, and boredom — and this despite the fact that the rising upper bourgeoisie (merchants, bankers, industrialists) were eager to join with the educated nobility, the members of *zemstvos*, university professors, lawyers, physicians, and white-collar workers, all of whom made up the effective working forces of the Gradualists. *The Russian Gazette,* of Moscow, and the respectable monthly, *Messenger of Europe,* directed by Arseniev and Pypin, were the rallying points of the Westernizers, who condemned the violent methods of the socialists and, without engaging in a direct political struggle, hoped to mitigate autocratic abuse through a defense of legality. They also had faith in a pale and uneffectual propaganda of constitutional doctrines and in 'small deeds,' and loved to repeat the proverb, *gutta cavat lapidem* — 'the drop hollows out the stone.'

The radicals and socialists were, meanwhile, undergoing a great change. The majority of the intellectuals had been hard hit by the de-

[3] See Slonim, op. cit. p. 205.

feat of the Party of the People's Will. Like Chekhovian characters, they felt bored, disgusted, and morbidly isolated. Some of them responded to Tolstoy's preaching of moral regeneration, since they had lost faith in political action, and particularly in the transformation of the regime through violence; the philosophy of non-resistance to evil found many followers. On the other hand the doctrine of 'small deeds,' as opposed to extensive social activity, also appealed to people who had found disappointment in heroism and sacrifice, while a great many simply adopted an attitude of utter resignation.

Weariness, opportunism, and boredom also greatly affected the periphery of the radical circles. There was, however, a minority which was determined to carry on the revolutionary traditions of Populism. Despite arrests and executions, various attempts were made to revive the party and between 1882 and 1887 new conspiracies and certain terroristic acts gave proof of the underground activity of the intransigents. In 1887 a group led by Lukashevich, Chevyrev, and Alexander Ulianov began laying the groundwork for the assassination of Alexander III, but all were arrested and executed. In signing the death sentence of Alexander Ulianov the Czar could hardly have foreseen that Vladimir, the terrorist's younger brother, then aged seventeen, was destined to become the leader of Communist Russia thirty years later, under the name of Nicholas Lenin.

Despite the defeat of the party, however, which definitely disappeared from the Russian scene by the end of the 'eighties, the Populist circles continued to exist and to spread their ideas. Paradoxical though it may seem, the period that saw the triumph of reaction and the quelling of revolutionary activities was also the time of an extensive diffusion of socialistic ideas. What was lost in intensity, force, and action was gained in scope. And while the ruling classes rejoiced at the apparent calm that finally descended upon the Empire, in thousands of clandestine circles the intellectuals, young and old, were discussing the problems of the revolution and participating in the controversies between the Marxists and the Populists.

IV   After the split in the Land and Freedom party, a young member of the Black Division group, George Plekhanov (1856–1918), a nobleman and a former officer in the army, went abroad to study the socialist movement in Switzerland, France, and Germany. In 1883 he founded the Emancipation of Labor party, the first Russian Marxist organization. His two books, *Socialism and the Political Struggle* (1883) and *Our Divergencies* (1885), in which he analyzed the reasons for the Populists' failure, evoked violent polemics in Russia and among Russian *émigrés*. These books, like most books by

Russian socialists, had as a matter of course been printed by the underground press, or had been smuggled in from abroad.

Plekhanov maintained that Russia was already following the path of Western capitalistic development, and rejected the Populist hopes of her non-capitalistic evolution. He also attacked the doctrine of the role of the individual in history, labeling it an idealistic illusion, and pointed to the principles of dialectical materialism according to which historical events are determined by forms of production and distribution and by the class struggle.

Political developments in Russia seemed to corroborate Plekhanov's point of view. Industrialization had brought into being a proletariat of peasant origin, which was constantly growing in numbers. The growth of the proletariat was accompanied by the strengthening of the bourgeoisie, which demanded the extension of its rights and often clashed with the landed gentry. Despite subsidies and special privileges, the land crisis seriously threatened the nobility. As a class the gentry was declining rapidly, although by the end of the nineteenth century approximately thirty thousand landowners possessed seventy million dessiatinas (a dessiatina is two and a third acres) while ten million peasant families had but seventy-five million. Land and agriculture still constituted the crucial problem of Russian life. It was also the pivotal point in the debates between the Populists and Marxists, groups of both of which had multiplied abroad and at home.

In 1885 *A Projected Program for a Russian Workmen's Socialist Democratic Party* was published by the *émigrés*. The Social Democrats rejected both the Slavophile and the Populist theories of a 'special way of development' for Russia's peasantry. Plekhanov criticized these 'dangerous delusions' with irony and vehemence: for him the *mir,* collectivistic psychology, and all that the Populists called 'socialistic tendencies' were just so many 'relics of a dated economic order' bound to collapse under the impact of advancing capitalism. Concentration of landed property in the hands of big holders and the exodus of poor peasants into the city would deal the last blow to the archaic way of life of the Russian masses. The majority of the peasantry would be 'boiled down in the cauldron of capitalism.' Thus, all hopes in the revolutionary role of the peasantry were sheer nonsense. The proletariat alone was a truly revolutionary class.

Plekhanov and his friends were convinced of the necessity for political struggle. 'The winning of democratic freedoms is the first step of the proletarian movement,' the Marxists affirmed in 1885, in apparent agreement with the stand of the Populists six years before. The Populists, however, had claimed that the political struggle would lead to a revolution strongly tinged with socialist reforms; the Marxists contended that the revolution in Russia would be a bourgeois one, 'with the help of the proletariat.' Thirty years later, after 1917, the tables were turned: the Bolsheviks, who were a faction of the Social Democratic party, were actually striving for a socialist revolution, while the Social Revolutionaries, the heirs of the Populists, contended that the revolution was political and bourgeois.

The Marxists tended to glorify the workingman, just as the Populists had idolized the peasant. At the First International Socialist Convention in Paris in 1889, Plekhanov surprised his audience by saying: 'The revolutionary movement in Russia can triumph only as a labor movement.'

The man who made this categorical statement was, however, far from being a utopian. His mind was clear and logical, and he fought relentlessly against 'vague Bakuninism,' 'socialism of the heart,' 'Populist falderals,' and 'revolutionary castles in the air.' This nobleman, who had abandoned a career in the army for that of a Marxist revolutionist, was a disciple of the French rationalists, and his materialism, like that of Marx and Engels, stemmed from Holbach, Helvetius, and Diderot. Thought, for him, was but a function of matter, and he saw in social life the expression of economic, material processes. He warned Russian intellectuals not to build their socialism on such notions as 'moral responsibility,' 'a debt to the people,' and 'Duty and Beauty'; he wanted them to comprehend the factors leading to an inevitable economic transformation of society. Their task was merely to help history in the accomplishment of what was already determined. It was imperative to make Russia open her doors to capitalism — and to accept all the consequences thereof.

Such formulas aroused the ire of intellectuals, the majority of whom were hostile to capitalism either on emotional and traditional grounds, as in the case of the aristocrats who were disgusted by the vulgarity of the newly rich and the ugliness of industrialization (Chekhov's *Cherry Orchard* pictures these unforgettably), or because of political considerations, as in the case of the liberals, Populists, and Slavophiles, who felt alarmed by the disintegration of the peasant way of life. They all labeled Marxism horrible and monstrous. The Populists were also worried by the irresistible progress, the boldness, and the scope of the Marxist movement. A small group of orthodox Populists took a firm stand against 'the capitalist plague,' still believing that salvation would come from the *mir* and the *artel;* most of the Populists, however, were forced to admit the validity of the scientific methods of the Marxists and of their criticism of Populist errors, and they felt the urgency of a revision of their own doctrines.

Between 1885 and 1895, under the onslaught of Marxism, Populism was supplanted by 'critical' Populism, as expounded by Nicholas Mikhailovsky (1842–1904). In the 'seventies and 'eighties, and even in the 'nineties, his position was similar to that of Chernyshevsky or Pisarev in the 'sixties. Sociologist, journalist, editor of influential monthlies, this socialist of noble birth had acquired considerable renown as a literary critic with his brilliant essays, such as 'The Right Hand of Count Tolstoy and His Left' (1873) and 'The Cruel Genius' (1872), dealing with Dostoevsky, and by his sociological studies, particularly *What Is Progress?* (1869), *Darwin's Theory and Social Science* (1870–73), *Struggle for Individuality* (1875–6), and *Heroes and the Mob* (1882), in which he displayed his talent as a witty polemicist.

Taking up Lavrov's anthropologism as a doctrine of 'socialist individualism based on moral values,' Mikhailovsky offered a system of ideas that reinforced the trend of non-Marxist socialism in Russia. The term 'system of ideas' is used advisedly. As in the 'forties, the Russians of the 'seventies and 'eighties were looking for an all-embracing doctrine, for some sort of secular religion, and they joined Populism or Marxism just as Christians of various denominations join their respective churches. Mikhailovsky, like Plekhanov, was a leader because he offered a faith, an amalgam of thought, emotion, and will-for-action; he was, not unlike Belinsky, a moral authority, and his articles taught men how to live as well as how to think. But he was neither a utopian nor a doctrinaire. A follower of Herzen, Chernyshevsky, and Lavrov, he blended various currents of Populism into a single stream. He fully recognized the merits of Marxism, particularly in economics, yet he refused to accept historical materialism and denied the possibility of explaining social and cultural evolution in terms of economic factors alone.

According to Mikhailovsky, moral, religious, psychological, national, and many other factors are as operative in human life as are the class struggle and economic forces. Man creates values of good and evil, of justice and injustice, which are ethical concepts; we judge everything and we set our goals in accordance with our ideals, which are also an expression of our moral consciousness. Individual and collective activity is inspired and guided by values we recognize as supreme. These values determine our interpretation of history (which interpretation is, therefore, subjective) and our attitude toward current conditions. In the course of human evolution there was a supreme value that had affirmed itself above all errors and passions: human individuality, the respect for and integral development of which could be defined as one of the highest aims of mankind. Social progress was the march toward such forms of collective life, by which the interests of the individual and the satisfaction of his needs were assured.

It is true that social progress does not always coincide with personal happiness. In modern society technical achievements and division of labor often act to the detriment of the individual, who is caught in the net of political and economic complexities. He is denied his human rights, he is a slave, a tag, a number, a cog in the machine.

This leads to what Mikhailovsky called the struggle for individuality. Man aspires to a regime in which the interests of the individual and those of society are harmoniously reconciled. Such a happy blending could exist only in a new social order based on co-operation and exclusion of economic competition. Socialism, which proclaims the solidarity of all who labor, is such a social order. Men are going to be emancipated by labor, since — and this was Mikhailovsky's famous 'formula' — 'the interests of labor coincide with the interests of the individual, and man manifests himself fully in creativeness and work.'

It is interesting to notice that this cult of labor, and particularly of manual labor, was typical of the repentant noblemen; Mikhailovsky's apotheosis of labor is similar to Tolstoy's; and since the 'twenties of our century, in Soviet literature, the same theme, although with different overtones, has been resumed.

Socialism, claimed Mikhailovsky, is emancipation by work and through work, since it liberates the people, the majority of individuals. Yet Mikhailovsky was careful enough not to lapse into a sentimental idealization of the people, or into any deification of the peasant. He pointed out that while the intellectuals are inspired by idealistic concepts, the masses are often deaf to ideas of justice, freedom, and beauty. The intellectuals, however, must adhere to these high values at any cost; they have the duty of defending the interests of the people, but that does not mean sharing the people's prejudices, backward opinions, and benighted attitudes.

One of the significant features of Mikhailovsky's doctrine was his identification of the objective scientific truth with justice and beauty. 'The truth of a theoretical heaven apart from the truth of the practical earth,' he wrote, 'was far from being satisfactory and always offended me. And on the other hand, the noble practice of life and the highest moral and social ideals seemed to me offensively helpless if they despised scientific truth.' He attempted to reach a synthesis of knowledge and morality; consequently his system was directly effective in determining the aims and behavior of his followers.

As a critical positivist, Mikhailovsky warned the Populists against any overestimation of the *mir* and the *artel* and he carried on polemics against the Old Guard of Populism — V. Vorontzov, P. Chervinsky, I. Kablitz-Yuzov, and others. He recognized that certain traditions of Russian peasantry contained positive elements that could be used in a future socialist transformation. Yet he was aware of all the changes capitalism and the increasing Western influence were bringing into Russian life. This did not prevent him from insisting on the peculiarities of Russian economy and history. While the Marxists spoke of the universal pattern of social evolution and claimed that the difference between Russia and Europe was due to the *gradation* of the same process, the disciples of 'Russian socialism' emphasized Mikhailovsky's discrimination of *types* of development, thus establishing a qualitative instead of a quantitative criterion of comparison. Mikhailovsky applied his distinction between the *type* and *degree* of development to many social and moral phenomena.

Without sharing the enthusiasm of early Populists and Slavophiles, Mikhailovsky believed that Russia would not copy Western standards, and that her revolution would be the result of an alliance between the peasants, the proletariat, and the intellectuals. Under a new guise, he brought Russian socialism to the fore again. This re-entry was fairly successful; Mikhailovsky's doctrine attracted many followers, and Marxism and Neo-Populism were the two main currents that divided the radical intelligentsia at the end of the 'eighties and the beginning of the 'nineties.

2

USPENSKY, GARSHIN, AND SALTYKOV

I   POPULISM as an intellectual influence was to transcend political programs and inform virtually all the literary activity of the period. Its emphasis on 'reunion with the people,' its dream of the unity of the masses with the intelligentsia, was to dominate the 'seventies and 'eighties. As Alexander Ertel put it, one might not share the illusions and ideology of Populism, but one could hardly escape the Populist mood.

This is true even of Tolstoy and Dostoevsky, who were going against the current and opposing socialism and the revolutionary movement. The peasant Platon Karataev in *War and Peace* warmed the hearts of all Populists; so did Levin's discovery, in *Anna Karenina,* of supreme wisdom in the peasant mentality and way of life; and the infallible peasant justice described in *Power of Darkness,* with the stammering, illiterate Akim representing the *muzhik's* high moral sense. Tolstoy's Populism was religious, but even those who did not share his faith accepted both his contrast between the peasant's 'healthy morality' and the shallowness and hypocrisy of the upper classes, and his criticism of capitalist civilization. Dostoevsky's vision of the 'simple people' as bearers of orthodox sanctity (e.g. *The Idiot, Notes from the House of the Dead*) and his messianic faith in the salvation of the world through Russia were other examples of the Populist trend.

Minor writers followed the dominant tendency in a more direct and obvious manner. Some simply idealized the *muzhik* as a social type of high moral standing. This idealization went hand in hand with the anti-capitalist trend and was also combined with a biased interpretation of all the evils of peasant life: the latter were represented either as consequences of a backward environment (superstition, ignorance, poverty) or as superficial ills on the otherwise healthy body of the peasantry (rugged individualism as exemplified by the *kulaks* and the exodus of villagers to the big cities). Others, however, were gradually cured of such illusions, and their pictures of the peasants were strongly colored by 'objective realism'; in the 'eighties most of them felt the disillusionment and the despair of defeat. A close link could be established between them and the writers of the 'sixties such as Pomialovsky and Reshetnikov.[1]

The Populist movement in literature encompassed many and various writers: the moralistic and sentimental Nicholas Zlatovratsky (1845–1911), whose major work — *The Foundations* (1878–82) — depicted the clash between the village commune and the *kulaks;* the ironical tramp Alexander Levitov (1837–77), author of *Sketches of the Steppe* (1866) and forerunner of Chekhov and Gorky; the witty Vassily Sleptzov (1836–78), a tireless defender of emancipation of women and a humorous recorder of peasant vernacular; a member of the Land and Freedom party, Nicholas Karonin (pen name of Petropavlovsky, 1857–92), a rather bitter chronicler of the village life (*Parashkino Villagers,* 1881); Nicholas Naumov (1838–1901), whose short stories (*The Forgotten Country,* 1882) were devoted to Siberian farmers; Paul Zassodimsky (1843–1912), who wrote lachrymose stories about the poor people of town and country; Kazimir Baranzevich (1852–1927) and the more talented Michael Albov (1851–1911) followed in Zassodimsky's wake. A new note was sounded in *The Gardenins* (1889), a vast panorama of country life by Alexander Ertel (1855–1908), a critical Populist and a Tolstoyan; his remarkable sense of language gave him a supremacy over other minor writers of the period.

A group of Populists who remained faithful to the traditions of the 'sixties devoted their attention to educated society and portrayed their generation. Some of them, such as Andrei Ossipovich-Novodvorsky (1853–82), described the failure of the movement; others centered their works around the burning issues of their times: emancipation of women, the struggle against social prejudices, the clash between the young radicals and their conservative environment in family and society. The favorites with the intelligentsia were Alexander Sheller-Mikhailov (1838–1900), author of the highly popular novel *When a Forest Is Cut Down Splinters Fly* (1871); Gregory Machtet (1852–1901), a roving idealist and a short-story teller; Konstantin Staniukovich (1843–1903), author of *Sea Tales* (1885), a widely read collection of tales about the Russian navy; and Innokenty Fedorov-Omulevsky (1836–83), a Siberian poet and novelist whose *One Step After Another* (1870) was highly praised by the Socialists.

[1] See *The Epic of Russian Literature,* ch. 10.

The Populist and radical literature found its counterpart in the writings of Serghei Terpigorev-Atava (1841–95), whose stark, realistic *Impoverishment* (1882) depicted the decay of the landowner class, and in the melodramatic novels by Boleslav Markevich (1832–84), Vassily Avseyenko (1842–1913), and Konstantin Golovin-Orlovsky (1843–1913). By the end of the 'eighties, however, this kind of conservative and anti-Populist prose was distinctly on the decline, despite political conditions favorable to it. The only truly anti-radical and 'reactionary' writer of the period — Dostoevsky — was himself in many ways a religious Populist.

II   The winding paths of Populism led from the idealization of the people to the more sober study of their life and mentality. This was the course followed by Gleb Uspensky (1843–1902), the most important author of the movement. He was highly representative of the radical conflicts of the 'seventies and 'eighties.

An unhappy childhood had developed a morbid sensitivity in Uspensky, the son of a petty official. After attending the University of St. Petersburg he became a contributor to *The Contemporary,* an influential monthly. In 1866 he published a series of sketches under the title *Life in Rasteryaeva Street.* Written in the manner of 'physiological naturalism,' these dealt with artisans, petty clerks, the poor, and the disinherited.

Like all Populist writers, Uspensky focused his attention on the 'humiliated and the wronged,' on their poverty, drunkenness, and brutality. *Rasteryaeva Street* presents every aspect of the idiotic, the vulgar, and the monstrous. Partly autobiographical, the book shows an evident Gogolian influence, although its realism is almost one-dimensional. It depicts downtrodden men and women, exhausted by hard work, by worry and the struggle for a daily pittance, whose only consolation is the oblivion of drunkenness. They pawn their shabby belongings and commit all sorts of petty larceny for a glass of vodka. The provincial 'acquirer' and pawnbroker Porfyrich exploits the misery and ignorance of his fellows, and makes their existence even more dismal.

Uspensky's radical and Populist inclinations were developed by contact with the socialist *émigrés* he met during a trip to Europe in 1872, and by the close ties he formed with members of the Land and Freedom party and the Party of the People's Will. Later Mikhailovsky was also to exert a strong influence on Uspensky.

His sensitivity, his exposed nerves, made him extremely susceptible to 'the travail and diseases of the conscience,' as Mikhailovsky put it. His 'social conscience' tormented him, and he saw injustice, poverty, and administrative abuses as personal affronts. He traveled extensively, living in villages and small towns and gathering material for his literary work everywhere. His great popularity was due mainly to his sketches of peasant life. He presented facts on an almost ethnographic level, but always related them to the larger social and political issues.

As a Populist, Uspensky tended to celebrate the moral stamina of the peasant; yet as a realistic writer and a keen observer he never failed to give a true picture of village life. As a matter of fact, he concentrated largely on its seamy side: the sordid existence of poor farmers burdened by taxes and fettered by cruel and stupid administrators; the tragedies of evictions and debts and lawsuits; the epidemics, droughts, and famines; the ignorance and prejudices of the peasants themselves, who persecuted the progressive elements in their midst; and the grim practices of predatory *kulaks,* who were growing into a caste of petty despots and were introducing capitalism in the villages (these accounts were to win him Lenin's praise).

He carried his realistic approach so far as to revise the intellectual's attitude toward the peasants; he warned the idealists against what they would find in the country. He believed that although the peasant was potentially a higher *type* of individual, he still remained on a very low *level* of development — a distinction that often escaped the Populists.

A humorist with a good ear for speech differences among various social groups, Uspensky was essentially a writer of sketches, part fiction, part sociological essay, part newspaper article. In this genre he was indubitably a master. His writings, however with some rare exceptions, resemble an enormous scrapbook in which a highly gifted artist has jotted down his observations and thoughts. Everything is tentative, incomplete, and rough, and the sketch, despite occasional passages of brilliant insight, never becomes a definitive artistic achievement.

That which bestows life upon them is the intensity with which the author responds to the suffering of men.

Uspensky was particularly sensitive to the moral effects of the autocracy and of poverty. He saw two main groups in Russia: the terrorizers and the terrorized. The lower classes were constantly crushed by fear: 'keep your mouth shut,' 'lie low' — these were the usual admonitions. In his wanderings he had learned that most common people were morally crippled by insecurity and servility — and he violently resented this distortion of human souls. His most significant sketch, 'She Put Me Straight' (1885), deals with a half-starved village schoolmaster, Tiapushkin, who sleeps on a wooden bench in a dirty hut, with a torn sheepskin coat for a blanket, and who is persecuted by the police, scowled at by the uncouth *muzhiks,* threatened by his enemies and the officials. But no matter how grieved and heartsick Tiapushkin may be, he finds comfort in a wonderful recollection: he had once gone to France and had seen the Venus de Milo in the famous Square Hall of the Louvre. The statue had given him joy and faith. He can now endure fear and misery, for the goddess had 'put straight' his warped soul. She had made him realize 'the happiness of being a human being, the possibility of being beautiful, all the infinite perspectives of human improvement, of a glorious future.' Inhuman conditions and cruel men can certainly oppress, offend, and distort humanity, but as long as the Venus de Milo stands triumphantly on guard in the Louvre, the ideal of harmony and freedom still lives in men's minds, and the village schoolmaster Tiapushkin will not go down before the 'disgusting reality.'

Uspensky's faith that the future would put everything straight could not fortify him against the ugliness and dissonances of his day. His restlessness and the fervor with which he reacted to all the evils of his society took a morbid turn. In 1889 Uspensky showed undeniable signs of insanity, and three years later he was placed in a mental institution, where he remained until his death in 1902, having had but few lucid intervals.

Uspensky's dream of an 'infinitely bright future' for the Russian people, his belief in the 'tremendous beauty of the human being,' and his ardent search for harmony and justice endeared him to hundreds of thousands of Russian readers.

Very similar to Uspensky in sensitivity was another popular writer of the period, Vsevolod Garshin (1855–88). But while Uspensky, with his conception of literature as a public service and his 'factology,' was fundamentally a man of the 'sixties who had carried his realism and his faith over to the Populist era, Garshin reflected the mood of the 'eighties after the defeat of the Party of the People's Will. There were two other differences: Garshin was an intellectual who made no attempt to step outside his social group and to 'unite with the people'; his poetic temperament led him away from Uspensky's naturalism toward symbolic images and psychological analysis. Most of the Populists described life realistically and attempted to give a faithful picture of social actuality: Garshin analyzed the psyches of the intellectuals, with their burden of doubts and woe. Both men suffered, of course, from the same disease of guilt, of hypersensitivity, of what Chekhov, speaking of Garshin, called a case of a 'sore conscience.'

The son of a small Ukrainian landowner and army officer, Garshin studied at the University of St. Petersburg. Although he was an antimilitarist by conviction, he enlisted in the army as a private in order to take part in the 1877–8 war against the Turks, because he wanted to share the dangers and sufferings of the people. This gesture was typical of the Populist 'mood'; the young men and women acted according to the proposition: 'If the people suffer, so must I.' Although Garshin left a comparatively small body of work, his literary reputation was very quickly established during his lifetime. This afforded him little satisfaction, however, since his fits of despair and the recurrent attacks of a mental disorder kept him from systematic work. In 1888, during severe depression, he committed suicide by leaping down a stairwell.

'Four Days' (1877), his first and perhaps his greatest short story, is partly autobiographical, written after he was wounded in battle. His hero, one of whose legs has been shattered by a Turkish bullet, lies for four days on a battlefield, close to the putrefying body of a Turk killed by a Russian bullet. Details and descriptions have a nightmarish quality; 'Four Days' is a story of quiet horror.

Garshin was always concerned with the problem of evil. In one of his best tales, 'The Red Flower' (1883), an inmate of a lunatic asylum comes to believe that all the evil of the world is concentrated in three red poppies growing in the backyard of the institution. He picks them and hides them in his shirt, close to the heart. He feels that the slow poison of these horrible plants is slowly killing him, but he is ready to make the supreme sacrifice, to save mankind by renouncing his own life. Thus he dies thinking he has eradicated evil forever; the three wilted flowers are found on his corpse. Evil and suffering seared the heart of Garshin, and he perished like his own hero, finding the burden of evil unbearable.

Each of Garshin's stories deals with pain, bloodshed, and dread. The painter Riabinin, in 'Artists' (1870), wants to paint a steel worker whose task is to use the weight of his body to buck the rivets on the inside of a boiler as they are being driven in from the outside. Garshin, like his Riabinin, was obsessed by these victims of human cruelty and greed; he wanted to provoke a feeling of pity and horror in the reader. His pangs of conscience were not relieved by any hope of immediate amelioration. This 'Hamlet of the heart' craved love and harmony but, like Gleb Uspensky, he knew that his dreams would never come true during his lifetime.

In 'Attalea Princeps' (1884), one of Garshin's symbolic tales, an exotic palm is stunted and warped by the low glass of a hothouse. In a supreme effort the proud tree breaks through the glass and rears its head in triumph over the roof, only to discover a leaden sky, biting frost, and the squalor of a northern city. In this story, as in all his others, Garshin was revealing his personal tragedy, and his contemporaries felt he was mirroring their impotence and pain as well. They did not realize that this mad artist differed from his fellow writers. He called himself a realist, yet his writings veered further and further from the realistic school. Details of physical suffering and the intricacies of moral torment attracted him as they did Dostoevsky; the dramatic plots and romantic spirit of his longer stories such as 'Nadezhda Nikolaevna' (1895), the tale of a prostitute murdered by her diabolical lover, who also shoots his rival and kills himself, reveal Garshin's kinship with the author of *Crime and Punishment*. On the other hand, in his rhythmic prose, his symbolic, allegorical style, and his sense of the uncanny, he pioneered in a new direction. This ill-starred writer undoubtedly anticipated Chekhov and the Decadents.

Garshin was paralleled in poetry — although on a much lower artistic level — by Semion Nadson (1862–87), the beloved bard of a generation of frustrated idealists. His father, of Jewish descent, died insane, his mother was a sickly aristocrat; after a sad and solitary childhood, he studied at the military school in St. Petersburg, and subsequently served in the army as a commissioned officer, but his poor health (he had consumption) compelled him to resign. The premature death of a young woman whom he adored made his condition worse, and he spent the rest of his life a semi-invalid in sanitariums and health resorts in Russia and abroad.

When Nadson was sixteen, and the Party of the People's Will came to the fore, he imitated Nekrassov and sang of 'the battle against darkness,' of the sufferings of the people. Later he became the spokesman for a generation that was rotting in the atmosphere of defeat and stifling reaction, and yet vividly recalled the heroic deeds and the sacrifices of its elder brothers. Nadson, with his quivering sensitivity and forebodings of imminent death, was able to express the exact mood of his contemporaries. They felt they were slowly disintegrating in a period of corroding compromise and betrayal, and they were delighted by the whining and highly idealistic stanzas of the dying Nadson. His verses, enhanced by the legend of his unhappy life (not unlike that of Lorenzo Stecchetti in Italy or John Keats in England), were extremely popular — his collected poems were reprinted fourteen times in twelve years. He addressed himself to youth in its own naïve language of generalities: idealistic, melancholic, highly individualistic, although filled with generous altruistic flights. Though he was wordy, inflated, exclamatory, his lines were moving, and his readers seemed unaware of the triviality of his expressions and similes.

In the 'eighties such poems had a contemporary relevance and the immediacy of a living voice. Now that the voice is no longer audible and the times have changed, we do not respond to the pathetic intonations of this poet of weakness, sobs, and sickly dreams. His bad taste and cheap lyricism are hardly compensated for by his sincerity and longing for beauty. That Nadson for decades remained a favorite with young intellectuals is a phenomenon of social rather than literary significance.

It is noteworthy that the three most popular writers of the period — Uspensky, Garshin, and Nadson — all had a tragic fate: insanity, illness, premature death were their common lot. And in this they seemed to symbolize for their contemporaries the doom and melancholy of a whole generation.

III   The greatest writers of the 'seventies and 'eighties — Tolstoy, Dostoevsky, Goncharov, Turgenev, Leskov, Fet — did not identify themselves with the socialist intelligentsia. There were, however, two prominent men of letters — Nekrasov in poetry and Saltykov-Shchedrin in prose — who were acknowledged leaders of the left wing. Saltykov's position was unique: he belonged to the generation of the 'Natural School' and his were the methods and spirit of the critical realism that had characterized the literary climate of his youth. In this sense he continued a tradition; at the same time he originated and developed a special genre of social and political satire.

Saltykov's place in Russian literature is comparable to Swift's in the English. Although he drew upon all the currents of Russian satire, specifically upon Griboyedov and Gogol (the latter's influence is evident even in the sentence structure of his early works), he was much angrier and much more programmatic than his predecessors. 'Saltykov alone,' said Chekhov, 'knew how to express openly his contempt; two thirds of his readers disliked him, but all trusted and believed him.' Chekhov's comment suggests three salient characteristics of Saltykov: the accuracy of his realistic descriptions, his scrupulous fidelity to facts, and the Biblical wrath of his satire.

Mikhail Saltykov (1826–89), who wrote under the pen name of N. Shchedrin, and who is often referred to by the double name, Saltykov-Shchedrin, was born into a family of ancient nobility on an estate in the province of Tula. In his childhood he had ample opportunity to witness family despotism and the abuses of landowners. He was educated at Pushkin's alma mater, the Lyceum of Czarskoye Selo, and after graduation entered the civil service. His association with the Petrashevsky circle and his interest in the French utopian socialists, especially in Fourier, formed his political views. His first tales ('An Involved Affair' and 'Contradictions,' 1848), in which he wondered why some people drove in carriages while others must slog through the mire, provoked administrative reprisal: the young author was exiled to Viatka, in the extreme North, where he was compelled to live until 1856. By one of those inconsistencies then current among the administrative authorities, he was allowed to resume his civil-service activities. Saltykov described Viatka as 'a world of stinking vapors, swamps, gossip and greasy pies, card games, mounds of red tape, and papers.' He recorded his impressions in *Provincial Sketches* (1856–7) — a caustic exposé of administrative abuses and stupidity. No one since Gogol had assailed bureaucracy and the vices of the regime so effectively, and the progressives, including Chernyshevsky and Dobroliubov, hailed the new writer with enthusiasm.

The wide popularity of the books by N. Shchedrin, the writer, did not affect the career of Mikhail Saltykov, the official. He rose in the bureaucratic hierarchy and was appointed Deputy Governor of Riazan and Tver. He had achieved the rank of State Councillor by 1862, when he resigned to devote himself entirely to writing. After the arrest of Chernyshevsky he became one of the editors of *The Contemporary;* from 1868 he shared with Nekrasov the management of *Notes of the Fatherland,* in which he published most of his works. His role in rallying liberals and radicals around this influential monthly was very important. In 1884 this publication, to which he had sacrificed sixteen years of labor and anxiety, was suppressed by government order. Saltykov, whose pugnacious genius needed an outlet, was thus deprived of his most powerful weapon in the struggle against hypocrisy, ignorance, injustice, and perfidy. He spent the last five years of his life writing his astringent satires and autobiographical novels.

Saltykov's writings may be divided into three main groups, the first of which includes his masterpiece, *The Golovlev Family.* Saltykov worked eight years on this novel, which was published in 1880. It is a chronicle of the life and gradual decay of a noble family on their ancient estate. Goncharov, Aksakov, and Turgenev also described the disintegration of nests of the gentlefolk, but they did so with nostalgia, lyricism, and sympathy. Saltykov did it with contempt and disgust. An implacable foe of the regime that supported the nobility as a ruling caste, he saw in the manorial estate the source of all evil: 'all death, all poisons, all sores derive therefrom.' The decay of the Golovlevs is drawn with the most repellent details; it becomes the symbol of the disintegration of a class that is driven toward madness, baseness, and degeneracy.

Arina Petrovna, the domineering and rapacious head of the family, rules her husband, her sons, and her serfs with an iron hand — and is loathed by all of them. Bent on the accumulation of wealth, she sacrifices herself, torments her children, and ruins her husband's life — and all 'for the sake of the family.' When her predatory instincts are satisfied at last and she has accumulated a fortune by acquiring land and villages with many *souls* (i.e. serfs), it becomes apparent that the fruits of her labor are so many grapes of Sodom, and she finds herself living in a void; in the end her son Porfiry, through a series of well-planned frauds and schemes, divests her of land, serfs, and money, and the old matriarch dies a sad and lonely death.

The figure of Porfiry Golovlev belongs among the great creations of Russian fiction. His nickname of Yudushka (Little Judas) has become a symbolic colloquialism; as a type, he ranks with Pecksniff, Uriah Heep, and other arch-hypocrites of world literature. This Russian Tartuffe is ingratiating and suave to his mother, although he actually is a beast of prey and a vampire. Unctuous to his victims, he ruthlessly pursues his avaricious course. His devotions are never of the closet: he is forever invoking God, and never undertakes a swindle without uttering a prayer and making the sign of the cross.

But after his successes in fleecing his mother and his relatives and becoming sole master of a large fortune, there is very little for him to do. To fill the vacuum created by his idleness Porfiry gives free rein to his evil imagination, and plays all sorts of nasty tricks under the guise of morality and fear of the Lord. He wastes his time in futile account-ings, petty worries, senseless litigations. These give him an illusion of activity — just as his prayers and the repetition of quotations from the Bible or of the most trivial sayings give him a veneer of religion and re-spectability. This obsequious hypocrite is also a liar and a babbler. He talks continuously; he conceals all his moral degradation, all his evil doings, behind a screen of chatter. His end is, nevertheless, as tragic as that of any of his victims. Abandoned by all, sickened by his drunken-ness, surrounded by filth and heaps of dusty papers, he lives in his den like a savage; loquacity and sanctimoniousness are of no avail against his inevitable physical decay.

This horrifying family chronicle records nothing but frustration, fail-ure, and death. Few novels in Russian literature are as gloomy and un-relieved as this, in which even the descriptions of nature are keyed to the general atmosphere of doom and decay: clouds shrouding the earth, rains that turn everything into morasses, blizzards and frost that kill all life, the destroying blaze of summer with its 'darkness of heat.' The qual-ity of tenseness in the novel suggests Dostoevsky, who, by the way, also tried to create a type of hypocrite and parasite in Thomas Opiskin, the hero of *The Village of Stepanchikovo;* Opiskin, however, is benign and innocuous in comparison with Yudushka.

A realistic treatment of the family and private ownership of property, two of the institutions the autocratic regime sought to defend, *The Golovlev Family* showed the moral and physical decadence of the nobility as a class. This was accomplished through the psychological analysis of the main characters, a method that distinguished the novel from family chronicles written by other realists. Saltykov's use of realistic details is highly functional. The author chooses them deliberately, and they all serve a sharply defined purpose, fitting into a well-ordered design. Turgenev, who compared Saltykov to Juvenal and Swift, pointed out 'the grave tone of his frightening humor; his realism remains lucid and sober amidst the wildest display of fancy.'

These qualities, although with less psychological insight, are also present in his last book, *Old Times in Pochekhonie* (1887), a semi-autobiographical chronicle of pre-Reform Russia. It lacks the power and unity of *The Golovlev Family,* but contains masterful descriptions of customs and life on a typical country estate and striking portraits of the landed gentry and their peasants. Some of its episodes have a highly dramatic quality.

The second group of Saltykov's works includes his satires, for the most part drawn as caricatures in broad, dashing strokes. Their sarcasm often turns into harshness and loathing. Saltykov's scornful pages crackle with the bitterness of his civic indignation and contempt for stupidity. The imps and demons of iniquity and greed, of narrow-mindedness and conservatism, are alike impaled by the stabbing attacks of his humor. Among many works of this sort *The Story of a Town* (1870) is probably the most characteristic as well as the most popular. Following Gogol's example of attacking the present through the past, Saltykov represented the history of Russia as the history of the imaginary town of Glupov (Fooltown), the inhabitants of which accept their rulers with a kind of oriental fatalism.

The Glupovians, like the characters of Uspensky, are frightened for all time; they are destined to tremble forever—just as their administrators are destined to inspire life-long fear through floggings and mistreatment. The townsfolk are sluggish, submissive, and apathetic: their rulers are mad, willful, ignorant. One of the administrators of Glupov has an empty receptacle instead of a head but apparently nobody seems to mind this, since his regime is precisely like every other regime: 'The citizens are nabbed and jailed, beaten and flogged, framed and sold.'

Readers had no difficulty in recognizing in this extravagant gallery the individual features of the Czars and their favorites. Negodiaev (Good-for-nothing), who blasted the streets paved by his predecessor in order to use the material for building monuments, was a thinly disguised portrait of Paul I, while the lustful mystic Grustilov (Grieving), who flogged his subjects 'melancholically,' was a parody of Alexander I. A devastating caricature of General Arakcheyev, Alexander's favorite, was drawn by Saltykov in his famous Ugrium-Burcheyev, a governor who entered Glupov on a white horse, burned down the school, and abolished all learning. His dream was to make the straight line triumph everywhere — in men's minds as well as in streets. With the coming of his reign 'the course of history ceased.' Certain chapters of the book were so obviously aimed at famous historical events and were interspersed with such bold allusions and impertinent hints that the censors never dared to recognize the truth, lest they be accused of irreverent inferences about Emperors and Empresses. The fact is that the authorities preferred to play deaf and dumb, and *The Story of a Town,* published in 1870 as a serial in *Notes of the Fatherland,* was subsequently issued in book form and enjoyed a tremendous success. Of course, this parody on history (including the historians themselves, particularly the representatives of the official Slavophiles, such as Pogodin, whom Saltykov tore to shreds) was but a method by which Saltykov lashed out at his own times. He was right when he wrote: 'I have nothing to do with history; I deal only with the present.' When Saltykov recounted the adventures of Glupov's administrators, whose reforms consisted of planting bay trees and encouraging the cultivation of cucumbers, or when he told of the occasional revolts of the burghers against the leadership of the bandits, quacks, and swindlers, his allusions to contemporary life were perfectly clear.

The same holds true of his remarks on the national characteristics of Glupov's citizenry: its inhabitants, said Saltykov, had had a number of potentialities in ancient times before the name of the town was changed by Jupiter from Umnov (Braintown) to Glupov, but their sleep had lasted for too many centuries and now they could only 'bow and sweat.'

This political satire hit out not only at the rulers with their coarseness and despotism, but also at the Russians in general for their passivity and timidity. Saltykov called himself a party man; he meant that, unlike other writers, he had firm political convictions. He expressed the temper of the revolutionary democracy of his times. His onslaught was deliberately virulent, and in his attacks on autocracy he went much further than any of his literary predecessors, such as Gogol, had gone. *The Story of a Town* was not merely an exposé of certain isolated phenomena, of certain specific ills of the regime: it questioned the Russian state in its entire historical structure; it radically rejected everything that had grown out of Czarism. While his forerunners had in the main merely aroused laughter, Saltykov provoked disgust and a violent desire to fight against all the Ugrium-Burcheyevs of Russia. The great satirist himself said that his intention was to dig beyond gaiety and fun. Indeed, one might add, Saltykov should be read by all who wish to comprehend the forces of hatred and cruelty that brought about the terrific explosion of the Russian Revolution and Civil War. Turgenev, who had attended public readings of Saltykov's satirical pieces, tells us that the laughter of the audience sounded uncanny: the satirist's lash stung sharply and spared nobody. 'Saltykov was intelligent, honest, austere, and never failed to tell the truth, no matter how painful it might prove,' wrote Gorky. 'He is a gigantic writer; the range of his creative effort is astonishingly wide, his laughter does not resemble Gogol's — it is far more stunning, truthful, deep, and powerful. Without Shchedrin one cannot grasp Russian history of the second half of the last century.'

After the publication of *Provincial Sketches* (1856–7), the sarcastic exposé of provincial officialdom became one of Saltykov's principal concerns. Instead of concentrating his fire on the bureaucracy of St. Petersburg, as had been the custom in the literature of critical realism, he devoted his attention to local despots who administrated the remote regions of the immense empire. Just as Ostrovsky had studied and pictured the *samodurs,* the stupid, willful merchants,[2] Saltykov wrote the natural history of the *samodurs* among Czarist officials. His *Pompadours and Pompadouresses* (1863–73) is a series of character sketches of the stupid, crass administrators who formed a close caste, lived on bribes, legislated through whims, perverted the law, and carried on vulgar love affairs.

The Tashkentsians, a sequel, describes the greedy and empty-headed young men and women who regard government jobs as sinecures and opportunities for graft. 'We are ruled by morons, nincompoops, foul swindlers, and unscrupulous bribetakers — all of them venal, hypocritical, and vulgar' — this was the inevitable conclusion Saltykov's contemporaries drew from his works.

His later writings, *The Reign of Moderation and Order* (1874–7), *The Refuge of Monrepos* (1879–80), *Letters to an Aunt* (1881–2), and others, were conceived in the same spirit of political caricature. In all of them Saltykov also attacked the provincial gentry and the new bourgeoisie. He pictured the rising class of homespun capitalists in the ridiculous figures of the merchants Derunov and Razuvaev, and of the saloon-keeper Kolupaev, whose names have since become symbolic. Saltykov contended that all the new businessmen had inherited the lack of conscience and the greediness of Czarist bureaucrats; like their predecessors of noble birth, they were intent on robbing and exploiting the 'flocks of Russian sheep.' Saltykov had no illusions about the peasantry, but he shared the prevailing fear of capitalism. Closely associated with the Populist movement, he fully supported its struggle for 'freedom and human dignity.' His chief target was the narrow-mindedness of the middle class, and he was convinced that rapacious capitalism would seek support largely among the vulgar, ignorant, and predatory elements of the Rus-

[2] Slonim, op. cit. pp. 194–5.

sian population. Thus his progressive and radical views were combined with a strongly negative attitude toward the development of capitalism in his country — although at times he perceived its inevitability. In this he was simply following the general current: the anti-capitalist tendency of Russian literature (including its right wing) is well known.

In his satires Saltykov resorted to what he called an Aesopic language: his pages were filled with hints, allusions, neologisms, distortions of colloquialisms, Frenchified peasant expressions, and all sorts of verbal tricks, the purpose of which was to make the reader see between the lines and grasp the political meaning of complicated and disguised material. This original, cryptic, and extremely rich style apparently presents an almost insuperable barrier for translators; it may account for the fact that Saltykov, one of the world's greatest satirists, is scarcely known outside Russia.

This Aesopic language — the delight of his readers and the despair of his censors and translators — was used most extensively in the third group of his writings, the *Fairy Tales,* which contain some of his most successful political allegories. Saltykov began writing them in 1869, with 'How One Muzhik Fed Two Generals,' but for the most part they were published in the 'eighties, when the suppression of *Notes of the Fatherland* made the Aesopic language a necessity. Some of these 'naïve tales,' as the author described them, were banned by the police, but found a large circulation in manuscript copies. In one way or another all of them lashed out at autocracy and exposed the lack of freedom in Russia. The zealous official (in the tale of the same name), who stopped all food supplies, disregarded public health, and burned all science books and scattered the ashes, reminds us of Ugrium-Burcheyev; in the same tale Saltykov gives us a concentrated form of the philosophy of Russian despotism: 'The more obnoxious any official is, the more useful he appears to be to the Fatherland. He abolishes education — good; he burns down a town — very good; he terrifies the population — excellent!' In 'The Satrap-Bear,' the boorish governor orders the destruction of all printing plants — as a security measure. The Czar's attempts to patronize the arts in a country of servility and police terror are ridiculed in 'The Eagle as Maecenas'; drones living on the backs of the peasants are pilloried in 'The Savage Landowner'; others of the *Fairy Tales* ridicule the moderates and parlor-pinks. Saltykov scorned all these 'self-sacrificing rabbits' (to quote the title of one of the satires) who talk big but lie low when a policeman is close at hand. He compared the moderates who act 'delicately and slowly' within the bounds set by lawful authority to 'An Idealistic Flounder' who preaches Spiritual Uplift and hopes for the Amelioration of Things until he is almost swallowed by the reigning Pike.

Saltykov's vehement criticism of conditions derived from his passionate desire to transform life in Russia. This may explain his great popularity in the Soviet Union, where critics document their own eulogies with quotations from Lenin and Stalin, both of whom have expressed great admiration for the master satirist. Present-day Russian critics and readers see him as the representative of 'active realism,' which uses literature as a means of transforming social reality. Because Saltykov had set definite political and social goals for himself in his writings, his work is cited as an example of militant art, in which all the techniques are subordinated to a definite political aim. Whatever the reasons, his popularity is extraordinary: while only sixty-five thousand copies of his works were allowed to be printed between 1897 and 1916, five and a half million copies were published in the three decades after the Revolution — 1917–48.

There can be little doubt that Saltykov, who in the 'sixties had been strongly influenced by Chernyshevsky, regarded literature as having a social function. He was a political reformer who scorned the theory of art for art's sake, laughed at the poets who were busy with 'sentimental nonsense,' and was ever ready to maintain that ideological content was the very essence of a work of art.

Saltykov's temperament, his realism, and the excellent knowledge of Russia he had acquired through extensive travels and in his administrative practice saved him from the sentimentality and exaggerations so prevalent in the 'seventies. His fight for the interests of the people was a matter of justice and reason, not an emotional transport. He was aware — even more than Uspensky was — of the backwardness and ignorance of the masses, and his satire was often directed against the 'slavish' patience of his people. Why did the peasant humbly accept his poverty? Why did the average Russian let himself be oppressed and exploited? Why did the crowd laugh when huge-fisted policemen (Saltykov called them 'dentists') smashed the jaws of minor 'law violators'? His pity for the downtrodden was mingled with contempt for their passivity and lack of gumption. His satire was particularly scornful and stinging when it strove to awaken a sense of human dignity in the cowed Russians and to destroy the reflexes of serfdom. At the same time, he loved the 'common folk,' recognized their potentialities, and always supported the peasants against officialdom, the landowning gentry, and the petty bourgeoisie — the three castes he singled out for his most pitiless attacks.

The emotional source of his Populism was his elemental love for the people of his own great Russia, for their physical type, their mentality, their colorful talk and gay songs. He liked even their poverty-stricken villages and the melancholy landscape. 'His love of the Russian people and the Russian land had nothing to do with logical analysis,' wrote Mikhailovsky in his essay on Saltykov. 'It was spontaneous, since Saltykov was a true grass-roots Russian, and as such, was instinctively attracted by everything that had the flavor of Russia.' Few writers knew Russian customs, traditions, fairy tales, and proverbs as Saltykov did, and very few members of the intelligentsia had succeeded in remaining so close to the soil of the country. In this respect at least, Saltykov had much in common with the Writers of the Soil, although he vigorously opposed their conservatism and their Slavophilism.

It is the consensus that *The Golovlev Family* and *The Story of a Town* alone among Saltykov's works have endured. Many of his other works, although they provide an extraordinary record of Russian life between 1848 and 1888, are too topical to be of more than historical interest to the modern reader. The present writer believes, however, that *Old Times in Pochekhonie,* that penetrating study of serfdom, should also be ranked among Saltykov's best works. Some of his satires, and particularly his *Fairy Tales,* are as relevant today as they ever were, since they point out evils still to be found in Russian life. "Do you imagine,' Alexander Herzen wrote in the 'seventies, 'that you can now throw all of Shchedrin's tales overboard, together with *Oblomov,* and thus be rid of them? Fellow citizens, you are too smart for that.'

3

Novelists of the Soil and Patrician Poets

I   THE 'SMELL OF THE SOIL,' which the critics of the 'fifties had discovered in Pisemsky, was pervasive in the literature of the 'seventies. It was found in the works of the most diversified writers — in the novels of Leo Tolstoy, the titled landowner; in the sketches of Gleb Uspensky, the Populist bohemian; in the satires of Michael Saltykov, the revolutionary bureaucrat. The Slavophiles and, as we have seen, the Populists were promoting the writers of this school. In their opposition to the 'genteel' tradition of the Karamzin-Turgenev school they eschewed the word-paintings of the upper-class writers and proclaimed a national independence of style — which was, in effect, a somewhat anti-Western attitude. The Writers of the Soil were 100 per cent Russian in their portrayal of types and environment and, particularly, in their language, which was based largely on the vernacular of the peasants. Whatever their political opinions, most authors in this vein strove, to use the then current phrase, for a 'reunion with the people.' Even the anti-radicals and anti-Populists preached a 'resumption of the lost unity' between educated society and the masses.

In some instances this trend took the form of regionalism (always in the realistic tradition). This was the case with many minor writers, such as Paul Yakushkin (1820–72), the famous collector of peasant songs; the explorer, Sergei Maximov (1831–1901), with his *A Year in the North* and *Roaming Russia;* and the historical novelist Gregory Danilevsky (1829–90), whose first books, *Fugitives in Novorussia* (1862), *Fugitive's Return* (1863), and *The Ninth Wave* (1874), dealt for the most part with the south of Russia and are filled with ethnographic details. A much more important representative of the same school was

Pavel Melnikov (1819–93), who wrote under the name of Andrei Pechersky. Critics have compared the eight volumes of his epic novels, *In the Woods* (1875) and *On the Hills* (1881), with the best works of Goncharov and Pisemsky, but Melnikov never achieved the wide popularity of some of his contemporaries. Most of his rather long descriptions, which still delight the ethnographers, seem heavy and dated to the modern reader; nevertheless the historian Bestuzhev-Riumin was right in saying that in Melnikov's works 'the Russian spirit speaks in Russian about the Russian people,' just as Alexis Remizov was correct in considering this author one of the wellsprings of the 'national stream' in Russian letters.

Like Saltykov, with whom he has a great deal in common, Melnikov was an author-bureaucrat. A petty squire by birth, he was graduated from the provincial university of Kazan, on the Volga, and became active as a teacher and archaeologist. But history, archaeology, and ethnography, to which he devoted all his time, could not secure him even a modest income, and Melnikov abandoned scholarship for a post in the Ministry of the Interior. From 1847 almost until his death he worked for the government and traveled on official missions throughout the vast regions of the Volga and the Urals. As an authority on religious sects he took an active part in the campaigns against the Old Believers. In the 'fifties and 'sixties armed raids, imprisonment, floggings, and the destruction of their chapels were considered the best means of persuading and converting the 'heretics,' and Melnikov in his turn employed these inhuman measures, giving the liberals the right to call him a heartless reactionary and to reproach him for his ruthless practices.

But while Melnikov the bureaucrat persecuted the Old Believers and called their sectarian doctrines morally perverse and a deviation from the true religion, Pechersky the writer described them not only with objectivity but with sympathy and love. *In the Woods* and *On the Hills,* his two monumental novels, unrolled a sweeping panorama of the life and customs of the Old Believers, or Old Ritualists, who had fled from persecution to the forests of the Urals, where, guided by the elders of their cult, they founded communities, chapels, and monasteries, and tenaciously preserved their ancient way of life. Melnikov discovered that they were something more than mere fanatics who regarded Byzantine traditions and their copper-clasped liturgical 'ancient books' as infallible sources of wisdom — these puritanical searchers after truth were also the keepers of a mystical flame. Their chants and legends had an unexpected ring of virile poetry. In the large wood houses of the rich as well as in the huts of the poor, the manners and beliefs of seventeenth-century Muscovy were kept intact. Austere, long-bearded patriarchs and their heavy-breasted and wide-hipped women listened to spirituals about the invisible City of Kitezh, spread over the bottom of a lake, or about the glowing beauty of the miraculous Kingdom of Opon.

A double barrier of mountains and forests guarded the Old Believers against the intrusion of civilization. Not unlike the American Puritans and pioneers, they had to battle against inhospitable nature and were forced to lead a strenuous life of incessant struggle; this made them tough, physically and morally — they became ruthless and practical.

Melnikov held that many contradictory traits of national psychology had been preserved in all their primeval force in this realm of the Old Believers. Their isolation in time and space helped them to maintain prejudices along with profound faith, superstitions close to the virtues of primitive Christianity. The Almighty of the sectarians was a merciless Judge, who frowned at the smallest infraction of the established rules and condemned every pleasure and whim. The strict family life of patriarchal rule corresponded to his Law, and Melnikov told of the tragedies of the young whose bodies and souls were warped by the rigidity of the ancient canon. One of the main themes of Melnikov's novels is the struggle between this canon and the desires and yearnings running counter to it.

Melnikov's shorter novels, including his first tale, *The Krassilnikovs* (1852), and *Poyarkov* (1853), are also impressive. It is true that the slow pace of his somewhat old-fashioned realism, his method of objective narration, and the abundance of ethnographic details in his works suggest antique mezzotints. But the magnificent descriptions of nature, the sculptural types, and finally the full-bodied, flavorful language all belong to a great literary tradition. Melnikov was deeply attached to the language of medieval Russia and tried to recapture its expressiveness. Together with Vladimir Dahl (who wrote also under the name of The Cossack Lugansky) he spent days and nights studying chronicles, hagiologies, and old legal documents; pre-Petrine manuscripts constituted their favorite reading. Melnikov, like Leskov, was also interested in 'artificial language': shop clerks, coachmen, thieves, shepherds, artisans used different argots in various parts of Russia; they twisted bookish words, invented new expressions, changed foreign terms to conform with Russian linguistic patterns, or resuscitated archaic turns of speech. Among the Old Believers the language of the seventeenth century was pure and alive; it was a tongue filled with peppery expressions and words enriched by Church Slavonic quotations and colored by old oaths or lyrical flights, and Melnikov attempted to reproduce the originality of this speech. In this respect, some chapters of *In the Woods* must be rated with the best of Russian prose. It is not surprising that a succession of writers, from Leskov to Andrei Bely and Alexis Remizov, who have attempted to infuse the native spirit into the literary idiom of their times, hold Melnikov in high esteem and often quote from his works. Undoubtedly Melnikov influenced Gorky's style, and it is regrettable that this aspect of Gorky's work has not been sufficiently studied. In the unusual subject matter of his novels, and the objectivity of his ethnographic approach to an environment seldom dealt with by other realists, Melnikov is one of the pioneer regionalists in Russian literature.

In the 'eighties and 'nineties regionalism was also represented by Dmitri Mamin (1852–1912), whose father was a country priest in the Urals. He studied in a seminary in Perm, in the Urals, and later went to St. Petersburg, where he became a journalist under the name of Sibiriak (The Siberian); he is generally referred to as Mamin-Sibiriak. Less gifted than Melnikov, he composed his novels according to the formula of naturalism. They are inchoate and wordy, abounding in details, episodic figures, and subplots, and often heavy to the point of formlessness. Yet they possess a certain power, very much like that found in Zola and Dreiser. Mamin's works are hastily and badly written; their raw material does not rise to the artistic plane; yet his characters are drawn with a firm hand, and most of his rather complicated plots are vital and dynamic. Most of his novels picture the growth of capitalism in the Urals, where it assumed particularly wild and rapacious forms. Mamin sympathized with the Populists, and he dealt at length with the exploitation of peasants by greedy speculators, or of workers by predatory lawyers and unscrupulous engineers. Capitalism had spread far and wide in the Urals and through Siberia, and consequently all the attempts of the idealists, such as the rich industrialist Privalov, who wanted to preserve the patriarchal honesty of the peasant community, were bound to fail. Mamin's best novels — *The Fighters* (1883), *Privalov's Millions* (1884), and *Bread* (1895) — show the moral decadence resulting from the power of money. In *Bread,* for instance, the grain merchants do not stop at forgery and murder in their accumulation of great fortunes. In *Traits from the Life of Pepko* (1894), Mamin attempted to prove that the same process of moral disintegration takes place in the middle class when it is contaminated by the capitalist mentality and ruled by the law of the survival of the fittest. *The Brothers Gordeyev* (1891), one of his best novels, is also an example of Russian naturalism, of the *tranche de vie* genre.

Despite his lack of craftsmanship and form, Mamin played a significant role in the development of regionalism; his were strictly Ural and Siberian novels, and he heralded the day when the supremacy of Central Russia in literature was to be shaken by poets and novelists dealing with other regions of their vast land.

II   The writer who called himself a disciple of Melnikov-Pechersky, but who was to prove much greater than
his master and was to found his own school, was Nicholas Leskov
(1831–95), contradictory and controversial, and one of the last representatives of the great tradition in Russian literature.

His literary career was unusual. In the 'sixties his name was taboo
among the progressive intelligentsia, who hated him as the author of
No Way Out (1864), an attack against the Nihilists, and of *At Daggers
Drawn* (1871), a long novel in the style of pulp serials, in which the
revolutionists were portrayed as melodramatic bandits, while aristocratic intellectuals were dubbed 'liberal drums' or 'bearded and bespectacled babblers.' Pisarev called for his excommunication, and after a
series of vicious attacks against this 'agent of reaction,' the critics con-
sistently ignored him. For many years Leskov felt he was being persecuted, and he encountered many difficulties in following his vocation.
There was no objective evaluation of his work during his lifetime. Only at
the turn of the century was he ranked close to Pisemsky, Ostrovsky, and
even Dostoevsky; since then his reputation and popularity have grown
steadily. Even before the Revolution he had found his place among Russian classics, and during the Soviet era various writers, from Zamiatin
to Gorky, have expressed their admiration for his work.

The Leskovs were a family of priests and merchants; the writer's
father was a petty official and his mother a noblewoman. He received only
a scanty education; unlike most of his contemporaries, he was shaped as
an author by his experiences rather than by books. As a civil servant
in Orel and Kiev, then as estate-manager and supervisor of a stud farm,
a salesman, and a businessman, he traveled throughout the country, meeting an amazing variety of people and accumulating an enormous body of
material.

In his thirties, at the insistence of friends who had been impressed by
the wit of his business letters, he began to write. After the appearance in
1863 of his first tale, 'The Sheepbull,' and, in 1864, of his first novel,
No Way Out, he wrote novels, chronicles, tales, memoirs, articles, and a
single play (*The Spendthrift*). The posthumous edition of his collected
works (1902–3) ran to 36 volumes.

Leskov was a man of various and strong interests, of turbulent passions and a physical exuberance that often conflicted with his religious
dispositions. He spent a great deal of time studying ancient popular art,
folklore, folksongs, and restorations of old paintings; he became a
specialist in old watches and English prints, in precious stones and the
literature of the Old Believers. The intensity of his artistic feeling and his

excellent knowledge of painting and architecture were blended with hedonistic and sensual elements. He found great joy in the motley incidents of life; he loved odd characters, bizarre customs, nonsensical comedy, unexpected situations, and surprise endings. This love for the colorful contributed to the anecdotal richness of his plots and the extraordinary vividness of his unique style. Yet he was deeply concerned with the sublimation of passions, and he repeatedly shows how the primeval instincts are purified by love, by sacrifice, and by the search for truth.

A central theme is found throughout most of his tales: that of the sinner who reaches righteousness through a purgatory of crime or lust. Very often Leskov underplays the initial sins, whereupon his hero becomes a Slavic Don Quixote. He was one of the few Russian writers who deliberately set out to portray positive types, and he always looked for a saintlike embodiment of goodness. Quite a few of his best short stories picture simple, naïve men who try to lead honest, truthful lives despite their abominable environment.

The hero of Leskov's greatest novel, *Cathedral Folk* (1872), is also a man of virtue. The priest Tuberosov, a man of probity and moral strength, fights a losing battle against the red tape of the Church. He despises religious bureaucrats; though his attempts to revive faith and Christian morality clash with the political and secular interests of his superiors, to his dying day he fanatically refuses to back down from his convictions, not unlike Avvakum, whom he resembles in many respects.

Except for a section caricaturing radicals (reminiscent of the author's earlier anti-Nihilism), which disrupts the unity, this chronicle of provincial life and the minor clergy is a remarkable work — vigorous, humorous, and pathetic. Its characters belong among the highest creations of Russian realistic fiction. Especially successful is the portrayal of the mighty deacon Achilla, a former Cossack, whose physical strength and fiery passions are devoted to the defense of religion. Another of Leskov's Upright Men, he is a symbol of the latent power of the Russian people and emerges as one of the most vivid characters in Russian literature. Some of the secondary characters of the novel — the dwarf Nicholas, Tuberosov's wife, and Father Benefactov — are also drawn with wonderful craftsmanship and humor.

A novel without an amorous intrigue, *Cathedral Folk* has a rewarding blend of human warmth and sharp wit; it is built on several levels and its implications go beyond the simple contours of plot and story. It deals, among other things, with the same problem of the Christian in modern society that haunted Dostoevsky in *The Idiot* and *The Brothers Karamazov*. Leskov's Tuberosov is one of the few 'positive' heroes in nineteenth-century Russian prose. He is a man not only of faith and integrity but also of superior intelligence and learning; his fight against formalism and rigidity and his craving for reform stem from his interpretation of the nature of truth and of Christian law. Simple souls such as his assistant or the deacon Achilla are instinctively drawn to him. Here, despite the tragic accents of the last chapters, lies the hopeful intent of the novel. Tuberosov's admirers sense his spiritual power; they respect the fearless defender of pure Christianity but at the same time they love him as a genuine representative of Russian character. Thus religious and patriotic emotions merge, and Leskov seems to agree with Dostoevsky's formula that a good Russian means a good Christian.

Ironically, the very works in which Leskov, inspired by Christian ideals, tells of ancient saints or modern honest priests made him suspect to the conservatives: they accused him of having exaggerated the miserable conditions of life among the lower clergy and of grotesquerie in dealing with the stuffiness and stupidity of high church dignitaries. Later, his anecdotes of life among the archbishops, although perfectly innocuous, also provoked the ire of clerical censors: Leskov was declared a 'secret Nihilist,' a 'subversive spirit,' an 'agent of the revolution,' and in the 'eighties was dismissed from a government job he had held for many years. He thus found himself repudiated by the Right as well as by the Left, and it was a long time before his works were judged independently of political moods.

Leskov's novels, with the exception of *Cathedral Folk*, are not so distinguished as his other writings, although they are often exciting. Some of them, such as *The Circumvented* (1865), belong among his early polemical works: they depict the disintegration of Nihilism and abound in melodramatic effects and journalistic allusions. Leskov never missed a chance to relate his plots to actual events; he made extensive use of the scandals of the day and of courtroom chronicles. (See 'A Winter Day,' 1894.) *The Islanders* (1867), in which he portrayed youth in a bohemian quarter of the capital, has many striking passages, and the style is very similar to Dostoevsky's. Another group of novels includes historical narratives, in which Leskov demonstrated a remarkable knowledge of the documents, manners, and language of remote periods. *Old Days in Plodomasovo,* the publication of which was begun as early as 1869, and *A Family in Decline* (1874) contain an extraordinary gallery of decaying aristocrats, peasants, and officials. They indicate Leskov's interest in the historical roots of national idiosyncrasies; he goes back to the source in an attempt to determine the foundations of Russian customs and Russian thought. His last work, *Hare Park*, which he left unfinished, was written in 1894 but was not published until 1917. It differs from his other novels, and despite its complicated plot it is rather like one of the long tales in which he manifested all his sparkling humor and literary crafts-manship.

Leskov is at his best in stories and novellas; in most of these he in-troduces a narrator, whose mannerisms and personality are revealed through his diction and linguistic peculiarities. The most important of these shorter works is *The Enchanted Wanderer* (1873). This master-piece belongs to a category rarely found in nineteenth-century Russian letters: it is picaresque. Ivan Fliagin, the wanderer of the story, is a former serf, driven by restlessness of body and soul to ramble all over Russia. He is imprisoned by the Tartars, escapes, becomes an actor, a traveling salesman, a horse dealer (or, as he calls himself, 'a judge of horseflesh'), a soldier, a gallant; finally, after many vicissitudes, he becomes a novice in a monastery. At the time he is telling his story, he is on a pilgrimage to Northern Russia. The pilgrim recounts his incredible life in an idiom that delights all lovers of Russian. In linguistic texture the novella is amazingly vivid and humorous, full of puns, jingles, folk expressions — yet at the same time its composition is compact and expressive. Despite his coarseness, his occasional cruelty and explosive passions, Fliagin loves nature, is kind to children and animals, whom he understands intuitively — and can lose his head over 'beauty, the perfection of nature.' In his case it is the gypsy girl Grusha, whose kiss was the touch of an aspergill dipped in venom, sending a 'searing pang through all the blood to the very heart.' Fliagin goes through suffering and crime for her sake.

Like the Bogatyrs in the epic songs of Russia, Fliagin is a giant, and his travels are the wanderings of all mythological heroes. He is also akin to the deacon Achilla. In a way *The Enchanted Wanderer* deals with the same problem raised by Dostoevsky in relation to Mitya Karamazov and Stavrogin: the problem of Russian extremism, of that elemental, wild force which is a manifestation of the physiological youthfulness of the nation, as well as of its rich moral potentialities. Fliagin symbolizes the Russian people, and the end of the short novel is most revealing: when Fliagin hears rumors of war he forgets that he has decided to become a monk and atone for his sins; he wants to enlist. 'I want, very much, to die for the people,' he tells his astonished listeners. The fundamental ideal-ism of this simple heart is, according to Leskov, the most important trait of Russian character; the search for an 'upright, virtuous way of life' has never ceased in Russia. It is noteworthy that Tolstoy's religious preach-ings greatly appealed to Leskov, and that in the 'eighties he was for some time under the influence of Tolstoyan morality.

The Enchanted Wanderer demonstrates all the major traits of Les-kov's literary manner: swift pace of narration, thrilling variety of epi-sodes, profusion of action and dramatic movement (another similarity to Dostoevsky), and a 'chain structure' of the story, presenting a succession of events with subplots and astonishing incidents. This 'drama-comedy of life,' as Leskov called it, is also a picture of Russia, with its descriptions of various regions: the steppe, the Volga, the Caucasus, Central Russia, the Lake of Ladoga. Fliagin's travels and his love of horses give Leskov an opportunity to introduce us to all sorts of people, from vagabonds, cattle rustlers, and gypsies to army officers and aristocrats, and to describe country fairs, horse markets, stables, barracks, country estates, and so on.

Ranking close to this masterpiece is another long tale, *The Sealed Angel* (1873). Marc Alexandrov, the narrator, an artisan and a lover of ancient religious art, recounts the misfortunes of a group of Old Believers who work at the construction of a bridge over the Dnieper, and whose icons are seized by the Imperial police. Ignorant officers put seals upon the holy images, and the Schismatics weep as they see the hot wax melting and covering the face of a beloved angel. Only a miracle performed by a saint succeeds in restoring the sacred object to the pious workers. In the end, which was probably inspired by Katkov, and which is the only unsatisfactory part of the tale, the Sectarians are converted and join the Orthodox Church. An interesting plot is enhanced by the vividness of visual and auditory details and by a profound knowledge of ancient religious art and Sectarian customs.

Leskov's sharp wit, his Gogolian bent for linguistic grotesquerie, his delight in twisting and playing on words, and his feeling for the intricacies of popular speech and its historical and social changes are at their best in 'The Tale of the Squint-Eyed Left-Handed Smith from Tula and the Steel Flea' (1881). The story is told by a jester at a fair to an audience of *muzhiks,* small shopkeepers, and soldiers, who roar at the puns and adaptations of highfalutin foreign words or technical terms. The story deals with an almost microscopic steel flea which the British present to Alexander I during his tour after the defeat of Napoleon, in order to impress the Czar with the skill and cunning of British craftsmen; the tiny flea actually dances after being wound up. Alexander's successor, Nicholas I, is convinced that no Russian can produce such fine work, but Platov, a rough, tough Cossack general, eager to defend national honor, finds an illiterate smith in Tula, a town long famed for its armorers and smiths, and the squint-eyed, left-handed fellow goes the British one better: he puts horseshoes on the steel flea's feet. The British invite him to London and try to lure him into staying there, but he finds the climate too foggy, the whiskey too weak, the puddings too slight, and the girls too thin. He returns home, goes on a Homeric toot, drinking against an Englishman on a bet, disembarks in the throes of delirium tremens, is beaten up and robbed by the police, and dies in a charity hospital. This masterpiece of humor does, however, strike one serious note, that of the latent talents in the Russian people: the heroic left-handed smith astonishes the foreigners in the same way as the *muzhik* Maroy in *The Sealed Angel* astonishes British and German engineers by showing them a new method of cutting steel, or as Sebastian, an artist, amazes everyone by painting a miniature icon in record time. It was to be expected that when the story was dramatized by Eugene Zamiatin, the play had a tremendous success in Moscow and throughout the Soviet Union in the 1920's and 'thirties.

First-hand experience and research contributed to the verbal virtuosity of Leskov's stories. 'This popular, pretentious, vulgar slang in which many of my pages are written,' he wrote, 'is not of my invention: I heard it from peasants, from the semi-educated, from wind bags, from half-wits and half-saints. For many years I collected words, expressions, sayings, picking them up in the streets, on river barges, in recruiting offices, in monasteries. For many years I studied attentively the pronunciation and manner of speech of Russians on various social levels.' Leskov was a specialist in 'popular etymology' (as a Russian philologist has called the habit of misspelling and mispronouncing words and names of foreign or scientific origin) and in macaronic language; he excelled even Ostrovsky in the faithful reproduction of the speech and manners of the middle class. His stories of the merchantry range from the grimmest tragedy to the broadest comedy. At one extreme we have the remarkable sketch, 'Lady Macbeth of the Mtsenk District' (1865), a tense story of passion, which Shostakovich used as the libretto for his opera and which also enjoyed a great success on the Soviet stage when it was dramatized in the 'thirties. Katharine, its fascinating heroine, murders her father-in-law, her elderly husband, and a young nephew who is to inherit the fortune of the trading Izmailov clan — committing all these crimes for the sake of her lover. The lovers, caught *in flagrante delicto,* are tried and sentenced to penal servitude in Siberia. Despite all Katharine has undergone for her lover, he humiliates and tricks her, finally forsaking her for a petite, white-skinned tart by the name of Sonetka. As the convicts are being ferried across the rain-swollen Volga, Katharine seizes Sonetka and plunges with her into the 'dark waves' — thus ending everything by a fourth murder and suicide. This melodramatic, Dostoyevskian story is extraordinarily compact and forceful.

At the other extreme we have the hilarious 'Night Owls' (1891), written for the most part in dialogue, and dealing with the 'miracles' performed by Ivan of Kronstadt, a highly revered priest, and the credulity of his flock of middle-class merchants. 'A Slight Error' (1883) deals, in an exceedingly droll way, with another miracle-worker, Ivan Koreisha, who is actually a madman, while 'Chertogon' (The Devil-Drive, 1879) tells of the spirituous and spiritual jag of a merchant prince.

Leskov's humor is down to earth and devoid of mystical undertones. He smiles at the jumble of life, and is thoroughly amused by imbroglios of every sort, by the hodgepodge of characters and situations. He was delighted by fuss and feathers. He confessed to an 'innate slyness' in his nature, and was often crafty, alternating cunning with kindliness. This attitude accounts for a certain duplicity in his humor. He was not a real satirist, since satire needs passion; Leskov's smile was condescending and he excused human frailties. Leskov preferred to the righteous indignation of a Saltykov, or to the bitterness of a Gogol, his role as a story-teller enchanted by the playful pattern of an anecdote, by the fireworks of a jest, and particularly by the clownish mirth of a funny word. 'I am merely a crossings-sweeper,' he once said, 'and I will stick to my broom.'

This collector of witticism, conundrums, and puns, whose language is as bright as a colored print or as modern chintz, is certainly one of Russia's finest humorists, and his influence on Chekhov, as we shall see later, is obvious. Soviet writers, especially Zoshchenko and Zamiatin, also owe a great deal to the author of *Cathedral Folk*.

The diversity of Leskov's interests as well as the special features of his style have provoked both admiration and objections. In Tolstoy's opinion Leskov had 'an excess of talent,' while Dostoevsky reproached Leskovian heroes for speaking in 'well-turned sentences.' Menshikov, a rightist critic, contended that Leskov's style was over-rich; Chekhov, on the other hand, enjoyed Leskov as a 'combination of a graceful Frenchman with an unfrocked priest.' The best description of Leskov, however, is given by Gorky, who had himself been greatly influenced by Leskov: 'He did not write about the *muzhik,* the Nihilist, the landowner — he wrote about the Russian. Each of his heroes is but a link in the chain of men, in the chain of generations. One feels that in each of his tales Leskov was mainly preoccupied with the destiny of the whole of Russia rather than with that of any individual . . . He is one of the foremost Russian writers — and his work took in all of Russia.'

III   Under great and minor poets, from Nekrassov to Polonsky and Pleshcheyev, civic poetry flourished in the 'seventies. Yet the Patricians and Aesthetes remained faithful to the tradition of Maikov and Alexis K. Tolstoy, and to what they called Pushkin's Cult of Beauty. In the 'eighties the Patricians, with their conventional lyrics in classic meters, gained in importance and influence.

A typical poet was Grand Duke Konstantin Romanov (1858–1915), who, under the initials K.R., published three collections of poems between 1886 and 1901, wrote *The King of the Jews,* a play in verse, and made good translations of English and German poets.

More expressive of the gloomy atmosphere of the 'eighties was Konstantin Sluchevsky (1837–1904), nobleman and civil servant. He started to write in the 'sixties but was upbraided by the radical critics for his 'lack of content' and remained silent for two decades. Between 1880 and 1890, however, he published four volumes of poems. Their mood was dull and pessimistic, and some reviewers compared their rhythms to the monotonous litany of an autumnal rain.

In the same way that radical youth idolized Nadson, the upper classes and the educated bourgeoisie admired Alexis Apukhtin (1841–93), a well-known poet of the non-political, Aesthetic group. A nobleman of old stock, a civil servant, and a society man, Apukhtin was a popular figure among high officials and pretty women. In the mid-eighties his poetry became still more popular and he acquired a nation-wide reputation. He wrote in simple meters, following in the wake of Alexis K. Tolstoy, and played on cheap musicality and trivial emotions. His drawing-room ballads were melancholy without lapsing into actual grief, humorous without going much beyond a polite chuckle, or dramatic — within the bounds of good taste. He sang of the delights and deceptions of love, of lost youth, of the little dramas of everyday life. A number of his songs in the gypsy style deal with the sad fate of the *demi-mondaine* and otherwise convey the atmosphere of the *café chantant.* Apukhtin was a schoolmate of Tchaikovsky and a friend of Mussorgsky: these great composers wrote music for his lyrics, and the songs remained favorites for many years in the repertoire of amateurs and at popular concerts.

Far above other minor poets was Konstantin Fofanov (1862–1911). He belonged to the group of Patrician poets not by birth (his father was a small shopkeeper) but through artistic conviction. An opponent of civic poetry and a firm defender of art for art's sake, Fofanov devoted his songs to descriptions of nature and to nuances of the emotions. Some of his lyrics have unusual musicality and, despite their extreme unevenness, reveal remarkable craftsmanship. The Decadents and Symbolists regarded him as one of their forerunners.

The truly great poet of the period, ranking with Lermontov, Nekrassov, and Tiutchev, was Athanassy Shenshin (1820–92), better known under the name of Fet. His contemporaries, with a few exceptions such as Turgenev and Tolstoy, were hardly fair to him. He lived in an era when poets were supposed to demonstrate civic concern and to deliver social messages. Fet's poems about nightingales, about forest scents or the magic of moonlight upon the face of one's beloved seemed so much rubbish to the zealots of Purposeful Poetry. He was made the target of devastating parodies, and his rare admirers were labeled nincompoops and intellectual snobs. Even later, when his reputation was established, the general public saw in him a poet of fleeting impressions, of idyllic landscapes and superficial eroticism. Nobody questioned the charming musical quality of his graceful verse, but he was considered somewhat shallow.

Only at the beginning of the twentieth century, after the re-evaluation of Russian poetry by the Decadents and Symbolists, was Fet conceded the place he deserves. The Symbolists were only too happy to inherit Fet's impressionism, his visions of nature, and the elusive quality of his verse, but they also pointed out the philosophical significance of his work. They claimed that the reason for his lack of popularity lay not in shallowness but actually in a metaphysical depth that the vulgar could not plumb. This judgment seemed paradoxical to a number of critics and readers — but then there were many paradoxes in Fet's poetry as well as in his life.

His mother, Charlotte Fet (or Foeth), married Shenshin, a Russian nobleman, in her native Germany, but the marriage, solemnized according to Lutheran rites, was not recognized by Russian law, and Athanassy had to bear his mother's name and to accept the status of a natural son. He struggled for a reversal of his case for many years, and did not acquire the right to be called Shenshin, with all the accompanying advantages, until the age of fifty-three. The two names corresponded to the different aspects of his personality. The poet Fet admired the plastic beauty of Hellenic art, adored nature, music, love, knew the inebriation of creativeness, translated Goethe and Hafiz; while the stingy landowner and slave driver Shenshin was so absorbed in the management of his vast household and in the accumulation of money that he could hardly find any time for writing. In his old age he was prouder of his title of Chamberlain (which Pushkin loathed so violently) than of his literary reputation. In everyday life this grasping, greedy, flint-hearted acquirer never demonstrated the idealism that pervaded his poems. Even his intimate friends gave up the attempt to solve the riddle: how was it possible for this materialistic, energetic man of property, whose wealth was mainly the fruit of his own endeavors, to detach himself from all earthly preoccupations and transmute the simplest feelings and scenes into the radiance of poetry?

Fet himself did not suffer from this ambivalence but found it perfectly natural. He always stressed the fundamental difference between reality and poetry. The latter represented for him an escape from the material world into the ideal: the two were on completely separate planes and could never meet or blend. Even in his youth he contended that all the charm of art lay in the illusion it created, in its 'sacred lie,' and wondered whether 'the crown should be awarded to the Goddess of Beauty or to her reflection in a mirror.' Later he arrived at the conclusion that this 'lie' of art was probably the supreme truth, since it revealed the very essence of the world. The poet in his moment of inspiration catches a glimpse of what is hidden from the crowd. In a poem written when he was over sixty (his best pieces were composed either in early youth or in old age), he compared the poetic revelation to the flight of a swallow whose wing barely skims the waters of a lake. Fet refused to remain merely 'an idle onlooker of nature.' Of course, most of his lyrics present unabashed pictures of forests, steppes, dawns and sunsets, formal gardens under the moonlight, the shy beginnings of spring, or the sensuous fullness of summer. But these impressionistic flashes always point at the unity and wholeness of the universe. In his pantheistic vision he caught the connection between 'the dark delirium of the soul and the vague scent of herbs.' Souls and plants were for him identical manifestations of Divine mystery and universal Beauty. Human life, he maintained, is but a dream, and only the artist 'discovers the trace of the Beautiful everywhere.' The 'living altar of the Universe' is beyond our perceptions; the earthly or unearthly rays we see are but the refractions of the Sun of the World — 'they are but a dream, a fleeting dream.' [1]

It was under the influence of German idealistic philosophy in the 1840's that Fet was formed as a poet. He translated into Russian the works of Schopenhauer, whom he greatly admired; he did not, however, share the pessimism of the author of *World as Will and Idea*. Fet's poetry is in a major key, the pantheistic wisdom of his inspiration is often colored by a strong hedonism, and he not only accepts but celebrates and enjoys the 'fleeting dream' of life. This intimate friend of Tolstoy and Turgenev lacked their horror of death and annihilation. In one of his most penetrating lyrics he said: 'It is not life I regret — what are life and death in their eternal rotation? — I regret the flame that once lit all the universe, and now is dissolving into night, and weeping even as it fades away.' Fet was strongly attracted by nature and life, and the overtones of his poetry are bright and joyful. The emotional overflow of his verse and its inner vitality are, however, expressed with a great delicacy of touch, in an almost ethereal form. A master of poetical virtuosity, Fet made a great contribution to Russian poetry: the variety of his rhythms, the translucent quality of his lines, and their melodiousness found many followers among them, Balmont, Blok, and Sologub.

In the Soviet era Fet, however, did not enjoy popularity: he was labeled a formalist, a 'mystical aesthete' who deliberately avoided correlating concrete reality with poetry. Even those of his poems that have

---

[1] These words open the first of the four volumes of Fet's best books of lyrics, published between 1883 and 1891, under the title *Evening Lights*.

been put to music (there are a number of them and their popularity has never waned) were accepted with a shrug by Soviet critics. The reactionary convictions and practices of Shenshin the landowner also handicapped Fet the poet. Yet many of his descriptions of nature, or such classic pieces as 'I come again with greetings new, to tell the sun is high in the sky,' are included in textbooks and are known by almost every educated Russian. He who does not love Fet does not love poetry, said Turgenev. Political considerations and changes of poetic fashion cannot alter the fact that Fet is one of Russia's great poets. Sensitive readers will always feel the charm of the ardent and subtle lines of the poet who saw the mystery of the world behind the 'gold lashes of the stars,' and who 'looked straight from time into eternity, perceiving the blaze of the Sun of the World.'

In historic perspective Fet represents not only the end of the great Pushkin tradition but also the beginning of a new trend. Although most of his poems were written in the lucid language bequeathed by Pushkin, he lacked Pushkin's preciseness and concreteness. Fet was as remote from Pushkin's realistic rationalism as he was from Nekrassov's social restlessness or Lermontov's moral quest: his was a poetry of nuances, of mystical allusions, and of musical sweetness expressed in enchanting, plastic forms; it signified that the great movement in Russian poetry that had begun in the 1820's had come to an apex and then had exhausted itself. A renovation of poetic methods and style was imminent, and Fet — although he belonged to the Golden Age — heralded it in his ambivalent work. The same phenomenon occurred in prose: in the 'eighties the great drive of Russian realism was completed; the movement begun in the time of Pushkin and Gogol had produced its highest achievements and had come to an end. The Classical period was about to close, and the approach of new times made itself evident in the tales of Chekhov. Decadents and Symbolists in poetry, and Chekhov in prose, were about to open a new chapter in Russian literary evolution.

4

CHEKHOV

I   IN 1880 a certain young medical student, who was to write under a dozen or so *noms de plume* before making famous his own name of Anton Chekhov, became a regular contributor to various comic periodicals issued in Moscow — *The Dragon Fly, The Alarm Clock, Splinters,* and so on. He turned out quips, topical comment, squibs, cartoon captions, nonsense, sketches — he had no qualms about punning and was not above even the mother-in-law joke. His sparkling wit and spontaneous humor enabled him to turn out a constant flow of copy, and this meant money badly needed for his family, which was as poor as it was large. Some of the pen names he resorted to were My Brother's Brother, Physician without a Practice, The Man without Spleen (originating in a printer's error), and his own favorite, Antosha Chekhonte, a nickname that had been bestowed upon him by one of his school teachers.

The son of a small grocer and grandson of a serf who had bought his family's freedom for seven hundred rubles a head, Anton Chekhov was born in 1860 in Taganrog, a minor port on the sea of Azov, in the south of Russia. His childhood was none too happy: he was brought up under strict paternal discipline, in an atmosphere of middle-class Orthodox piety and provincial tedium. The grocery business did not prosper and, after its bankruptcy in 1876, Chekhov's father decided to move to Moscow with his family. The sixteen-year-old Anton was left behind in Taganrog to finish his studies in the local gymnasium; he had to earn his living and tuition the hard way, by tutoring backward children and doing odd jobs for the town merchants. The depressing environment in his native town and the tawdriness of his own circumstances affected him greatly, but fortunately he was a lively youth of gay disposition, with a remarkable sense of humor and a lucid mind.

After finishing the gymnasium in Taganrog he joined his family in Moscow. Here the domestic atmosphere was far more cheerful; we have the testimony of Maria Chekhova that the household was fun-loving, and that Anton led her other brothers in playing practical jokes, writing jingles, and organizing amateur theatricals. These, apparently, assured the success of his literary debut: his first published production, 'A Letter to a Scholarly Neighbor' (1880), was a burlesque very much in the Gogol-Leskov vein, with a great deal of playing upon — and with — words. He was an excellent parodist: 'The Thousand and One Passions, or the Terrible Night' (1880) was inspired by *Notre Dame de Paris* and other works of Hugo, while 'An Unnecessary Victory' (1882) mimicked the then-popular Hungarian novelist, Maurus Jokai; he parodied Jules Verne in *The Flying Islands* (1883); in 'The Mysteries of the One Hundred and Forty-Four Catastrophies, or the Russian Rocambol' (written about 1884, first published in 1923) he burlesqued the endless French novel of adventure, and 'A Drama of the Hunt' (1884–5) was a take-off on the murder mystery story.

He disdained no targets, no matter how battered: lovelorn youngsters and sex-starved old maids, absent-minded professors and bragging hunters; he compiled comic almanacs, made up comic advertisements, composed answers to correspondents and wrote topical comments — the last necessarily not too vitriolic, since even the jester had to contend with censorship. It was dangerous, in the Russia of the 'eighties, to make fun of even such innocuous subjects as bald heads and beards, since Alexander III was both bald and bearded. And yet, however ephemeral this material, much of it is indicative of what the writer was to become and remains readable to this day.

His earnings as a humorist enabled Antosha Chekhonte to become Anton Chekhov, M.D. He received his diploma in 1884 and, in the same year, published (at his own expense) *The Fairy Tales of Melpomene,* his first collection of stories, many of which are gay and delightful.

In his search for material Chekhov frequented courtrooms, markets, race tracks, barrooms, and places of popular entertainment, constantly adding to his first-hand knowledge new insights into the character of bohemians, clerks, minor officials, priests, peasants, and workers. He attached little importance to his literary work and wondered in his letters how comic stories could bring fortune and fame to a certain American who was writing under the name of Mark Twain. His own sketches, however, were improving steadily, even though years later (1899) he refused to include most of them in his collected works.[1] 'Chekhonte,' he declared, 'wrote lots of stuff which Chekhov cannot acknowledge.' Today, when we reread the Chekhonte stories, we find in them all the elements that are so obvious in Chekhov's more mature work. The main themes show the characteristic concern with the triviality of life and the exposure of human pettiness.

Critics usually overlook the process of self-improvement Chekhov underwent during his university years. That process had been a long one and comprised a double growth: the formation of the writer and the intellectual, and the moral liberation of the individual. There are few examples in Russian literature of such a successful personality development. It was achieved at the cost of much effort and sacrifice, after an inner struggle and conflict with his environment. In a somewhat self-deprecatory letter to Alexis Suvorin, dated 7 January 1889, which gives the clue to the story of his life, he writes: 'What the Genteel Writers used to take from nature gratis, the Raznochintsi had to buy at the cost of their youth. Write a story, do, about a serf's son, a young man who once worked as a grocery clerk, who sang in a church choir and went through high school and university, who was brought up to respect rank, to kiss a priest's hands, to submit to the ideas of others, to give thanks for every piece of bread; who was often flogged; who as a tutor made the rounds of his pupils without galoshes, who used to fight, to torture animals, who loved to dine at the homes of rich relatives, was hypocritical to God and man without any necessity — simply from a feeling of his own insignificance — write how this young man is squeezing the slave out of his system, drop by drop, and how, on awakening one fine morning, he feels that the blood in his veins is no longer a slave's, but real, human blood.'

After receiving his medical degree Chekhov began his practice in Moscow, but he never became a professional physician. He was so strongly attracted by literature that he decided to devote all his time to his writing. But he loved medicine and used to say that it helped his art: in fact, his powers of observation, the accuracy of his 'clinical' analyses, and his way of listing the symptoms of human frailties all reveal him as a keen diagnostician.

In 1885 the writer Grigorovich, a veteran of the realistic renaissance, wrote to Chekhov begging him not to waste his talents but to turn to serious literary work. Much the same pressure was brought to bear upon him by his friend Alexis Suvorin, influential editor of the *New Times* daily. Chekhov disregarded Grigorovich's advice about writing novels,

---

[1] Out of 117 of the longer pieces he had written between 1880 and 1883 he selected only 20.

but he realized and admitted the 'light heartedness, carelessness, and lack of respect' he had for his own work. His second book, *Motley Stories* (1886), although entirely in the Chekhonte vein, plainly indicated the direction his development was to take: from the sketch he had gone on to the short story; two years later he had passed from the short story to the *povesti,* so beloved of Russian writers and so often used by them. This form, in which Chekhov excelled in his mature years, is not simply a long short story as we know it in Mérimée, Poe, or O. Henry; it differs in scope, since it presents not merely an episode but a continuity of events and extensive characterizations; probably it comes closest to the short-novel form — the novelette or *novella.*

In the Twilight (1887), the third collection of Chekhov's stories, wherein a few rather melancholy pieces were included with the purely comic material, won him the Pushkin Prize of the Academy of Sciences in 1888. The prize was only five hundred rubles, but it was the first step toward an expanding literary reputation. In 1889 there was an exceedingly successful production, at the Alexandrinsky Theater in St. Petersburg, of the revised version of *Ivanov,* the first performance of which (Moscow, 1887) had had an exceedingly tumultuous and mixed reception; the previous year was marked by the publication in the *Messenger of the North* monthly of 'The Steppe,' Chekhov's first long tale. Enthusiastic admirers, such as Garshin, called Chekhov a first-rate artist; they praised the lyricism of his descriptions of nature in 'The Steppe,' his subtle understanding of a child's psychology, as well as his water-color realism. Some critics, however, reproached him for his 'aloofness' and the lack of social significance in his work, unaware that Chekhov deliberately avoided all moralizing. In a letter dealing with 'The Horse Thieves,' one of his best stories, he jeers at those who wanted him to point out that stealing horses is wrong. His aim was simply to show men and customs as they were, without assuming the attitude of a judge; he had, moreover, a profound distrust for broad generalities and Pollyanna precepts.

At the same time he was passing through a period of restlessness and introspection. His one-act 'curtain raisers' — *The Bear, The Wedding, The Proposal* — and his short stories had won him general recognition; editors and publishers were paying him well and he could write without financial worries. He was traveling extensively, constantly adding to his wealth of knowledge about Russia. By the end of the 'eighties he had come under the influence of Tolstoy and was seeking some worth-while project. This led him to undertake in 1890 a voyage to Siberia and the Island of Sakhalin to study the life of the convicts and exiles. The journey was adventurous: the trans-Siberian railroad had not been built and

Chekhov had to travel thousands of miles by stage; he returned from Sakhalin by way of India, Indo-China, Suez, and Odessa. 'After having been in India and China,' he wrote to friends, 'I do not see any great difference between Russia and other European countries.' This remark was revealing: a typical Westernizer, he refused to accept the romantic illusions of the Slavophiles and Populists.

The Island of Sakhalin,[2] superb as a penological study, excellent as reportage, and merciless in its objectivity, was not the only result of this journey: 'In Exile,' 'Gussev,' and several others of his later stories were definitely inspired by his travels in Asia.

Chekhov had noticed his first symptoms of pulmonary tuberculosis toward the end of 1885; by the beginning of 1892 the progress of the disease obliged him to buy a farm close to the village of Melikhovo, not far from Moscow, and to settle there. Despite his worsening health, however, the period between 1889 and 1897 was, on the whole, a very productive one; it was then that he published his best *povesti,* such as 'The Duel,' 'A Dreary Story,' 'Anonymous Story,' 'Ward No. 6,' 'Peasants,' 'My Life (A Provincial's Story),' and 'The Black Monk,' as well as the plays *Uncle Vanya* and *The Sea Gull.* He had attained his spiritual heights and the apex of his fame; his simplicity and sincerity had won him many friends. Unassuming, gentle, modest, he had a unique charm; the regular features of his rather handsome face, his intelligent eyes in which sadness mingled with irony, his even, somewhat hollow voice, his sedate manners — all expressed genuine kindliness and a melancholy wisdom. Yet this seemingly acquiescent intellectual, the very incarnation of the good-hearted Superfluous Man, could be very firm when contending against anything he rejected or felt to be opposed to his basic principles of decency and human dignity. When, in 1902, the Academy of Sciences rescinded its election of Maxim Gorky as one of its fellows, only two out of the many Academicians had the courage to protest by resigning. One was Chekhov; the other was Korolenko. And that protest was not so much against the Academy as against the direct wishes of the Czar himself.

Chekhov's declining health compelled him to undertake several journeys abroad and (beginning in 1899) to make protracted stays in the Crimea, where he and Tolstoy became close friends. Chekhov also formed a friendship with Gorky; other writers, such as Bunin, Kuprin, and Mamin-Sibiriak, were frequent visitors. At the turn of the century his plays were staged by the Moscow Art Theater and were the hits of several seasons. In 1901 *The Three Sisters* was produced, and he married the star Olga Knipper, who created the role of Masha in the

[2] The first 19 chapters were serialized in the *Russian Thought* monthly in 1893–4; published in book form in 1895.

play. It was a strange marriage, since she continued her artistic career in Moscow, while Chekhov's tuberculosis confined him to the Crimea. His correspondence with her is a remarkable example of epistolary literature. Chekhov's letters are, in general, of exceeding interest, and not only from a biographical or psychological point of view: in literary value, they compete with some of his best writings.

In 1903 Chekhov finished *The Cherry Orchard,* his last play, and a new novelette, 'The Betrothed.' By 1904 his condition had become desperate and in May of that year he was sent to Badenweiler, a German health resort, where he died on 2 July. His body was brought to Moscow and buried in the cemetery of the New Convent of the Virgin, the resting place of many Russian writers.

At the time of his death Chekhov was one of the best-loved authors in Russia; that popularity, with only a slight decline between 1912 and 1922, has not ceased growing to this day, nor does it seem likely to do so. In the USSR it assumed overwhelming proportions. Soviet critics canonized Chekhov as a classic, as the last great figure of the Golden Era of Russian literature, and readers confirmed these judgments by an undeviating devotion to his works. Between 1918 and 1947 the total publication of his books passed the eighteen-million mark (in Russian and in translations into the various languages of the USSR). If statistics can be said to prove anything, they show that with the exception of Gorky, and such older classics as Pushkin and Tolstoy, Chekhov is the most widely read author in contemporary Russia. The excellent edition of his complete works and letters in 20 volumes (53,000 copies each), undertaken by the State Publishing House in 1944 and completed in 1950, is tangible proof of the love the Russians have for Chekhov.

Chekhov had no great hopes that his writings would have a lasting appeal. He maintained that they were merely a reflection of his times: 'They won't be calling us Chekhov, Tikhonov, Korolenko, Shcheglov, Bezhetsky, but "the 'eighties," or "the end of the century." ' For the most part time has sustained his judgment: scarcely any one today reads the novels of the brothers Tikhonov, Vassily and Alexis, or the short stories of Ivan Shcheglov (the pen name of I. Leontiev), or the sketches of Bezhetsky — all minor and rather mediocre writers of the period. Korolenko, however, is still remembered, while Chekhov is more alive today than ever.

What Chekhov meant was that the range and the subject matter of his stories and plays were strictly limited by the conditions of his era; he considered himself a chronicler of the 'eighties and 'nineties. Many critics during his lifetime believed him, and fell into a trap. A good many books in Russia as well as abroad labeled Chekhov's works 'a mirror of Russian life toward the end of the nineteenth century.' There is no doubt that they do reflect the dullness and drabness of the reign of Alexander III. His characterizations of the clergy, of the middle class, of the peasantry, and, in particular, of the intelligentsia are indisputably realistic and could be of use to the historian. Chekhov, like his contemporaries, could not escape belonging to a defeated generation: hence the melancholy tone of his writings, the sluggishness of his heroes, the general impression of futility conveyed by most of his stories. But even though Chekhov's intellectuals, who pine and whine without ever doing anything, his bored and sloppy officials, his wistful and unhappy women, and his dour and ignorant bestial peasants all belong to Russian life in the 'eighties, this hardly explains his universal appeal. For his fame has spread not only through Russia but to many other countries, particularly England, Germany, Scandinavia, and the United States. He transcends the limitations of his period: like all great writers, Chekhov reveals the hidden springs of our actions and gives us an original interpretation of human behavior.

II   From the very beginning of Chekhov's literary activity certain *leit-motifs* appeared in his stories, and their persistence gives unity and consistency to his works.

Antosha Chekhonte laughed at fools and at the triviality of life; subsequently the pettiness and tedium of ordinary human existence provoked sadness rather than mirth in Anton Chekhov. And while the young humorist yielded to his gaiety, the mature writer evinced a melancholy tolerance of human frailties.

Chekhov's early humor is the spontaneous chuckle of a spectator who finds amusement in living marionettes and their posturings. His first stories may well be likened to mere candid-camera angle shots. They abound in farcical situations and nonsensical plots and quite often are no more than anecdotes, with their laughter directed at drunken coachmen, hapless vacationists, unfaithful wives, and complacent husbands. These sketches — usually no more than three or four pages long — deal with people from almost every walk of life; for the most part, however, the characters are the small fry of provincial towns. A young clerk who had been run over by a carriage forgets his injuries in the delight of seeing his name in print in a brief newspaper report of the accident ('Bliss'). The mayor of a small town walks about its streets with his fur coat wide open — and does not feel the bitter cold in his glowing pride at flaunting a decoration he had wrangled out of a transient Persian of some importance ('Lion-and-Sun'). Erast Ivanych Yagodov drops in at the wretched little barbershop of Makar Kuzmich Blestkin, one of his daughter's suitors, for a free haircut. When half the head has been cropped exceedingly close, the barber finds that he is definitely rejected as a son-in-law by the old man; heart-broken, Makar Kuzmich cannot go on and puts off cropping the other half of the head till the morrow. Next morning Makar, erstwhile suitor, now all barber, insists on being paid in advance for finishing the job; Erast Ivanych, who regards it as a sin to squander good money on haircuts, refuses — and dances at his daughter's wedding with his hair half-long, half-cropped ('In a Barbershop').

Some of the stories have a more obvious leaning toward the grotesque, Gogol's 'bitter laughter.' Cherviakov (meaning worm-like), a minor government clerk, sneezes while seeing a show and, to his horror, discovers that the bald-head in front of him, which he has bespattered, belongs to a general. He apologizes so profusely and so insistently that the general, wearied with forgiving him, at last tells him to go to the devil. Cherviakov crawls home, takes to his bed, and soon dies from sheer fright ('Death of a Government Clerk'). The young son of a minor official, on his father's instructions, plays the clown at a party given by his father's superior; at the whim of His Excellency, the father and son have to trot around the table and crow like roosters; they succeed in making His Excellency laugh, and the young aspirant is wild with joy: 'I'm surely slated for an assistant clerkship' ('The Victor's Triumph'). An ex-sergeant is so used to army ways that he keeps on bullying people and ordering them about even though he is long out of the regiment ('Sergeant Prishibeyev'). While a group of lawyers are waiting, before going out to dine together, for the presiding judge to finish writing a dissenting opinion, the court clerk begins talking of good things to eat and drink in such a way that listener after listener, unable to resist the temptation, rushes out to a restaurant; finally, the presiding judge, after spoiling several sheets, follows in their wake, leaving the clerk to worry about the unfinished opinion ('The Call of the Siren').

Chekhov is established as a great humorist by scores of stories out of the hundreds he himself chose for preservation, as well as by dozens of items from the copious material collected after his death. The funny names, the droll expressions, the comic phrases he invented have passed into Russian speech, even though they may have originated in a squib of less than a page. In the same way, many of his characters — even minor ones — have become common points of reference: the harassed banker Shipuchin, and that unforgettable 'defenseless' woman Merchutkina, in the one-act play *The Jubilee;* the hapless Epikhodov and his two-and-twenty misfortunes, and Yasha, the flunky — both from *The Cherry Orchard;* and so on. Although Chekhov may have been influenced by the popular writers Uspensky and Levitov, who reported dialogue with naturalistic accuracy, his own dialogue does not follow the vernacular; it is selective, functional, and possesses that *sec* quality which is so typical of Chekhov's style. He was a humorist throughout his life, and maintained, not without reason, that *The Cherry Orchard,* his last play, was a comedy. After 1886, however, melancholy accents became perceptible in his stories; his comic figures more and more often betray a touch of the pathetic. The humor is either modulated or relegated to the background, while the themes of futility and of the gloominess of life come to the fore. He still deals with average men and women surrounded by drabness and enmeshed in triviality, but they are no longer mere marionettes: they have changed into cranks, neurotics, or generally unhappy creatures. The tawdriness and narrowness of their daily lives assume tragic tones.

In his innumerable pictures of Russian provincial life Chekhov shows ordinary people doing ordinary things. They play cards, gossip, philander, drink vodka, and go to their offices without ever being able to overcome their ennui. The monotony of routine is a law of their existence: the same stupid parties, the same old jokes, the same compliments paid by the officers of the garrison to the pretty girls who will lose their prettiness after marriage, the same useless discussions about education and municipal affairs among the local intellectuals — the doctor, the druggist, the teacher, and the judge. All are sick to death of their own emptiness, of their words and gestures, but they resume them again and again with exasperating regularity.

These characters are non-romantic. They are all alike, and they will leave nothing behind them on earth except the crooked wooden crosses marking their graves in the provincial cemeteries. Hamlets, Fausts, Don Juans, or even Childe Harolds may lay claim to immortality, but Ivan Ivanovich Ivanov is a candidate for neither Heaven nor Hell. There is very little excitement about spending a rainy evening in a stuffy room playing whist, or bickering with one's wife, or wondering whether or not it is worth while to get up from one's chair for another drink of vodka. Long before Sherwood Anderson or Sinclair Lewis, Chekhov probed the dullness of middle-class life and described boredom as the most prevalent disease of modern times. He felt acutely the despair of spiritless work and stereotyped diversion, and he showed how the weight of habit transforms life into a series of conditioned reflexes, whether in love-making or in drinking or in conversation.

Chekhov's men and women are isolated individuals, and the mediocrity and wretchedness of their daily existence prevent them from participation in anything that would take them out of themselves. Nor are most of the people drawn by Chekhov aware of their own pettiness and insignificance. They are simply engulfed in the mire of triviality, buried under an accretion of unimportant things which hides all that might possibly be worth while.

Even their cruelty and vices stem from boredom and shallowness. Banality breeds evil. Pedestrian desires and narrow minds produce distorted existences. The police official Prachkin, who is a poor loser at cards, evens things up by thrashing his son for a window pane the boy had broken some time before ('Out of Sorts'). Laevsky, in 'The Duel,' behaves abominably to his mistress Nadezhda, simply because he is bored stiff. And in 'Anonymous Story,' Orlov, a St. Petersburg bureaucrat, is ready, together with all his friends, to deceive, to play any vile trick, merely to create diversion and to relieve the monotony of life. All the petty officials who are so disgustingly obsequious and servile to their superiors, all the high dignitaries who value a piece of stamped paper far above a human being, all the simple-minded merchants who fight ferociously over a penny, or all the bearded peasants who act as viciously as savages when it comes to a foot of land — all of them, as well as their counterparts among the intelligentsia, are victims of triviality and emptiness.

By the end of the 'eighties and the beginning of the 'nineties Chekhov is more and more concerned with the effects of this emptiness and this triviality — these 'enemies of mankind.' He finds that pettiness destroys human dignity, that mediocrity turns men into living caricatures. Such is the fate of Belikov, the hero of 'The Man in a Case,' one of Chekhov's finest stories. Belikov, a teacher of Greek, wears galoshes and carries an umbrella even in the finest weather; the collar of his coat is always turned up, a huge muffler swathes his neck, his ears are stopped up with cotton, and dark glasses protect his eyes. He is afraid of life, and seeks refuge in the monotony of a regulated existence. This automaton stuffed with Greek quotations lives in an emotional desert: nothing real concerns him, ethics are replaced for him by grammar, he is withered by the aridity of his own fear. Dr. Startzev, in 'Yonych,' was once an energetic, idealistic young physician, but has sunk lower and lower: he never notices how slackness, minor compromises, cards, alcohol, heavy food, laziness, and hundreds of insignificant trifles of everyday life have changed him into a mummified, irritable, miserly egotist.

III While some of Chekhov's people are vitiated and distorted by banality, others, although unable to struggle, are disgusted by their lot. The Moody Man is the victim of his environment. He suffers from its impact but is too weak or sluggish to revolt against it. The Moody Man is, as a matter of fact, the chief Chekhovian hero. The writer himself has said that his aim was to sum up all the characteristics of this variety of Superfluous Men, as he studied them in the 'eighties and 'nineties. Of course, this hero reflects the era of uninspiring 'small deeds'; his plight is that of a generation devoid of dreams or passions. The Moody Man differs, however, from his literary predecessors. Russian writers, who excelled in such portraiture, have left us a whole gallery of Superfluous Men, most of them of noble extraction, such as Pushkin's Eugene Oneghin, Turgenev's Rudin, and Goncharov's Oblomov. Still, none of them was as melancholy and dejected as were Chekhov's heroes. The Moody Men of the 'eighties have no energy and force, and are resigned to letting themselves be suffocated by the ennui of their environment; they degenerate into philistines or, at best, become eccentrics. Like Laevsky, the hero of 'The Duel,' they are sluggish and make a mess of everything. Weakness and moral laxity mark Laevsky's behavior. He has no capacity for work or love; papers from his office (he is a government employee) are brought to his bedroom and he signs them without ever glancing at their content; he is sick and tired of his mistress Nadezhda, who is betraying him, yet lacks the courage to get rid of her and lies to her endlessly. His adversary, the zoologist Van Koren, hates him and finally challenges him to a duel; yet despite all his Nietzschean readiness to 'weed out' superfluous individuals, Van Koren is also infected by the disease of Oblomovism: the scientific expedition he is forever talking about will never take place, and he is wasting his time in a sleepy little seaport without being of much use to himself or to anyone else.

The Moody Men belong to educated society, for the most part to the intelligentsia, and Chekhov is highly critical of them. As Trofimov puts it in *The Cherry Orchard:* 'The intellectuals seek nothing, do nothing, are unfit for work of any kind. They call themselves intellectuals, but they treat their servants as inferiors and the peasants as animals, learn little, read nothing seriously, do practically nothing.' And in the same monologue he also contends that the great majority of the intellectuals are ignorant: 'They read nothing, have little taste in art, and they talk, talk, talk while surrounded by dirt, vulgarity, and Asiatic backwardness.' Chekhov voiced similar opinions in his letters: 'I have no faith in our intelligentsia — it is hypocritical, false, hysterical, half-educated, lazy . . . Our soul is a great empty space . . . we have no politics, we do not believe in revolution, we have no God, we have no fear of ghosts . . . staleness and dullness is our lot.' It would be an error, however, to accept these criticisms as a comment on the national character: Chekhov, not unlike Saltykov, despite the difference in their temperaments and general outlook, was disgusted by the vile, servile, and sluggish spirit of his times. He disliked the Moody Man for his passivity and resignation.

Most of Chekhov's intellectuals are at a loss what to do, and therefore accept their status as inevitable. Silin, in 'Fear,' is so afraid of everything that he dares not lift a finger to help himself; though the girls in *The Three Sisters* are forever talking about going to Moscow, they stay right where they are, because they know perfectly well that the change will not bring about any real transformation in their lives.

This general passivity of Chekhov's characters makes them appear woeful failures. Yet he always doubted if the matter of failure or success was of any actual importance. 'One must be God to be able to tell successes from failures,' he wrote to Suvorin. 'To divide men into the successful and the unsuccessful is to look at human nature from a narrow, preconceived point of view. Are you a success? Am I? Is Napoleon? Is your servant Vassily? What is the criterion?' Some of his heroes are not failures in the accepted sense as long as they reach an enviable social standing, yet they all suffer from neurasthenia and deficiency of will power, and complain of tedium and loneliness. The trouble with them is not so much the lack of success as the lack of successful living. They are all, in one way or another, unhappy. Something is definitely wrong with them — and the fault lies in their temperaments or their environment.

Nicholas Stepanovich, the professor of medicine in 'A Dreary Story,' comes to the conclusion that he has never been really happy and that he knows nothing of life. He is a stranger in his own home, his wife and daughter are as remote as if they were miles away; the only person he really cares for, his ward Katya, ruins her life; yet when she begs him to help her, he merely hems and haws. The sense of futility and despair envelops his days like a shroud; his is a tragedy not of old age but of a life that lacks central values. Therefore the professor, who has apparently won success and fame, is nevertheless a failure, while the insane hero of 'The Black Monk' dies with a smile of happiness on his lips: his life had had a meaning, it had found fulfilment, even though only in dreams and hallucinations.

Life for Chekhov's characters is entangled in lies. Volodia, the adolescent in the story that bears his name, hears his mother boasting about their family — all barons and generals — and although her facts are correct, he shouts 'It's a lie!' because her way of speaking, the expression of her face, and all things about her are false — the whole world is a sham and a deception. Orlov, in 'Anonymous Story,' seduces a married woman by making her believe he adores her, and she even leaves her husband for him. Actually Orlov started the whole affair out of sheer boredom, and he tells her lie after lie and laughs at her behind her back. Other characters try to fool themselves by refusing to face reality: Ranevskaya in *The Cherry Orchard* talks of her numerous lovers in highly romantic terms, although they are really only after her money; the Princess, in the story of that name, is convinced that she is conferring a favor on the monks when she visits their monastery and that everybody adores her, yet people fall to cursing her as soon as her carriage disappears down the road.

Those who observe the rites of religion do so mechanically: Chekhov's characters make the sign of the cross, baptize their children, celebrate Easter, and are married and buried according to the ritual of the Orthodox Church, yet they have no faith and care nothing about Christianity. 'It is terrible to become nothing,' wrote Chekhov in one of his letters. 'They haul you off to the cemetery, and then come home, drink tea, and make hypocritical speeches. It is disgusting to think of.' Many things taken for granted are disgusting, and some people who see the truth cannot stand it — the student Vassiliev in 'The Fit,' who had a 'talent for human feelings,' became hysterical when he realized that the women in a brothel, sold and treated like chattels, are nevertheless real human beings.

In truth or falsehood, man always remains alone. Lack of understanding between men is the central fact of life. In that magnificent story, 'The Lady with a Dog,' Gurov, who calls women 'an inferior race' yet cannot be a day without them, falls genuinely in love while on a holiday. Upon his return to Moscow he feels the need of confessing to someone — but the only person he can find is a bureaucrat. As they are leaving their club one night, Gurov cannot help telling him: ' "If you only knew what a charming woman I met in Yalta!" The bureaucrat seated himself in the sleigh and started off, but suddenly turned and called back: "Dmitri Dmitrich!" — "What is it?" — "Do you know, you were right the other day: the sturgeon they served wasn't any too fresh!" '

Most of Chekhov's main characters, particularly in his plays, are really reciting monologues, since nobody listens to anybody, and the audience hears only voices crying in a wilderness. In 'The Enemies' the doctor who has lost his son and the landowner whose wife has run off are both unhappy, but each talks only about his own troubles, and each remains isolated in the cell of his own loneliness and misery. The bishop, in the story of that name, is desperately lonely; his only confidant is a septuagenarian monk; despite the bishop's pleasant nature he inspires fear — even his own mother feels awkward in his presence and recovers a sense of intimacy with him only when he falls seriously ill. The nine-year-old Vanka, apprenticed after a happy country boyhood to a shoemaker in town, writes a letter to his old grandfather, telling of his loneliness and the general abuse he suffers; then, filled with a child's hopes, he addresses his letter simply 'To grandfather, in the country,' and, sneaking out, drops it, without a stamp, in the nearest mailbox ('Vanka'). The thirteen-year-old Varka (in 'Sleepy'), who unwittingly strangles a restless baby because she is worn out and frightfully sleepy, is, like so many other children in Chekhov's stories, thrown helpless into a hostile world and tortured by loneliness.

Loneliness, futility, despondency: these drawn-out themes in Chekhov's writings convey a very special mood. His tales seem to float in an aura that makes ideas of secondary importance. Picture a chilly autumnal twilight; it is drizzling; the road is miry; a gaunt horse is agonizingly pulling along a peasant cart in which a poor country schoolmistress huddles on damp straw; the coachman lashes the poor animal pitilessly, while the young woman thinks of her village school, of the cold winter nights, of the damp wood that fills the shabby room with smoke without giving any warmth; the road is long, desolate, monotonous; the drizzle never ends; the whip swishes through the chill air; the breathing of the horse is labored; everything is unrelieved gloom ('The Schoolmistress'). This is what is usually called the Chekhovian Mood. Yet it would be a complete error to assume that this mood is uniformly one of despair. Chekhov is indulgent toward human failings; when he condemns the Moody Men, cranks, and liars, or makes fun of them, it is because he is convinced that life can and should be better. This conviction seems to shed a diffused glow over most of his works.

Although critics called Chekhov a pessimist, and although many of his stories do convey a feeling of doom and futility, they seldom lack an element of hope. A nineteenth-century man, a positivist, and an agnostic, Chekhov, after a long and painful process of doubting and seeking, arrived at a system of positive values. He believed the maturing of the human personality, in progress and education. In 1902, writing to S. Diaghilev about the revival of religion among Russian intellectuals, he defined modern culture as 'only a working start toward a great future . . . Interest in religion is but a survival, practically the last vestige of something that has ceased or is ceasing to exist.' Like Turgenev, to whom he is so much akin stylistically, Chekhov is one of the most 'secular' of Russian storytellers: his realism has even fewer mystical accents than the older master's, and is more pointedly anti-religious. His hopes, therefore, all revolve about social and earthly matters, although his characters are often absorbed in dreams and inchoate aspirations. 'My holy of holies,' Chekhov wrote in the much-quoted letter to Suvorin, 'is the human body, health, intelligence, talent, inspiration, love, and absolute freedom — freedom from coercion and falsehood, no matter in what form the last two manifest themselves.' He reaffirmed this credo repeatedly, putting above all other things freedom of thought and expression, life, science, the right to enjoy and to create art; he valued love, friendship, quick understanding, physical fitness, and beauty.

This painter of sluggish and spineless people had a hearty dislike for passivity and resignation. There was, it is true, a period in his youth when Tolstoy's doctrine of non-resistance to evil had appealed to him greatly. Tolstoy's search for truth and his blasting of various illusions and prejudices had likewise left a profound impress on Chekhov's mind. 'I am not a believer,' he wrote in 1900, 'but of all beliefs I consider Tolstoy's the nearest and most kindred to mine.' Nevertheless he refused to accept Tolstoy's practical conclusions, and rejected the norms of behavior that the Sage of Yasnaya Polyana imposed on his followers. 'My Life,' a novelette, is revealing in this respect. Between 1890 and 1896 Chekhov made direct attacks on Tolstoy's doctrines. 'Tolstoy's philosophy,' he wrote to Suvorin in 1894, 'possessed me for six or seven years . . . But now something in me protests; reason and justice tell me that there is more humanity in electricity and steam than in chastity and vegetarianism.'

This feeling was stressed in Chekhov's earlier works as well. The young Tatar of 'In Exile' (written in 1892) argues with old Semion, who preaches aloofness and resignation: 'God made man to be alive, to know joy and sadness and misfortune, yet you do not want anything. This means you are not alive; you are like clay, like stone . . . Stone does not need anything, and you do not need anything. No, God does not love you.' In 'Ward No. 6' (also dated 1892), one of Chekhov's most significant stories, Dr. Ragin points out: 'A sage is . . . distinguished precisely for holding suffering in contempt; also, he is always content, and is never surprised by anything,' to which Gromov, an inmate in the lunatic ward, retorts: 'All I know is that God created me out of warm blood and nerves — yes! And organic tissue, if it be imbued with life, must react to every irritant. And I do react! To pain I react by screams and tears; to baseness by indignation; to vileness, by revulsion. According to me that, precisely, is what they call life.' Ragin is gentle and dreamy and he cannot get things done; he makes little effort to improve conditions in his hospital, which lacks even a decent thermometer and where the patients are beaten by brutal orderlies. Ragin tries to justify his passivity by such rationalizations as these: 'I am serving an evil cause, and receive my wages from those I dupe: I am dishonest. But then I, by myself, am nothing; I am but a particle of an inescapable social evil . . . Therefore, it is not I who am to blame for my dishonesty but the times . . . Were I to be born two hundred or so years from now, I would be an honest man.' [3] External reality, according to him, does not

[3] The quotations from 'Ward No. 6,' used here by permission of the publishers, are from *The Portable Russian Reader,* translated by B. G. Guerney, The Viking Press, New York, 1947.

matter; contentment is to be found within one's self — Tolstoy's 'The Kingdom of God is within you' dictum. Ragin's opponent, the madman Gromov, calls this a philosophy admirably suited to a Russian sluggard; it is an excuse for shying away from life, and it leads to disaster. As a matter of fact, Dr. Ragin himself impresses his provincial friends as a madman, and he is finally put away in Ward No. 6 of his own hospital, where he dies, a broken man, after being beaten by the guard Nikita. In 'Gooseberries' Chekhov supplies an almost perfect answer to Tolstoy's didactic tale, 'How Much Land Does a Man Need?': 'It is customary to assert that man needs but seven feet of earth. That, however, will suffice only for a corpse. A human being needs more than seven feet, more than a whole estate — he needs the whole world.'

This growing anti-Tolstoyan tendency corresponded to Chekhov's indictment of conditions in Russian life and to his desire to change them. 'Such an incongruous, unwieldy country — this Russia of ours,' Gorky reports him as saying. Chekhov wanted Russia to find reformation through logic and hard work. Such tales as 'The Thieves' (1890), 'The Wife' (1892), 'The Peasants' (1897), and 'In the Ravine' (1900) presented critical and almost naturalistic pictures of the lower classes. 'During the summer and winter there had been certain hours and days when it has seemed that these people lived worse than cattle; to live with them was horrible: they were coarse, dishonest, filthy, far from sober; they did not live in amity, were forever quarreling; inasmuch as there was no mutual respect, they feared and suspected one another. Who kept the inn and ruined the folk through drink? The peasant. Who embezzled and drank away community funds, school funds, church funds? The peasant. Who stole his neighbor's goods, set his neighbor's house on fire, swore falsely against his neighbor, all for a bottle of vodka? The peasant. Who was the first, at county and other meetings, to fight against the interests of the peasants? The peasant.' But the author loses no time in giving the other side of the story: 'Yes, it was horrible to live with them, yet they were human beings, for all that; they suffered and wept as human beings do, and in their life there was nothing of such a nature that one could not find some justification for it. Hard work which made the whole body ache at night, cruel winters, poor crops, no room to turn round in—yet there is no help, and no quarter to expect help from' ('The Peasants').

Of the middle classes, and educated society in particular, Chekhov becomes even more critical and, on occasion, indignant: 'To be forced to see and hear how they all lie, to endure insults and humiliation, without daring to declare openly that you are on the side of honest, free people, and to lie to yourself, to wear a smile, and all for the sake of a crust of bread, of a snug corner, of some sort of official rank not worth a copper — no, we can't go on living like that.'

Many characters in the later works recognize this impasse — but even the most despairing among them nurture some vague hope for the future. These weak and melancholy men and women do not, however, venture beyond nebulous dreams. Sonia, in *Uncle Vanya,* finds consolation for herself and her unhappy uncle in the thought that they will find repose after death and will behold angels and a diamond-studded sky (just as the little girl Sasha, in 'The Peasants,' insists that she can see cherubs flitting across the sunlit sky — provided she can keep from blinking). Vershinin, in *The Three Sisters,* daydreams: 'After the lapse of two hundred, three hundred, or even a thousand years, let's say — since the point does not lie in the actual period of time — a new, happy life will come. We will have no part in this life, of course, yet we are living for the sake of that life now, we are working for it — yes, we are even suffering for it; we are creating it, and in that alone lies the aim — and, if you like the happiness — of our being here on earth.' 'I want our life to be holy, lofty, and triumphant, like the vault of the heavens,' confesses the narrator in 'Anonymous Story.'

This longing for a better and richer life held, in the 'nineties, little more than the lyrical quality of a prayer; at the turn of the new century, however, it became something besides a vague hope. When the rising tide of political activity replaced the reactionary doldrums of the reign of Alexander III, Chekhov conveyed the new expectations in his stories and plays. His main characters talked of the imminence of a storm that would change everything. In 'The Betrothed,' his last story, he wrote: 'It seemed to her that everything in the town had long since grown old, had lived its day, and was constantly waiting either for the end, or for the beginning of something youthful, something fresh. Oh, if this new, radiant life would but come as speedily as possible, when one would be able to look one's fate in the eyes, straightforwardly and unafraid, to realize one's self in the right to be happy and free. For sooner or later, such a life is bound to come.' Trofimov, the Eternal Student in *The Cherry Orchard,* and Ania feel that mankind is striving for 'a higher truth, for a higher happiness,' and that they are in the ranks of fighters for this beautiful future. And, according to Trofimov, 'All Russia is our garden.' Tuzenbach (*The Three Sisters*), like other Chekhovian characters, hopes that work will transform everything. Through these vague aspirations for a future of work and integrity, the creator of the Moody People, the chronicler of the 'eighties and 'nineties, expressed the feelings and hopes of Russian society on the eve of the 1905 Revolution. Chekhov was indirectly foretelling the great upheaval that was to change the entire structure of his native land.

IV   There is no doubt that, as a writer, Chekhov followed in many ways the rich tradition of the past. It could be maintained that most of his characters are a new version of the Common Man as portrayed by Gogol in 'Overcoat' (hence the blending of pity with humor), or that his Moody Intellectuals are direct descendants of Turgenev's Rudin or Goncharov's Oblomov. His humor is often akin to Leskov's, although Chekhov subdued the latter's lushness and histrionic richness. In style Chekhov carries on the tradition of Turgenev: his touch is light and sure, his artistry restrained, and his writing has a definitely rhythmic structure — he shares the elegance of phrase that was the heritage of Turgenev's school. Chekhov, the physician, the positivist, and the admirer of symmetry, rejected the exuberance and the extremes of the Writers of the Soil. He disliked the Slavophiles and, in his general outlook as well as in his concept of control and harmoniousness in art, was certainly a Westernizer. The influence of Tolstoy did not affect his style, but he most assuredly responded to Tolstoy's search for complete truth and to his method of unmasking men and women through the device of psychological realism. Sympathy for the victims of life — the basic humanity that gives such warmth to Chekhov's humor and such depth to his melancholy — is one of the general traits of Russian literature, and in this Chekhov carried on the great tradition of the Golden Age, of which he, together with Gorky, was the last product. His sensitiveness to and awareness of the ills of the day are similar to those of writers of the 'eighties; in this respect Uspensky, Garshin, Albov, and Levitov may be regarded as his predecessors.

Beginning in 1886 Chekhov had a definite artistic objective: 'To depict life faithfully, and at the same time to show to what extent life deviates from the norm.' (Norm is used here in the sense of ideal rather than standard.) While representing life as it is, he intimated that it ought to be different. He called himself a realist, since he dealt with everyday experiences and strove for a faithful rendering of reality. 'Familiarity with natural sciences and with scientific methods,' he wrote in 1899, 'has always kept me wary, and I have always tried . . . to be consistent with the facts of science.' The 'absolute and honest truth' which he proclaimed to be the goal of conscientious writers was in his work based upon direct observation. His notebooks and letters bear witness to his incessant labor in this field; he painstakingly collected anecdotes, expressions, peculiar or amusing words, names, incidents, themes, traits of character, and put this copious material to good use. Yet he condemned the photographic or naturalistic approach. The writer must be as objective as a chemist, Chekhov maintained, but he also 'selects, conjectures, combines, and this in itself presupposes a problem: unless he sets himself a problem from the very beginning, there will be nothing to conjecture and nothing to select.'

In other words, the moral idea that Leo Tolstoy believed to be a prerequisite of true art seemed to Chekhov to be the *conditio sine qua non* of good writing. He did not believe in art for art's sake. 'Great writers,' he affirmed, 'head somewhere and summon us thither; they have a goal . . . . He who does not want anything, does not hope for anything, and does not fear anything cannot be an artist.' 'Some have more immediate objectives,' he wrote in 1892. 'The abolition of serfdom, the liberation of their country, politics, beauty, or simply vodka, like Denis Davydov. Others have remote objectives — God, life beyond the grave, the happiness of humanity, and so on. The best of these are realists and paint life as it is, yet in addition to life as it is you feel life as it ought to be, and this captivates you.' Because Chekhov exercised self-restraint in making didactic and social judgments, critics reproached him for his aloofness and lack of a 'philosophy of life.' Shestov, the philosopher and critic of the 'nineties, called Chekhov's work 'a creation out of nothing,' and accused him of 'destroying everything: art, science, love, inspiration,' and of reducing them to dust. And yet behind the formal objectivity of his fiction and the disintegrating effect of his irony, a definite core of moral values is discernible in all of Chekhov's writings. Although his moral attitude seldom shows itself, it gives the true perspective to all the fleeting moods, the casual conversations, and delicate tracings of characters which fill his stories, short and long, with such motley and apparently random details.

Chekhov's chief aim was to divest men of their pomposity and pretense. He detested sham, stilt-walking, tinsel, and bombast in life just as he loathed rhetoric, fustian, and high-falutin style in literature. The memoirs of his friends (those by Gorky and Korolenko are the best) recall the many visitors who came to Chekhov to talk to him about Art, Beauty, and Life. After listening to them for a while, he would suddenly ask them some such irrelevant questions as 'Do you like fishing? Do you like marmalade? Do you play checkers?' So kind and understanding was he that the visitor would forget all about lofty matters and begin talking about whatever really interested him: fishing, or games, or food. Chekhov's literary method is similar to the one he used to stem the artificial flow of eloquence in his visitors. This deflation of man is perceptible in all his work. He strips the individual of lies, illusions, and tricks of the imagination, and shows us his true anxieties and real moods. In Chekhov's mature writing his mischievous smile became ironical without being sardonic and, still later, it changed into sadness and was blended with tolerance and compassion.

'In the same way as the savage adorns himself with shells and fish-teeth,' Gorky wrote, 'the Russian puts on the showy trappings of cheap bookish words.' Chekhov knew how to make a character shed these tawdry embellishments; he wanted to free him from all such vulgar trash. A merciless judge of banality, an enemy of dissimulation and coarseness, he has repeatedly proclaimed, as man's supreme aim, 'freedom, absolute freedom — freedom from coercion, prejudice, ignorance, and the devil.'

His almost clinical analysis of motivation and behavior increased in clarity as he progressed from the sketch to the short novel; at the same time his realistic method presented a certain element of novelty by comparison with earlier techniques. A master of the short story, he is as concise as Merimée and as astringent as Maupassant, but he rejected the plotted narrative and discursive psychological analysis or physical description. Instead of accumulating data in the manner of naturalist writers, he resorts only to the 'significant detail,' used as sign and symbol. 'If you have a gun hanging on a wall in your first act,' he once told a young playwright who sought his advice, 'you will have to shoot it off later on.' The entire structure of his short story is based on a small number of expressive details, on a few hints, on a not too extensive array of external characteristics indicative of an inner life — especially of moods. Instead of describing incidents, or explaining a situation, or rounding out his characterizations, he merely cites a few facts and focuses attention on the atmosphere and on the passing sensations of his characters. Thus bits of conversation, casual thoughts, fleeting impressions come to the fore. Seemingly insignificant touches, glimpses of landscape, elusive sounds and shades, all create the mood of his stories and plays. 'Chekhov, like the Impressionists, has a style all his own,' Tolstoy has pointed out: 'At first glance it seems as if the painter has merely daubed his canvas with any color that came to hand, using no discrimination, so that his strokes do not appear to have any relationship. But as soon as one steps back and looks from a distance, one gets the remarkable impression of a colorful, irresistible painting.' This impressionistic method is what makes it so difficult to summarize Chekhov's stories: the most important things in them are rendered by shadings and nuances.

His character-drawing also differs from the classical realism of the nineteenth century. His people have none of the solid qualities of flesh and mind so minutely described by Goncharov, Pisemsky, Tolstoy, and even Turgenev. They are painted in light, sometimes pale watercolors, not in oils. The full-length portrait is replaced by a few sure strokes, carefully selected to be representative. The contours of the characters are almost vague; we know more about their moods and changing attitudes than about any of their salient traits. We even suspect that they lack such traits, since they are average men and women, and, as has been pointed out, Chekhov describes the species *homo sapiens* as all baked from the same batch of dough, rather than as highly individualized specimens.

Understatement is Chekhov's favorite device: he tells merely a few things, gives fragments of conversation about some trivial thing, while all the rest is left to the reader's conjecture and imagination. The pleasure we experience is an active one: we are reconstructing a whole drama or comedy on the basis of the few hints the writer wishes to convey. The composition of the tale avoids climaxes: the story usually lacks a punch — at any rate no obvious point is made. Finally we realize that the denouement takes place outside of the narrative; it comes to us in a flash after we have closed the book, after the whole succession of images and hints has become firmly lodged in the mind. Thus the effect of not a few of Chekhov's stories is that of a delayed-action bomb. The overwhelming horror in 'Sleepy' is conveyed by just two words in the last sentence; a single vital but vain question put by a man on trial for his life occurs only four brief paragraphs from the end of 'In Court.' Yet a number of critics regarded this as little more than a literary trick and refused to see the perfect consistency and logic of the author's technique.

This method proved particularly daring and novel when applied to the stage. Chekhov the playwright at first startled and shocked his audiences, but by degrees won them over. In addition to the farcical one-acters — *The Bear* or *The Boor* (1888), *The Proposal* (1888–9), *The Wedding* (1889–90), *A Tragedian despite Himself* (1889–90), *The Jubilee* (1891) — the dramatic monologue *The Swan Song* (1887–8), and the tragi-comic monologue *On the Harm of Tobacco* (1902), he wrote five plays that became a turning point in the history not only of the Russian stage but of the theater throughout the world: *Ivanov* (1887–9), *The Sea Gull* (1896), *Uncle Vanya* (1897), *The Three Sisters* (1900–1901), and *The Cherry Orchard* (1903–4).[4] There is scarcely any plot in his plays, and even the most salient incidents — such as the suicide that occurs toward the end of *Ivanov,* or the one in *The Sea Gull,* or Tuzenbach's death in a duel (*The Three Sisters*), or Uncle Vanya's attempt to kill Professor Serebriakov — are devised as psychological rather than actually dramatic climaxes. All of Chekhov's plays are built on the relationships between the protagonists, and since the nature of these relationships is revealed from the very beginning, nearly all dramatic sus-

---

[4] Chekhov also wrote *The Wood-Demon* (1889–90), a four-act comedy, and *On the Highroad* (1885), a one-act dramatic sketch.

pense or element of surprise is excluded. We know almost immediately that Ivanov no longer loves his sick wife, who adores him, and that it is the young girl Sasha he loves. In *Uncle Vanya* Voinizky tells us right away that Professor Serebriakov is a parasite and a pompous, empty egotist; at the same time Voinizky confesses his love for Elena, the professor's wife. In *The Sea Gull* both the drama of the young actress Nina, whose life is going to be ruined by her love for the writer Trigorin, and the failure of the young playwright Treplev to win her, are fully outlined in the first act. The following acts do not develop any action but simply present a more detailed study of the characters and the fiber of their relationships.

The same holds true of *The Three Sisters,* in which loneliness and unhappy loves are not acted out but are merely talked about, and of *The Cherry Orchard,* in which the sale of their ancestral estate by the ruined patricians does not bring about any real conflict but simply gives rise to conversations, recriminations, and casual comedy. Very little actually happens in Chekhov's plays — perhaps it would be more nearly correct to say that what does happen is usually unspectacular and lacking in dramatic force.

Even when death occurs, it comes at the very end of the play (*Ivanov, The Sea Gull*) and in *The Sea Gull* it is not shown but is briefly announced by a minor character. In general, the most important events — the illness and death of Ivanov's wife, the drama of Nina's love for Trigorin and her failure as an actress (*The Sea Gull*), and the auctioning off of the cherry orchard — are merely referred to in passing. It may be said of Chekhov that he deliberately placed offstage what his predecessors would have used for highly dramatic effect. He replaced incident and action with undertones, lyricism, moods; he used transformations of tonality and successive changes of impressions to arouse the emotions of his audience, resorting to an elaborate setting that gave the atmosphere of the play, making use of the pause as a potent means of communication, and availing himself fully of sound effects as integral scenic devices, ranging from instrumental music (*The Three Sisters*) to axe strokes (*The Cherry Orchard*). What he sought to achieve was the illusion of the actual flow of life, of the texture of existence (the precise grounds for the critical condemnation of *The Wood-Demon*); both as storyteller and as dramatist, his aim was to make us sense the destiny of men and women through their casual talk and the irrelevant details of their daily lives. The objective of a realistic playwright was achieved, according to him, through media of poetic suggestion; hence the term Lyrical Drama, so often used to describe his work for the theater.

When *The Sea Gull* was first produced in 1896 at Alexandrinsky

Theater in St. Petersburg, it failed largely because the actors, with the exception of the admirable Vera Kommissarzhevskaya, played it as they would have played any other piece in their repertoire. New intonations and new ways of acting were needed to bring out the subtle qualities of the play, and these were supplied when the Moscow Art Theater, led by the pioneering Stanislavsky and Nemirovich-Danchenko, decided to produce the same play in 1898. *The Sea Gull* became a great success, and linked forever the name of the playwright with the Moscow Art Theater — the theater that opened a new era in the history of Russian culture.

The actors and directors of the Moscow Art Theater stressed the significance of the typically Chekhovian devices: the setting was superb; every movement, each bit of business, was thought out in minute detail; the actors were aware of the scenic impact of pauses, hints, changes in tonality, as well as of the necessity of acting in a subdued, natural way, without any external effects, without raising the voice or exploiting the sure-fire lines; they used the same method of understatement, of sober control, of naturalness and lyricism that was the foundation of Chekhov's art.

The enormous success of Chekhov's plays produced a veritable school of playwrights who attempted to carry on the trend of the Lyrical Drama. Some, like Andreyev and Gorky, merely followed the outward pattern of the Chekhovian plays, while dozens of minor playwrights (D. Surguchev, in his *Autumn Violins,* for example) simply imitated them. After World War I the impact of Chekhov's plays was strongly felt in Europe and America, where they have been repeatedly performed. Chekhov the playwright exerted a decisive influence on the development of dramatic forms both in Russia and abroad.

Although some critics, such as Prince Mirsky, denied Chekhov's influence on Russian prose, and represented him as completely alien to modern sensibility, the imprint he has left on Russian letters is unmistakable, and his popularity among Russians is steadily on the increase. The perfection, the finish of his stories, their combination of simplicity and complexity, the graceful artistry of all his work, its economy of means enlivened by the lyrical movement of his style, all acted upon Russian literature as a new stimulant. 'After Chekhov it is impossible to write carelessly.' This was a slogan for many pre-Revolutionary writers. Chekhov initiated a new phase of realism, and between 1900 and 1917 not only Gorky and Korolenko but a large number of writers of the young generation, such as Leonid Andreyev, Ivan Bunin, Alexander Kuprin, Boris Zaitsev, and others, joined what was then called the Chekhovian Trend. His influence on the art of the short story has spread far beyond the boundaries of Russia: in the 1920's many writers, such as

Katherine Mansfield and Virginia Woolf in England, and Ernest Hemingway, Dorothy Parker, Katherine Anne Porter, and others in America, have plainly shown their indebtedness to the Russian storyteller.

For a short time after the Revolution of 1917 Chekhov was seen as the embodiment of the 'destructive, negative' tendency in Russian literature; his works were criticized as 'not conforming to the spirit of the times,' since he always pictured 'the undoing of life' instead of creating an upsurge of vital impulses. But readers failed to follow the Communist extremists, and a new approach to Chekhov was devised in the 1930's. The party eulogized Chekhov as the writer who 'had foreseen the revolutionary storm,' and his complete rehabilitation, sponsored chiefly by Gorky, speedily followed. By 1931 Chekhov was a favorite not only with Soviet readers but with critics as well; today his plays are often performed and his works sell millions of copies. Chekhov, who was so typical of the intelligentsia under the Czars, who never was a revolutionary, never belonged to any radical groups, and never delivered any messages, whose 'moods' were so out of tune with official optimism — this same Chekhov has the love and respect of millions of Russians, from the rank-and-file worker to the highest Communist leader. Chekhov's popularity has strong emotional overtones. He is not only widely read but also greatly loved, as one loves an intimate friend or a member of one's family. Evidently his humor, his stories, and his plays still hold an irresistible attraction for his countrymen, despite the chasm that separates the Russia of his time from the USSR of Stalin. Time had also augmented his fame abroad: the Western world now sees in him the last representative of Russia's great tradition, although he has not yet achieved the stature of its other writers.

Those who knew Chekhov intimately point out, invariably, that he conveyed the impression of understanding everything, and that whoever met this gentle, quiet man with the keen twinkling eyes liked and respected him. Personal affection and confidence of much the same sort mark the relation between Chekhov and his readers — an attitude that assures him a special place in Russian literature. Chekhov held, and still holds, a particular significance for the Russians, and no one has expressed this better than his friend and admirer Gorky, in a survey of some of the characters this master storyteller created: 'A great, wise man, heedful of all things, has passed by all this dreary, drab crowd of helpless people, has looked upon these depressing fellow countrymen, and with a sad smile, in a tone of gentle but profound reproach, with hopeless melancholy on his face and in his heart, has said in a beautiful, earnest voice: "You live badly, ladies and gentlemen!"'

5

The Modernist Movement

The reign of Alexander III (1881–94), during which Chekhov became a major writer, was otherwise lacking in great works of fiction (with the exception of a few short novels published by Tolstoy). The mighty realistic current had run into tributary streams and rivulets. The few survivors of the 'forties were such minor novelists as Ilya Salov (1835–1902), the painter of provincial life, and Nicholas Akhsharumov (1819–93), who produced lengthy narratives dealing with the bureaucracy of St. Petersburg. Although the periodicals were filled with realistic stories, the dominant school was obviously on the decline. Some of its disciples sought a refuge in French naturalism, as in the case of Peter Boborykin (1836–1922), a widely read and well-educated nobleman, who played a limited literary role at the end of the century. A mild liberal and a convinced Westernizer, Boborykin felt drawn to the Goncourt brothers and Zola. In his novels — he turned out something like a hundred — he attempted to give a social history of contemporary Russia. Actually he succeeded in producing only fictionalized illustrations of various ideological changes among the intellectuals (*On the Wane,* 1890, *Vassily Terkin,* 1892, *The Pass,* 1894), or photographic panoramas of the rising capitalist class (*Businessmen,* 1872, *Kitai-City,* 1882 — one of his best works). Like European and American adherents of the naturalistic school of the same period, Boborykin lacked psychological insight and artistry; his works are overburdened with secondary episodes and unnecessary details, and are superficial and flat.

Less ambitious were the authors of light, entertaining stories, such as Ignaty Potapenko (1856–1929), who wrote innumerable tales and novels, all of them brimming over with fine feeling and cheap optimism, or Vas-

sily Nemirovich-Danchenko (1848–1936) who began as a war corre-
spondent in 1877, and subsequently published vivid descriptions of his
travels (*Sketches of the Volga, the Urals, and the Kama,* 1896, *In Spain,*
1889); he also turned out dozens of dime novels.

Much superior to either Potapenko or Nemirovich-Danchenko was
Nicholas Garin Michailovsky (1852–1906), an engineer who took up
literature as an avocation and became well known for his autobiographical
novels: *Tëma's Childhood, High School Boys, Students, Engineers,*
(1892–7). The life story of Garin's hero, Tëma Kartashov, appealed to
readers as being typical of that of the average intellectual.

The level of lighter literature can best be judged by looking at the
work of humorists such as Nicholas Leikin (1841–1906), whose laughter, devoid of any depth or satirical intimations, was merely coarse and
buffoonish: *Cheerful Russians* (1879), *Our Folks Abroad* (1890–99).
Somewhat better were the sketches of Ivan Gorbunov (1831–95), an
excellent monologist and storyteller, who created the character of General Dityatin, a brass-hat reactionary whose brain had been removed by
an operation and who delivered uproarious after-dinner speeches against
liberalism and general cussedness.

Among the younger generation (some of the new writers were to
demonstrate the full measure of their talent only later, after the turn of
the century) the most important was Vladimir Korolenko (1853–1921).
His father was an Ukrainian official and his mother a Pole. He joined the
Populists during his university years in St. Petersburg, was arrested, and
in 1879 was exiled to the Yakut region in northeastern Siberia. In 1885,
after obtaining permission to return to Russia, he published several tales,
one of which, 'Makar's Dream,' became widely popular. It deals with an
old Yakut who is freezing to death and dreams of disputing in Heaven
with the Lord about the hardships and injustices of earthly existence. The
kind humanitarianism that permeates this pathetic story is also to be found
in the author's other works: 'The Blind Musician' (1886), 'In Bad Company,' 'Prokhor and the Students' (1887), the short stories based on his
Siberian experiences and collected in a volume in 1893, and his novelette
'Speechless' (1895), about the adventures of a Byelorussian peasant in
New York and the American Middle West. Korolenko was both an excellent narrator and an expert at drawing northern landscapes in the suf-
fused manner of Turgenev. But it was his benign attitude toward mankind, his warm humor, and his faith in a better future that won him thousands of grateful readers. He was convinced that 'man was created to be
happy, even as bird was born to fly,' and nothing could impair his belief
in human progress. Plot or action plays but a secondary role in Korolenko's
work: most of his writings are character sketches of tramps, Siberian con-

victs, peasants, and 'seekers after truth.' These stories do not depart from the traditional realistic pattern, the author figuring as a witness of events or as a sort of father-confessor. In many other writers this device would seem flat, but Korolenko enhanced it by his emotional, lyrical quality. His concern for human sufferings and social injustice was so genuine, his love of common people so convincing, that conservatives as well as radicals respected this Populist and Socialist who wrote and lived in the manner of a good Christian. The moral authority of this typical humanitarian was accepted among the intellectuals, particularly among writers, to whom he had often extended a helping hand (the case of Gorky, though the best known, is but one of many).

At the end of the century Korolenko returned to the editorship of *The Wealth of Russia,* the Neo-Populist monthly, and devoted himself to pamphleteering. His articles in the daily press championing 'the wronged and the humiliated' had for their aim 'the defense of the rights and the dignity of man, in so far as it can be carried on with the pen.' In 1892–3 he published *The Cholera Year* sketches, and between 1895 and 1898 waged a vigorous campaign on behalf of the Votiaks, an Asiatic tribe falsely accused by corrupt and ignorant administrators of offering human sacrifices. He often acted as the champion of other mistreated national minorities, particularly of the Jews in his stories 'House No. 13' and 'The Day of Atonement'; and in 1906, in 'Everyday Happening,' he delivered a scathing indictment of mass executions of revolutionists by the Czarist authorities. His last creative work was *The Story of My Contemporary,* an excellent autobiography giving a vivid picture of Russian life between the emancipation of the serfs and the assassination of Alexander II. The first volume appeared in 1909, and two others were published posthumously, in 1922; the book, however, is incomplete. The ordeals of the Revolution and the civil war shocked and saddened this mild-mannered and sensitive veteran of Russian letters, and in 1920 he addressed an eloquent plea for humanity and the preservation of cultural values to Lunacharsky, at that time Commissar of Education. Soon after having written this declaration of liberal faith, Korolenko died.

Among other Neo-Populist writers mention must be made of Peter Yakubovich (1860–1911), Korolenko's friend and co-editor of *The Russian Wealth,* who signed his verse with the initials P.Ya., and used the pen names Melshin and Grinevich for his prose. His poetry was very popular with the radical youth at the turn of the century. In 1887 he was sentenced to death for taking part in attempts to resurrect the Party of The People's Will. This sentence was commuted to hard labor, however, and the poet spent many years in the mines and prisons of Siberia. The experience supplied him with material for his most important work, *In the World of the Rejected* (1895–9; the first complete edition appeared in 1911) — a moving and realistic description of convicts and their struggle for life and freedom.

II   By 1900 realism had lost its impact and freshness, even though it remained formally predominant in Russian letters; this contradiction created a favorable situation for an anti-realistic onslaught. There were, however, other and more complex reasons for the appearance of a new literary movement.

The evolution of Russian culture in the nineteenth century had been fairly consistent. Encouraged by the aristocracy, expanded by the gentry, and eventually developed by an intelligentsia that represented various social strata, it had gradually become more diversified and democratic. The intellectuals, after seeking, in the 'forties, for a national program among the Westernizers and the Slavophiles and, later, among sundry brands of messianism, had in the 'sixties and 'seventies turned toward Populism and Marxism, the two factions of Socialism. Politically, despite divergence and diversity of opinions, the intelligentsia remained liberal and radical throughout cyclical changes of reaction and reform; its character was anti-autocratic and, as often as not, anti-capitalistic; its activity was tinged with extremism, religious fervor, and revolutionary fanaticism.

Literature since Pushkin had plodded on at an even, measured pace; forms and poetic trends had been evolving in regular succession; the 'Natural' school had been predominant, since it stood for expression of realism in art, and emphasis upon social significance and didactic aims assumed the character of a national tendency. Since the days of Alexander I, several generations of intellectuals had grown up in this cultural atmosphere. Although they varied in their points of view and political allegiances, Populists and Marxists, liberals, and conservatives all took it for granted that literature should instruct and make readers conscious of social and political problems.

These commonly accepted norms were, however, challenged, questioned, and revised in the course of the revolt that broke out at the end of the century. The movement that undertook such a daring task and brought about such great changes opened a new era in poetry, fiction, criticism, the theater, the ballet, and all the branches of the plastic arts. It was labeled Decadent in its beginnings and Symbolist at its maturity. Whatever the tags bestowed upon it, it represented the most significant phenomenon in Russian literature and arts since the Golden Age of the classics; in fact, many critics are tempted to regard it as the 'last flourishing of pre-Revolutionary culture.' It might also be said that, just as the decade of 1830–40 forged the national consciousness, and that of 1860–70 the social and political consciousness of educated society, the 'nineties attempted to mold its aesthetic credo — and therein lies one of the main contributions of that decade.

The literary renaissance of the 'nineties in Russia almost coincided with, and partly depended upon, the romantic revival in Europe. The poetic movement in France, from Baudelaire to Verlaine and Rimbaud, the aestheticism of Ruskin and Wilde in England, the works of Wagner and Nietzsche in Germany, of Ibsen and Hamsun in Norway, of Maeterlinck in Belgium, as well as the expansion of Impressionism in art, all had strong repercussions in Russia. The aesthetes of Moscow and St. Petersburg looked to Europe to find support and inspiration for the new moods and ideas they strove to propagate at home.

The Decadents, as their opponents contemptuously called them, belonged to the intelligentsia: these sons and daughters of aristocrats, civil servants, merchants, or priests presented the same diversity of social origin as did any of the other groups of Russian intellectuals. In literature and art they sympathized with the main trends of the European *fin de siècle:* they exalted the refinement of form and the Cult of Beauty, defended the theory of art for art's sake, and attacked realism and social preachment in all phases of artistic creation. In poetry they tended toward the predominance of the musical and intuitive over the logical and rational; they preferred to intimate, to allude rather than to mirror or narrate; their vocabulary became vague or symbolic, and they were eager to toss overboard all the old rhythms and themes. Deliberately and consciously they were writing precious poems full of neologisms, sensuous alliterations, and cryptic meanings, while their ethereal prose sketched dreams and exotic or perverse emotions.

Ideologically the new movement signified more than a mere rejection of realistic tradition: its strong anti-social tendency was bolstered by haughty individualism, which often degenerated into narcissism. The poets of the movement enjoyed talking about themselves and about the minute details of their inner life. They had recourse to demonism, drugs, and sexual excesses in order to enter the 'artificial paradise' of hallucinations, mystical flights, and hypersensitivity. Plekhanov, one of the foremost Marxian art critics, saw in these traits the symptoms of the 'pallid disease of an anemic social class in decline.' Like other Marxists he contended that the exclusive culture of the aristocracy, after having reached the apex of refinement and artistry, had begun its downward curve and was disintegrating, while the Decadents invented their cooing rhythms and the Symbolists paraded their mystical experiences.

But even those who accepted this explanation of such a complex phenomenon had to recognize its extent, scope, and vitality. Whether or not it was the ultimate blossoming of the culture of Russia's upper classes, it had all the magnificence of late autumnal flowers, and it exerted a powerful influence on the further development of Russian art and literature. One fact, however, was indisputable: the Russian aesthetes hardly resembled their Western prototypes. Wildeian dandies with sunflowers in their buttonholes, the demon lovers of Sar Péladan, or the neurotics of Rodenbach lost a great deal of their languor and superciliousness upon being transported to Russia: under Northern skies they suddenly displayed the passion of iconoclasts and the ardor of pioneers.

The new movement passed through two periods or stages. The first, usually labeled the Decadent, started at the beginning of the 'nineties as a revolt and a revaluation of traditional concepts. It had strong romantic overtones and showed the overwhelming influence of the European *fin de siècle*. Its disciples proclaimed aestheticism, individualism, refinement; their attitude was strongly anti-social; they were unequivocal Westernizers and stressed their love for European culture. In the course of the changes that took place in the minds and hearts of individuals as well as in the general conditions of society, their mystical, philosophical, religious, and (subsequently) social tendencies, which had been weak or confused at first, came to the fore. This occurred mainly during the second period, the beginning of which coincided roughly with the foundation of the Religious and Philosophical Society (1902–3). At that juncture the movement was Symbolist rather than Decadent, and it reached its culmination soon after the Revolution of 1905, when recognition, popularity, and actual leadership in arts and letters. crowned the efforts of the Symbolists. This has brought about a curious error of perspective: readers and critics often forget that the favorites of 1905–12 had been established, and sometimes had written their best works, a decade or so before their names won general recognition. The second period was marked by two important trends: the Symbolists made a rapprochement with the Slavophiles and turned toward national tradition, while the Western influence declined and lost ground. They also — and this is the second outstanding trait — became concerned with politics and social problems. A reconciliation took place between the insurgent writers and the radical intellectuals: after 1905 revolutionary Modernism and modernistic revolutionaries came into being.

Two generations had promoted the new school: the older one included Merezhkovsky, Sologub, Balmont, Briussov, Hippius, Rozanov; they continued their work and played an important role throughout the first quarter of the twentieth century. The younger generation, influenced by Innokenty Annensky and Vladimir Solovyov, considered Alexander Blok, Andrei Bely, and Viacheslav Ivanov their leaders.

The first battle of the Modernists took place in the field of criticism. The traditions of sociological criticism, of Chernyshevsky, Dobroliubov, and Pisarev, had reigned unchallenged since the late 'fifties, and the aesthetic incursions of Apollon Grigoriev, Paul Annenkov, Konstantin Leontiev, and a few minor essayists could do little to alter the general picture. Novels and poems were judged on their social merits by men like Mikhailovsky or Plekhanov, who used them as a springboard for political and philosophical disquisitions. Nicholas Shelgunov (1824–91), the leading literary critic of the influential monthly *Russian Thought,* contended that 'the history of literature is nothing but a struggle of ideas, in which the authors acted either as propagandists or as tribunes.' Alexander Skabichevsky (1838–1910), another popular critic, also considered literature a rostrum and judged writers accordingly. In this respect the Populists and Marxists, the radicals and conservatives were in complete agreement. The talented Slavophile critic Nicholas Strakhov (1828–96), who wrote penetrating articles on Tolstoy and Dostoevsky, and whose three-volume work *The Struggle against the West in Russian Literature* (1887–96) is frequently quoted even by present-day critics, also analyzed fiction according to purely ideological standards.

But the young men and women who called themselves Modernists challenged such methods. Literature, they claimed, was to be considered merely a manifestation of art and a reflection of an author's individuality. Consequently they advocated two kinds of criticism: impressionism, in the Wildeian sense, designed to re-create the thoughts and emotions produced by a work of art on the reader or onlooker; and philosophical criticism, striving to establish the connection between Beauty and the 'essence of things' as reflected in a book, a canvas, or a piece of music. Later a third category was admitted: psychological criticism, which probed the mysteries of a creator's personality. In a long essay, 'Reasons for the Decline of Russian Literature and Its New Trends' (1892–3), Merezhkovsky demanded the rejection of traditional criticism as one means for the solution of the problems of that time. Peter Pertzov (1868) discussed the philosophical foundations of Modernism in *The Young Poetry* (1895), a collection of poems under his editorship, and concluded with a denial of realism and sociological criticism.

An even sharper note was sounded by Nicholas Vilenkin (1855–1937). In his early poems, published under the name of Minsky ('White Nights,' 'The Garden of Gethsemane'), he had imitated the melancholy spirit of Nekrassov, but by 1884 he had become a champion of art for art's sake; he battled for the revival of idealism ('The Light of Conscience,' 1890), elaborated mystico-ethical theories that blended Nietzsche and Oriental concepts of the Nirvana, and challenged contemporary critics by calling them 'old-fashioned mandarins.' The greatest sensation of all, however, was the campaign waged against such 'Positivists' as Belinsky and Dobroliubov by Akim Volynsky-Flexer (1863–1926). He made Mikhailovsky one of his targets and dubbed this highly respected writer 'the gendarme of Russian literature.' Though this onslaught provoked a storm of indignation, Volynsky did not desist. In his books, such as *Religion in Contemporary Literature* and *The Struggle for Idealism,* he claimed that the new school of criticism had achieved a 'shift from physical phenomena to the world beyond; it is convinced of the impotence of science when faced with the mysteries of the universe; it considers individuality a reflection of the Divine, and it wants to liberate man from all the restrictions of earthly morality and all the requirements of earthly society.' His essays in defense of idealistic philosophy and his violent polemics against 'materialistic methods of criticism' were written in an elaborate, rhetorical style studded with metaphysical jargon, Biblical imagery, and quotations from Nietzsche, Ibsen, and Plotinus. In 1900 he published his *Leonardo da Vinci,* which won him honorary citizenship in the city of Milan; later he became a ballet critic, and discussed the dancers and their performances with his usual mixture of erudition and mysticism.

The original works of young poets — the first poems of Merezhkovsky (1888) and the *Russian Symbolists* (1894) and *The Young Poetry* anthologies — were met with scorn and ridicule by the majority of Russian critics; parodies and quips on Briussov, Balmont, Volynsky, and others filled the columns of the humor magazines. Yet the Modernists persevered, and their ranks grew steadily. The St. Petersburg group (Merezhkovsky, Hippius, Sologub, Minsky, Volynsky) rallied round the *Northern Messenger,* a monthly edited from 1894 to 1917 by Liubov Gurevich (1866–1940). The Moscow group, which by 1899 had established the Scorpio publishing house, was led by Valery Briussov, Yurgis Baltrushaitis (a gifted but rather obscure and ponderous poet), and Sergei Poliakov, a rich man of wide learning and an excellent linguist. The two groups united in the publication of the literary annual, *Northern Flowers.* In 1904 Scorpio started its own review, *The Balance,* which played an important part in the Symbolist movement. Subsequently (1909–17) the St. Petersburg review, *Apollo,* edited by Serghei Makovsky (b. 1877), the son of a well-known painter and himself an art critic and a fine poet, became the rallying point of the younger generation of aesthetes. Another review, *The New Road,* founded by Pertzov in 1903, served as the organ of all the God-seekers, who represented the religious tendencies of Symbolism.

III   By the late 'nineties the impact of Modernism was already being felt in various fields of art, and the poets shortly received support and encouragement from painters, sculptors, and musicians, who had also rebelled against realism and the sociological tendency. It was at this point that the Itinerants [1] (realistic painters who stressed the social and the topical in art) began to lose ground, even though they numbered among them such masters as Ilya Repin (1844–1930), whose dramatic and imaginative paintings enjoyed wide popularity, and Vassily Surikov (1848–1916), the creator of powerful historical canvases of high emotional appeal. Valentin Serov (1865–1911), the master of portraiture who also excelled in pictorial evocations of the reigns of Peter and Catherine, and Ilya Levitan (1861–1900), a friend of Chekhov's, whose landscapes were impressionistic, were both in sympathy with the new movement.

In 1898, in St. Petersburg, a new magazine came into being through the efforts of Serghei Diaghilev (1872–1929); called *The World of Art*, it encouraged such young painters as Alexander Benois, Konstantin Somov, Leon Bakst, Eugene Lancere, as well as the followers of Modernism in literature, the theater, and the ballet. In the first issue of the magazine Diaghilev spoke of 'a new climate, and of new ideas which, like precious fragrance, fill the air.' An excellent organizer, endowed with energy, enthusiasm, and a lavish taste, he became a great force in the entire movement and organized exhibitions of young artists in opposition to the Itinerants, who by this time were called the Barbarians. The St. Petersburg group (Benois, Somov, Ostroumova, Lancere, Borisov-Musatov) showed their works next to those of such Muscovites as Serov, Levitan, Korovin, Vrubel, and Maliutin. All these men were destined to give new life and brilliancy to Russian art, and some of them to acquire international reputations. Other Moscow artists, from Victor Vasnetzov (1848–1926) to Michael Vrubel (1856–1910), were engaged in painting sets for Mamontov's theatrical circle, and later for a new venture: in 1898 the Moscow Art Theater opened its doors to the public. Under the guidance of Vladimir Nemirovich-Danchenko (1858–1943), brother of Vassily, the writer, and Konstantin Alexeyev-Stanislavsky (1863–1938), it followed in its beginnings the realistic, or rather naturalistic, tendency represented by the German Company of Meiningen Players, who visited Russia and influenced its theatrical art. However, the Moscow Art Theater was not long in finding its own pace and in creating a unique singleness of dramatic purpose, of unity of stage direction, un-

---

[1] Cf. *The Epic of Russian Literature,* p. 210.

surpassed team work, and inventiveness in stage effects; it brought to the Russian public, in addition to foreign and native classics, all types of modern plays, from Ibsen and D'Annunzio to Chekhov and Gorky. Although more cautious in adopting new methods than their reputation would suggest, the Moscow Art Theater was a sign of the times and represented a changing spirit. Under its influence new life came to other theatrical institutions.

The *World of Art* group was directly responsible for a renaissance of applied arts and crafts, helped greatly by the experiments that were carried on upon the estate of Savva Morozov, the wealthy merchant who acted as Maecenes to the Moscow Art Theater and to sundry Symbolist literary ventures, and by Prince Tenishev, who had given his name to a vocational art school in Moscow. *The World of Art,* sumptuously produced and illustrated, with star correspondents in Paris, Rome, Munich, and other cosmopolitan centers, was a new window opening onto Europe. The impact of its first issues upon the elite of St. Petersburg and Moscow was overwhelming. Its encyclopedic character (the publication dealt with poetry and literary criticism as well as with the visual arts) contributed to widening its influence. Not until 1903, when *The New Road* was brought out for poets, novelists, and philosophers, did *The World of Art* lean more toward music and other non-literary arts.

As we have seen, Russian Modernism in literature, which had in its beginnings turned toward Europe, in a comparatively short while began to look for inspiration to Russia's own past and to Russian soil. This pattern was even more obvious in painting, sculpture, and the theater than in literature. *The World of Art* initiated a revival of Russian eighteenth century art, laid the foundations for the Old St. Petersburg cult (Mstislav Dobuzhinsky, Lancere, and others), and contributed to the discovery of national medieval art — especially that of icon-painting. These efforts coincided with the researches of such archaeologists and historians as Ainalov and Nikodim Kondakov. The exhibitions of 1911 and 1913 revealed to the public all the pictorial riches of the icon and some of the unknown or neglected treasures of medieval painting and architecture. In general, the history of Russian art was greatly advanced by the members of the *World of Art* group, particularly by Igor Grabar (b. 1871), the author of a monumental *History of Russian Art* and many monographs, and by Paul Muratov (1881–1950), widely known for his *Images of Italy*.

The graphic arts also had a revival: engravers and illustrators, from Dimitri Mitrokhin to Ivan Bilibin, produced beautiful illustrated books and founded a veritable school of designers and craftsmen who practically revolutionized publishing. While the *World of Art* exhibitions, given in beautiful and festive settings, were offering examples of European painting, from Degas and Renoir to the latest Impressionists, the Evenings of Contemporary Music were introducing to steadily growing audiences the works of Franck and Strauss and, later, of Debussy and Ravel. The era of Peter Tchaikovsky, of his popular operas and symphonies, was definitely over, and young composers, such as Scriabin, Medtner, Stravinsky, Rachmaninov, and Prokofiev, were opening new paths. The whole modern school of Russian music developed from the movement initiated by *The World of Art* and its adherents.

The suspension of their magazine, in 1904, did not at all mean the disintegration of the *World of Art* group. Its exhibitions did not offer the works of the pioneering members only; in 1910 it presented such divergent painters as Kustodiev, Sudeikin, Borisov-Musatov, Grigoriev, Yakovlev, Petrov-Vodkin, Annenkov, Shukhaev, Sorin, Narbut, Chagal, Goncharova, and a score of others — the adherents of conflicting schools, from Impressionism to Futurism. They all were, nevertheless, in some degree the offspring of the *World of Art* movement.

As for Diaghilev, 1906 saw him abroad, where he formed his ballet company and launched it on its triumphant international career. The lavish staging of these ballets not merely influenced the theater in Russia, Europe, and the Americas before and after World War I but also served to introduce to the West Russian music, painting, and dance. For two decades the Russian Ballet in Paris rallied the representatives of new tendencies in the arts, from Stravinsky to Picasso, and won recognition and fame for its composers, stage designers, and choreographers. Diaghilev's theatrical venture was, in a way, a plastic epitome of *The World of Art:* 'We repaid the West with interest for what we learned from it in the 'nineties,' as one of Diaghilev's associates put it.

IV   The most important exponents of Modernism had been poets — and the diversity, as well as the clash, of their creativeness indicated the vast range of the new movement. Two of these poets soon became identified with the Decadent trend: Valery Briussov and Konstantin Balmont.

After the publication of the *Russian Symbolists* anthology in 1894, Briussov, then 21, became the leader of the Decadents. A small group of enthusiastic young men and women rallied round him; although they scarcely understood his esoteric patter, they felt that this slender scholar, with high cheek bones and a haughty gaze in his Mongolian eyes, represented a new artistic force. The grandson of a serf and the son of a rich Moscow merchant, Valery Briussov (1873–1924) had been brought up in the atheistic and radical tradition of the liberal intelligentsia; he had received an excellent education. At 20 he considered himself the disciple of Verlaine, Mallarmé, and Rimbaud. He owed his discovery of the French Symbolists to Alexander Dobroliubov (1876–?), a nobleman who lived in a room with the ceiling painted gray and the walls papered black, who discoursed on French poets, the occult sciences, and demonism, and who was one of the most complex of the young aesthetes. A religious mystic and a conscientious objector, he paid for his convictions with a prison sentence and later settled down 'among the people' in the Volga region. Interested in theological intricacies, he became head of the religious sectarians folk-sect, and during the revolutionary years simply disappeared in the anonymous multitude.

Another promoter of Modernism was Ivan Konevsky (Oraeus), who taught Briussov that poetry was 'the sanctuary of mankind' and conveyed to him an exalted idea of the poet's mission. From the start of his career Briussov created the impression that he was a master craftsman rather than the seer some of the Symbolists wanted him to be. The problem of form was for him crucial, and what he sought was 'a new body for the new art.' 'There are subtle ties between the shape and the scent of a flower,' Briussov proclaimed, thus coining one of the slogans of the Decadents. Other slogans of his had to do with extreme individualism: 'The personality of the artist is the essence of Art.' At the age of twenty-four he stated: 'I recognize no other obligations save a virginal faith in myself — and that is a truth which needs no proof.' His first poems shocked readers by their deliberately challenging tone, and he was made the butt of the newspaper wits. But insults and sneers could not affect him. A hard-working and obstinate man, he coldly and calmly persisted in transplanting exotic flowers to his inhospitable native soil. Some critics felt that only sheer assiduity and incessant labor made him a prominent poet. The brow of his muse often dripped sweat; 'Onward, my dream, my faithful ox,' he once wrote.

His whole life was one of devotion and service to the only deity he adored: literature. Like a hierophant officiating in a temple, he performed his poetic rites far removed from the contemptible mob. This haughtiness of Briussov always had a chill and somewhat pedantic touch. Many of his poems described the frenzy of the senses, of carnal passion, and the rapture of sex: in his *Chefs d'œuvre* (1895) he spoke at length of 'voluptuous shadows in an alcove' and of 'bodies intertwined like a pair of avid snakes'; but the erotic lines that delighted his readers after 1905 had the icy sheen of rational invention. He fancied the pose of an orgiastic Dionysian poet, of a perverse seeker after forbidden pleasures and esoteric delights — yet all his orgies were intellectual, and his Demon wore the robe of a venerable academician. Even in the varied and challenging rhythms of his daring verse there was a lack of spontaneity and the musty odor of a dusty library room prevailed. Ever the great *artifex*, Briussov 'checked harmony through algebra,' to use an expression of Pushkin's Salieri, and sang the praises of 'the invincible logic of mathematics.' He often talked about mathematical signs as reflections of the world above and beyond, and in revealing stanzas asserted that 'Dreamers, Sibyls, and Prophets follow paths forbidden to Thought; they penetrate to a distant Realm, far from the Conscious, where Imperial Numbers shine.'

Briussov never expressed in his works any truly mystical experiences, as did such Symbolists as Bely, Ivanov, or Blok. He was most successful in ornate pieces in which he used symbols as aesthetic signs of an orderly verbal system, just as the Parnassians did — Hérédia, for example, or Leconte de Lisle.

His collections of poems — *Me Eum Esse* (1897), *Tertia Vigilia* (1900), *Urbi et Orbi* (1903), *Stephanos* (1905), *All the Songs* (1906–9), *The Mirror of Shadows* (1912) — contained majestic histori-cal poems, among which the sonnet 'Assargadon' and such pieces as 'A Priest of Isis' and 'The Trireme Rowers' won him what amounted to notoriety. All the Egyptian priests and Babylonian sages, all the Roman galley-slaves and barbarian warriors, all the remembrances of past rein-carnations and of assignations on the shores of the Nile, the Tiber, and the Euphratus which cluttered the poems of amateurs and third-rate versi-fiers throughout Russia in the first two decades of the twentieth century can be traced back to the Briussovian influence. He made extensive poetic tours through history, and the titles of his poems resound with the mouth-filling names of Chaldaean shepherds, Pompeiian girls, Cretan builders, and Macedonian warlords. A lover of the heroic, he utilized myth and legend to depict strong characters and great men, thus bestowing solemn Wagnerian overtones to his writings.

Most of his poems show solidity of construction; their deliberate pace, together with adroitness in the use of archaisms, augmented the general effect of massiveness, of solemnity, which at best came close to grandeur and at worst resulted in crushing ponderosity. This iconoclast and rebel was almost invariably attracted by classical completeness of imagery and by the precision of clean-limbed rhythms. The Derzhavinian tradition can be felt in his poems, which are conceived in a major key and combine sonority with somewhat high-pitched overtones. Yet Briussov lacked the magnitude, the dynamic power, and the genuine grandeur of Derzhavin. His poetry far too often sounds rhetorically contrived and shallow. Both bookworm and savant, Briussov burdened his work with obvious or im-plied quotations. His prose works (*The Altar of Victory*, in two volumes, 1912, and *The Angel of Fire*, 1908), although written in the form of fiction, are actually erudite treatises on Roman life in the fourth century, on German demonology in the sixteenth century, and so forth. It has often been pointed out that Briussov was one of the pioneers of the urbanistic trend in Russian poetry. As a matter of fact, he had come under the influence of the great Belgian poet Emile Verhaeren, whose works he translated into Russian. (Briussov was in general a fine linguist and an excellent and prolific translator from many languages — including English.) Briussov's most popular poem, 'The Pale Horse,' has a peculiar undertone of dread: 'The street was like a storm. Throngs passed by as if pursued by an ineluctable Fate; cars, cabs, busses rushed on — and the frantic torrents of humanity flowed on without end.' Suddenly in the heart of the metropolis, the Pale Horse appears, ridden by Death — and life comes to an end. The vision lasts but a moment, and then the torrents resume their rushing; but a lunatic and a prostitute still stretch their arms toward the ghost. Other poems on city life, machines, and the fast pace of our age made Briussov a forerunner of the Futurists; it would be interesting to investigate Mayakovsky's debt to the older poet.

In 1905 Briussov wrote about the Huns and Scythians, whose trampling iron boots he heard coming. With masochistic gloating he predicted the destruction of cities and books, and the flight of 'sages and poets, those trustees of faith and mystery, into catacombs, caves, and deserts — to keep the torches burning.' This hymn of 'welcome to those who would annihilate' the poet was not, however, an expression of mere intellectual masochism, or of his Nietzschean contempt for 'barbarian multitudes' — it revealed Briussov's acceptance of a revolutionary mass movement. He disliked the existing Czarist regime, felt the inevitability of its collapse, and in 1905 sided with the socialists. His poem about masons building a prison for their own brethren became a classic of revolutionary poetry. In 1914, during the war with Germany, he wrote patriotic verse — and from 1918 on hymned the proletarian revolution as a new chapter in the world's history. All this civic poetry, however (including that of his last years, when he joined the Communists), is flat and unoriginal; its formalistic character is most patent.

In all probability Briussov was unable to feel strongly about anything but books. All the strength of his nature and all the fire of his temperament went into his literary research. Gorky called him, in 1917, the most cultured of Russian writers. He had traveled widely, could read in eight languages, and was an outstanding literary critic: his interpretation of Gogol's drama and his studies on Pushkin and Tiutchev are still of high value, as are many others of his essays. The Moscow Institute of Art and Literature, in which he lectured after 1920, was renamed the Briussov Institute by the Communist leaders. Despite all the favors the Soviet government was ready to grant this old Decadent who so openly supported the new regime, Briussov spent his last years withdrawn from the market place, in the splendid isolation of his dreams and his literary research. Actually he preferred his manuscripts to the tumult of life. Individualist and aesthete, Briussov took pride in the recognition granted to his craftsmanship. He died with the conviction of having accomplished on earth the three aims he set for himself in his youth: 'The first precept — do not live in the present; only the future belongs to the poet. Remember the second — do not sympathize with anybody, love yourself boundlessly. And keep up the third one — adore Art — and only Art — and do it aimlessly, heedlessly.'

v   The other great Decadent poet, Konstantin Balmont (1867–1943), the son of a noble landowner of Scottish origin, also belonged to the Moscow group. 'I experienced my first passionate thought about women at five,' he tells us in his autobiography, 'my first real love at nine, my first passion at fourteen, my first belief in the possibility and inevitability of universal happiness at seventeen, and, at twenty-two, I attempted suicide.' This attempt (he had jumped out of a fourth-floor window) incapacitated him for a year and left him with a slight limp the rest of his life. After his recovery the high-strung and turbulent young man became the Orpheus of Modernism and fought many of its memorable battles. While the cold and haughty Briussov planned and led the struggle as a strategist, Balmont made frantic forays against the 'philistines and obscurantists.' The critics of the 'nineties tagged him as a raving madman and quoted his highly musical but apparently meaningless stanzas as typical of the 'Decadent nonsense.'

Balmont's music was as spontaneous and effortless as Briussov's was laborious and cerebral. Even in his first books, *Under a Northern Sky* (1894) and *In Boundless Space* (1895), he displayed the lilting melodiousness of his verse, and all the enticements of alternating meters, sonorous rhymes, alluring alliterations, and subtle inflections of tonality. His feeling for words was extraordinary: 'Words are chameleons,' he declared in one of his early poems. They are in a haste to live, they obey laws of their own, they have their own souls, they hasten to change, they are of all colors, they fade and bloom — and therein does their beauty lie.

The slightly melancholic inflections characteristic of the first period of Balmont's work did not last long. 'There are two gods [he wrote], the god of serene repose and the god of movement. I love both of them, but I did not abide long under the sign of the first.' His harmonious musicality and aestheticism soon evolved into an ecstatic praise of life. Balmont celebrated all its manifestations, and hymned with equal rapture the sun and the grain of golden dust, the ocean and the drop of dew on a petal. He also asserted his individualism, his 'right to be unlike others' and 'to navigate alone on the seas of whim and fancy.'

In the preface to *Buildings on Fire* (1900), which he called 'the lyrics of a Modern Soul,' he declared that 'everyone has endless faces, but many men who help to form one's personality ought to be thrown into the fire.' This collection, as well as the following one, *Let Us Be like the Sun* (1903), were Nietzschean in tone and proclaimed Balmont's supremacy as a poet. He tossed away his 'moon-dreams,' 'the azure of soothing songs,' and made startling declarations: 'I want to be daring and insolent, I want to strip off your clothes . . .'

His gentle lyrical moods were now replaced by tempestuous desires: 'I want daggerlike words and lethal moans of death; I want to be first in the world, on earth, and on the sea; I want the purple flowers which I have created everywhere; I want buildings on fire, I want howling storms.' He exalted 'burning lives,' 'titanic deeds,' 'eruptions of the Soul,' 'the beauty in ugliness and the goodness in evil,' 'the contortions of sinful flesh and the temptations of demons.' And without fail he finishes up with self-adulation: 'Who equals my might in song? No one — no one!'

Before the Revolution of 1905, and during the years of reaction that followed it, Balmont was the idol of youth, his poems were put to music, his platform appearances throughout Russia were met with ovations. The provincial audiences saw the Poet in this red-haired little man who stood erect, tossing his head backward and jutting out his Mephistophelian beard. His magnificent and foggy talk, his unpredictable manners, his hauteur, like that of a Spanish grandee, alternating with the pathetic childishness of a myopic tosspot, all puzzled and charmed his thousands of followers. While Briussov reigned in Moscow over intellectuals and was faithful to the *odi profanum vulgus* adage, Balmont, despite all his Nietzschean attitudes, loved to be acclaimed by the multitudes.

During the years 1905 to 1907 Balmont wrote hymns to the Revolution, sent up paeons to barricades and uprisings, and had to flee abroad from the Czarist police, whereupon he reverted to exoticism and devoted his next books to Slavic folklore (*The Firebird,* 1907), to Mexico, to South Africa, and to the various other countries he visited on his extensive travels. The Pacific islands provoked in him exactly the same kind of poetic fervor as had the landscapes of the Moscow region. In general, this capacity of becoming infatuated with the most diversified lands, objects, men, or periods was Balmont's salient characteristic. He never discriminated but simply responded to any external stimulus, and this ability for lyrical and poetic response seemed inexhaustible. He wrote thousands of poems upon thousands of separate themes. Instead of channeling his own flow, he dissipated it into trickling rivulets. He could not help it — this uneven, multi-voiced, often noisy, and frequently enchanting poet. His chief trouble was that he lived and talked in verse, and this talk degenerated into shallow chit-chat. His repetitions and verbiage became tiresome. Briussov was annoyed by Balmont's ability to learn and to forget with equal facility. 'He can gulp down a library,' Briussov once commented angrily, 'and it will stick with him as long as water on a duck's back.' This ability made Balmont a prolific translator (he knew dozens of languages), but his translations of the collected works of Shelley (whom he adored), of Poe (whom Briussov also translated), of Whitman, of Calderon, of Lope de Vega, and ever so many others all too often turned these authors into so many Balmont phantoms; the translations were, nevertheless, highly popular in Russia.

He assumed a hundred guises, but two of his self-characterizations seem not inappropriate: he often compared himself with the wind,[2] or with a sun-shot cloud. The charm of his poetry melts away like a cloud, and only a few of his poems, out of the scores upon scores of his volumes, have remained impervious to time.

The peak of his influence was between 1904 and 1910. He was known and loved much more than were any of his fellow Decadents, and was imitated by many poets. Even those who called him superficial, grandiloquent, raucous, or shallow could not deny his unusual craftsmanship, his musicality, his iridescent imagination, and the great role he played in the rebirth of Russian poetry. Yet his popularity was not lasting, and he was the first victim of the anti-Decadent and anti-Symbolist movements in poetry that sprang up during World War I. Since then, and especially in Soviet Russia, where he was tagged as a White Guard and 'reactionary émigré,' his name has become a synonym for formalism and frippery in verse.

Probably the only person not to notice the change was Balmont himself. He was very much a poetic Don Quixote, and such trifles as the realities of life did not in the least perturb him in his incessant pursuit of dreams. Even in the 1920's he seemed an anachronism; Bely called him the Russian Troubadour, and he served Poetry with all the devotion of a medieval knight, ready to sacrifice himself (and anyone else at hand) for the sake of his Lady Noble and Fair.

After 1918 Balmont became an émigré, living for the most part in France. Some spring within him broke, and he could only imitate his former self. Poverty and oblivion sharpened his nervousness, and his last

[2]   'My song is free — like the wind,' said Balmont.
        'Yes — and as sterile,' remarked Merezhkovsky.

years were darkened by fits of insanity. He died in Paris during the German occupation, at the age of 76, a pathetic remnant and reminder of a forgotten though glorious past.

VI   Theodore Teternikov, better known under his pen name of Sologub (1863–1927), the third pillar of Russian Modernism, was a Decadent born. This son of a tailor and a peasant woman had a twisted and complex personality, in which morbidity and various pathological drives were combined with extraordinary literary gifts. For almost thirty years he lived in small provincial towns fighting against terrific odds of poverty and anonymity. In 1892 — when he wrote 'Shadows' — he settled down in St. Petersburg, and for fifteen years taught or occupied administrative posts in various high schools, until he was able to resign in 1907 and devote himself entirely to writing poems, novels, tales, and dramas. This bald, bespectacled bureaucrat who exuded middle-class respectability was inconspicuous and self-effacing in social gatherings; yet underneath his placid manner and dull appearance he concealed a haughty, passionate, and perverted soul. A man of ambivalence and ambiguity, he maintained a surprising lucidity in all his maddening attitudes, and his poems were written in short, precise, although highly melodious, lines. 'On the visible surface art must be transparent and understandable to all,' Sologub maintained, and he avoided vagueness of expression while attaching symbolic meaning to the actual content of his works.

The core of his philosophy derived to some extent from Manichaeus the Persian. Sologub believed in the power of the Prince of Darkness, that Satan ruled all mankind, which was descended not from Adam but from Satan's own union with Eve, and the poet accepted the Prince of Evil as his master.

Lilith, the lamia of Hebrew demonology, was one of Sologub's key symbols; throughout his poems gargoyles, vampires, and succubae whirl in a saraband under the hostile, arrow-like rays of 'that fiery dragon, the sun.'

Sologub rejected the world of phenomena as an evanescent illusion, but he also spoke of the inanity of dreams, even though he saw in them the only outlet from deceptive and oppressive reality. One of the recurrent themes of his poetry is the transformation of Dulcinea, Don Quixote's Beautiful Lady of Tobosa, into Aldonsa, the fat and coarse kitchen maid. He often called life 'that plump, red-cheeked wench-housewife.' Despairing of this earth he exclaimed, 'What a burden it is to be among men!' and glorified isolation, visions, and sleep: 'Nothing in the world is more desirable than sleep — it has charm and silence.' Deliberately he shut himself behind a 'flaming circle' (the title of his best collection of poems, published in 1908) and, like a sorcerer, performed weird rites, called up spirits, and made other efforts to escape 'the prison of being.' Sologub was a solipsist; he created worlds in his own image, and in this realm of witchcraft, filled with hallucinations and inhabited by benign or malicious demons, he discovered the kinship of Freedom and Death, as well as of Death and Sex.

He belonged to the same generation as Chekhov, and many critics did their utmost to interpret his despondency as part of the mood of the gloomy 'eighties. Sologub's pessimism, however, had a strong romantic flavor; he was the victim of the romantic split between the ennui of reality and the boundless soaring of the imagination. He always contrasted frail beauty — often symbolized by the slender bodies of adolescent boys and girls — with the coarseness of everyday existence and the bestial ways of men. The most striking instances of this contrast are to be found in his prose, particularly in *Petty Demon* (1905), a novel that made him famous and assured him of a place among the classics.

Peredonov, the hero of this remarkable work, is a provincial teacher who is clearly akin to Karamazov the father and to Yudushka Golovlyov, but surpasses them both in meanness and malicious mischief; cowardice, coarseness, and crass stupidity make Peredonov a demon-like figure. His every act is disgusting: he spits in his mistress' face; he soils and rips off the wallpaper in his apartment to annoy his landlady; he steals a pound of raisins from his own cook in order to charge her later with theft. He mistreats his pupils, and he loathes anybody who looks clean and decent. Filth is his element; his imagination is as foul as are his words and deeds. He enjoys bringing about destruction and tears. Peredonov would feel decidedly at home in our own day: he writes an anonymous denunciation of a woman teacher because she wears a red blouse — and is therefore suspect of subversive ideas; he torments a good-looking schoolboy by accusing him of being a girl in disguise. Hatred and isolation drive him closer and closer to madness, and his persecution mania makes him resent not only people but also the objects around him. Everything strikes him as hostile or treacherous: the playing cards make faces at him, and he gouges out the eyes of the kings, queens, and knaves. Nightmares assail Peredonov; he sees enemies in his own home, and is convinced that his mistress has forced him into marrying her through a diabolical trick; he paints the letter P all over his body, to safeguard himself against being kidnapped or losing his identity. But all this struggle is useless: the Petty Demon, the gray, elusive Nedotykomka, gibbers at him from every corner, defying and infuriating him, until in a fit of rage and delirium Peredonov slits the throat of his best friend.

This tragedy of viciousness and madness is relieved only by the presence of Liudmila, an attractive girl, and Sasha, the boy whose handsome face had aroused Peredonov's suspicions. At first glance one might be inclined to assume that these two figures, represented in poetic, rhythmic style, were created as a counterpoise to Peredonov's vileness and folly. But Sologub's manner of presenting these two characters is highly equivocal: Liudmila is a perverted *demi-vierge,* and her morbid relationship to Sasha is based upon sadism and erotic whim. Peredonov had fallen victim to the forces of evil, to the bestiality of existence as personified by Nedotykomka, whereas Liudmila and Sasha, the symbols of Beauty, adore Death and Sex which belong to the realm of Satan, the Ruler.

Petty Demon was Sologub's attempt to overcome realism in prose by reverting to the Gogolian tradition, in which realistic detail is blended with dream-like fantasy. The introduction of supernatural and erotic elements into the narrative certainly put the novel outside the usual literary run. Yet, strangely enough, its best pages were those depicting the manners and antics of provincial society: the realistic part of Sologub's picture outweighed the symbolistic. He must have been aware of this, since he attempted the opposite in his later fiction. He failed, however, to achieve the horror-inspiring intensity of the *Petty Demon,* which has remained his sole masterpiece in prose. In *Created Legend* (1908–12), a series of highly sophisticated novels, the combination of realism (including current political events) with poetic visions resulted in a peculiar and not at all convincing amalgam. Trirodov, the hero of the Legend, is a magician who is followed by 'pale boys,' half-ghost, half-human; his house is a haven for revolutionaries as well as the scene of torture, flagellation, depraved love-making, and black magic. The action of the last part of the Legend is laid in the beautiful and fantastic country of Oile, ruled by Queen Ortruda, who is a reincarnation of one of Trirodov's mistresses; intrigues and conspiracies at her court reflect the vagaries of men on earth. The success of this involved, lengthy, and occasionally tiresome work can probably be attributed only to its erotic passages and touches of Satanism.

The opening words of *Created Legend* sound like a clarion call of faith, and they gained wide popularity among the Modernists: 'Mayst thou rot in darkness, thou dull life of everyday, or blaze in raging fires — I, the poet, will build above thee my created legend of the beautiful and the enchanted.' The legends Sologub went about creating actually had to do with strange children, with suicide and blood; these visions, 'sweeter than poison' (the title of one of his collections of tales), were a mixture of sensuality and idealistic flights, of contempt for the weak and of morbid pity. The repetitious images of bare feet, of lithe naked boys, of lithe naked slender virgins, and of swishing whips are mingled with descriptions of Oile, the land of harmony and music, or with invocation to Freedom and Beauty. And crowning this weird world of poetic theurgy there is Death — the Supreme Consolatrix. It would not be difficult for a psychiatrist to discern all the pathological drives that underlie Sologub's work: his sado-masochism, his death instinct, his schizoid ambivalence, and the alternation of his attractions and repulsions, which revealed his fundamental fear of reality.

Such a facile interpretation would not, however, explain the subtle fascination of his art. The short meters, the simple rhythms, and the plain colloquial words Sologub used in his poems do not seem to lose their incantatory quality or their crooning, warped musicality. A second reading of these unadorned, almost barren lines reveals obliquity and depth under a glossy polished surface. The perfect craftsmanship of these stanzas of longing, despair, and eerie dreams assures them an important place in Russian poetry. Sologub's prose, with the exception of *Petty Demon* and a few delightful short stories and plays, is uneven and involved: next to passages written in a remarkably beautiful style are patches of the purplest hue; his novels, like his works for the stage, are too precious and contrived.

Some of his contemporaries maintained that Sologub would have been a Decadent even if the Modernist movement had never existed: 'He fell from the skies as a Decadent.' Others claimed he reflected all the pathological twists and morbid trends of the romantic revival. And, finally, the Marxist critics affirmed that this poet (of proletarian origin) was the embodiment of the degeneration and psychological complexities of a culture that had been created by the nobility and was now entering the stage of premortal agonies.

After the Revolution Sologub found himself isolated and unwanted. The psychological strain, the dire material conditions, and the struggle for official permission to leave Russia made his life miserable; his wife (known as a writer and a translator under the name of Chebotarevskaya) committed suicide, and Sologub died a few years later (1927). His last work was significantly unrelated to the times: it was a collection of eighteenth-century pastorals, songs, and love sonnets, which sounded very strange amidst the ordeals of famine and civil war: they were called 'flowers upon graves' ('Only Love,' 'Incense,' 'Flute,' 1921–2).

VII   Another poet of Decadent moods was Zinaida Hippius (1867–1945), who came from a family of noblemen of German or Scandinavian origin. In 1889 she married Dimitry Merezhkovsky, and her literary career became closely identified with her husband's. Yet she had a distinct and different personality and did not always share Merezhkovsky's mystical and religious theories; on occasion it was Zinaida who influenced his literary and political evolution. She began in the 'nineties as a poet of supreme individualism and aestheticism. In sharp aphoristic verse she voiced her longing for 'that which is not of this earth' and denounced 'the boredom of reality.' In order to escape her tiresome and routine life, Hippius turned toward Dreams and Evil, both of which held equal attraction for her. In a poem dedicated to Satan, she exclaims: 'O wise Seducer, thou Spirit of Evil, art thou not the misunderstood Teacher of Great Beauty?' She compared her soul to a dread-inspiring snake, and glorified serpents as 'things devoid of shame.'

The Satanism that was genuine in Sologub was, however, nothing but a pose with Hippius. She was coldly intellectual; her ambiguity was deliberate and held obvious overtones of malevolence, almost of viciousness. Her intimate verse was divested of eloquence; it crept along like a snake and had the metallic sheen of certain reptiles. The poetess took delight in abstract questionings, in moral and psychological paradoxes framed in mellow and verbally elusive lines. She affirmed that 'only that which cannot be explained or understood gives joy,' yet her own writings, despite all their complexity, were cerebral; this can be seen particularly in her critical essays written under the pen name of Anton Krainy (Anton the Extreme). Her mordant remarks, her frequently unpleasant characterizations and wry humor, and her sense of the bizarre made these articles highly appreciated, though seldom liked, by the literary elite. Her collection *Living Faces,* published in 1928 and including sketches of Blok, Rozanov, Rasputin, and others, is the best specimen of her work in this genre.

After 1903 she displayed great interest in religious problems, but her writings of this period (*The Scarlet Sword,* 1906, and *Literary Diary,* 1908) can hardly be called successful. She was too cold and paradoxical and resorted too often to various devices of understatement for the purpose of stressing a hidden ambiguity of thought, setting traps for her reader to make him susceptible to any kind of religious affirmation. Her mind had a strong negative bent and she enjoyed the attitude of an onlooker who prefers moral and intellectual equivoque to clear-cut decisiveness. Plain colors scarcely existed for Hippius, but she knew all the shadings well. 'I pity men, I am ashamed of children,' runs one of her poems, written in 1906; 'the former will not believe me, the latter will not understand me; there is bitterness beneath, there is injury above, and I am between both, caught in a net, neither here nor there.' This mood is the *leit-motif* of her work, and that she was well aware of it is indicated by her poetic self-portrait: 'I am on the brink of a precipice — and I cannot fly into the skies above me. What am I to do — rebel or surrender? I have no courage to die or to live. God is close to me, yet I cannot pray; I yearn for affection, yet I cannot love.'

For a long period, between 1905 and 1917, her salon in St. Petersburg was an important literary center, and she exerted a definite influence on the second generation of Symbolists, who were attracted by her unusual intelligence, exceptional beauty, graceful and sophisticated personality, and inexorable critical sense. Although she maintained that she cared only for abstractions, for solitude, for all that is cryptic and not obvious, she attempted to enter the political scene.

A strange mixture of snobbishness, psychological interpretation of revolutionists, symbolism, and political innuendoes characterize her two novels: *Devil's Doll* (1911) and *Roman Czarevich* (1914), both done in a rather Dostoevskian manner. Her play, *The Green Ring* (1916), dealing with the emotional undercurrents of the youth of her time, was somewhat more interesting. A fierce anti-Communist, whose hatred of the Soviet regime is fully shown in her *Diary* (1921), she became an *émigré*, living most of the time in Paris. The articles, memoirs, and occasional poems she published in exile were all in her usual sophisticated manner, and added nothing new to her work. She outlived her husband by four years and died in 1945.

An intermediate position between the Decadents and Symbolists was occupied by Innokenty Annensky (1856–1909), an exquisite poet and the beloved teacher of the younger generation. His influence grew steadily; by 1917 he was recognized as one of the masters of Russian poetry. Son of a nobleman and brother of a highly respected Populist writer, Innokenty was an educator: for ten years he was headmaster and professor of Greek literature at the gymnasia of Czar's Hamlet. An outstanding scholar, he spent fifteen years translating Euripides, producing superb versions. No less remarkable were his translations from the French (*The Parnassians and the Accursed Poets,* 1904) and his fine critical essays done in an Impressionistic manner (*Books of Reflections,* 1906–9). But his main work was *The Cypress Casket* (complete edition, 1910), a collection of highly subjective and original poems of enchanting, filigreed craftsmanship.

The three themes of poetry, Annensky maintained, are suffering, death, and beauty — and to these he devoted his murmurous rhythms. He felt intensely 'the pangs of being,' the decay of things, and that subtle melancholy which a flutter of beauty — a woman, a flower, a quotation from Aeschylus — evokes in those who are disturbed by the coarseness and inanity of the world. With a refinement bordering on snobbishness he returned again and again to the same themes: the 'venom of poetry,' the 'intoxication of creative work,' the 'opium of dreaming' — to the tedium and futility of life, which can be dispelled only through art and love. This aesthetic attitude was, however, strangely blended with a sense of genuine compassion for 'all things that suffer." Annensky felt compassion not only for men and animals but also for objects, and his poems on vernal landscapes (he hated spring) or on flowers cease to be mere descriptions: in the light of pity and preciousness things start to move and distill a sweet poison of resignation.

The delicate insinuating musicality and the emotional symbolism of his lines are conveyed in changing, though perfectly constructed, meters. Nothing is loose in his poems; poignancy and concentration are blended. This poet's formal achievements were so varied that their echo resounds not only in the works of such Symbolists as Blok, but also in such anti-Symbolists as Gumilev, Pasternak, and Mandelstamm. Annensky's works never reached a large public but they had an indisputable place in the revival of modern Russian verse.

6

MYSTICS, PHILOSOPHERS, AND MARXISTS

I   THE AESTHETIC REBELLION of the
'nineties was concerned primarily with problems of form, and its main
impact was felt in poetry and the arts. Briussov, Balmont, and (to a certain extent) Sologub represented stylistic innovations and a new sensitivity. Yet the revolt against rationalism had a much wider range: the
Russian Decadents became the Symbolists. The influence of Nietzsche was
replaced by an allegiance to idealistic philosophy; the individualists and
literary aesthetes turned into God-seekers, mystics, and reformers of Christianity. At the beginning of the century they merged with various groups
of philosophers and theologians and a religious movement began among
the intellectuals.

The roots of this movement were manifold. There was a revival in
the Greek Orthodox Church, partly linked to the cult of the mystic saint,
Seraphim of Sarov (1759–1833), and to the activities of Father John of
Cronstadt (1829–1908), who advocated general confessions during religious services, with thousands of people shouting out their sins and sob-
bing for forgiveness. The Slavophile tradition of religious messianism
was not yet completely exhausted, and three great Russians attempted
to renew faith in Christianity: Dostoevsky made an appeal for the expansion of the national creed into a universal one; Tolstoy preached primitive
Christianity free from the pressure of any particular denomination; and
Solovyov strove for the union of all Churches. The trends in Western philosophy that were about to lead to Bergson and neo-idealism also created
a favorable atmosphere for a religious renaissance. The heritage of Hegel
and the German idealists was still alive in Russia: it had been preserved
by the Slavophiles and certain mild liberals. Various religious trends had
been latent in Populism. Two other features were typical of this religious

revival: its leaders were not only thinkers but poets and writers, and belonged to literature as much as to religious philosophy, or even more; and all of them had progressed from metaphysics to sociology, thus moving in the general direction of cultural evolution in Russia. Moreover, they hoped to 'meet the people' on religious grounds just as Populists and Marxists endeavored to meet them on the roads to Socialism.

These traits are exemplified in Vladimir Solovyov (1853–1900), the man whom some Western scholars consider the first and only Russian philosopher of the nineteenth century. The son of a prominent historian and related on his mother's side to the Ukrainian philosopher Skovoroda, Solovyov was born into a family of highly cultured noblemen. He received an excellent education, mastered eight languages, and at the age of twenty-seven, after extensive study at home and abroad, was appointed to teach philosophy at the University of Moscow. His academic career, begun so brilliantly, was interrupted, however, in 1881 because of a speech he made against the execution of the terrorists who had assassinated Alexander II, and by his plea for clemency in a letter to the new Emperor. After his resignation from the university Solovyov devoted himself to writing and published a number of treatises — among them *The God-Man* (1881), *Religious Foundations of Life* (1884), *Russia and the Universal Church* (1889), *Justification of Good* (1897) — as well as literary, political, and historical articles and collections of poems. A philosopher who led the life of an ascetic, a writer who aroused violent polemics in the daily press, a poet who held the younger generation of Symbolists under his spell, he left a profound imprint on many fields of Russian life and thought.

Solovyov's personality was complex and often contradictory and, according to Andrei Bely, his physical appearance betrayed his inner conflicts: he was a giant with weak arms and hands; there was a disproportion between his long legs and short torso; his inspired eyes hardly matched his heavy, sensual mouth; he spoke like a prophet, lived the life of a monk, yet, like a child, could not resist the temptation of a bonbon or a jelly tart.

Solovyov's metaphysical doctrine, in which Plato and the Gnostics were blended with the German idealistic philosophy of Hegel, Kant, and (in part) Schopenhauer, was profoundly religious and mystical. As a philosophy it may be considered eclectic — for which some critics have reproached him — yet nobody could deny its broad sweep and its ecstatic intensity. His main task was to prove the conformity of Christian faith to universal and eternal truth and the oneness of knowledge with being. One of the crucial points of his system (of which we are summarizing but a fragment) was his concept of man as a link between nature and God.

In Christ's incarnation he saw the evidence that man can be redeemed and become divine. The purpose of human history, which Solovyov conceived as part of a cosmic process, is the marriage of humanity to divinity, by which the duality of the divine and human, of the spiritual and the natural, would be overcome. This process, which also encompasses man's regeneration, is conceivable only as a collective endeavor within the framework of family, nation, or mankind; individual striving for the Supreme Good and communion. with God has to be fulfilled through collective unity.[1]

This fundamentally optimistic conception of the future deification of mankind was bolstered by Solovyov's faith in the objective existence of Good. From the doctrine of divine incarnation and atonement he derived the conclusion that evil and strife in man were overpowered by the Son of God and the Son of Man, and that history, despite all the deviations and temporary victories of the forces of darkness, will come finally to its mystical fulfilment. These basic principles determined his social and political opinions. He wanted to blend the practical and the ideal, and affirmed that 'the soul cannot remain in contemplation alone; it lives in practical reality.' In the same way that mysticism, in his system, underlies all creation, and theology underlies all knowledge, the Church was for Solovyov the foundation of all social institutions, and a 'moral society' could be built only as a spiritual union. Theocracy was bound to become the next stage of the development of mankind. This, however, is hindered by the conflict separating the various Christian denominations.

Like Chaadaiev,[2] he pointed out the negative influence of Byzantium, with its contradiction between monastic saintliness and secular corruption, upon the Russian Church, and contended that East and West should not always be opposed to each other. In one of his poems he asked those who spoke about the 'twilight of the West' and praised the virtues of Eastern Orthodoxy: 'Which East do you want to become — the East of Xerxes, or the East of Christ?' This intransigent idealist also refused to find nothing but virtues in Greek Orthodoxy and nothing but faults in Roman Catholicism. On the contrary, he was strongly attracted by the universality of the latter, and acknowledged its doctrinal and organizational strength. A scholarly analysis of the doctrine and ritual of the two Churches made him advocate their reunion. At one time he dreamed of some sort of Pan-Catholicism under the aegis of the Russian Czar. This put him in a very difficult position. After he had received a Papal benediction in 1886 for his efforts toward the reunion of the two Churches, the Procurator of the Russian Synod (the highest administrative organ of

[1] The Russian term *sobornost* is translated as 'congregationalism' or 'conciliarity.'
[2] See *The Epic of Russian Literature*, pp. 144–8.

the Greek Orthodox Church) forbade him to take part in any public activities, deeming him 'harmful both to the State and to the Church.' His former friends, the Slavophiles, resented his attacks against their beliefs in Russia as the Third Rome and in the messianic role of Greek Orthodoxy, 'the sole beholder of truth.' Solovyov criticized Slavophilism as a doctrine of 'zoomorphic nationalism' since he always considered religious and moral values to be far superior to any nationalistic sentiments and insisted that national problems would find their solution in free theocracy. The only concession he was ready to make was that 'the Russians are a theocratic people and seekers after the truth.'

Toward the end of his life he became more than ever convinced that the final victory of the Good would be preceded by wars, tribulations, and the temptations of Antichrist. The highroad of history was, in his opinion, 'coming to a dead end,' and Europe, Russia, and Asia were approaching a crisis. In *Three Conversations* (1900), and particularly in the chapter called 'The Tale of the Antichrist,' which may well be compared with Dostoevsky's 'Legend of the Grand Inquisitor,' Solovyov unrolled apocalyptic visions and spoke with a prophet's voice. Expectation of the Second Coming runs throughout the 'Tale,' which tells how 'Christ will come amid clouds, clad in great might and glory,' and will be met by Prester John, Pope Peter, and Paul the Confessor, symbolizing Greek Orthodoxy, Roman Catholicism, and Protestantism. The Second Coming would, however, be preceded by the reign of Antichrist, which would in its turn be ushered in by the Yellow Peril: Asiatic hordes led by the Japanese and the Chinese would overrun Russia and Europe. Pan-Mongolism seemed to him the next manifestation of evil and an imminent threat to Christianity.

Solovyov dealt the final blow to religious Slavophilism and to the official smugness of high ecclesiastics, thus putting a close to an entire chapter of romantic nationalism. His appeals for the universality of Christendom and his theories of the deification of mankind, as well as his doctrine of salvation through collective effort (especially his insistence upon the 'realization of self in and through humanity'), led to a renascence of Russian philosophy and particularly of Russian religious thought. Berdiaev, Bulgakov, Florensky, Ern, Elchaninov, and scores of other major and minor thinkers followed, and the whole religious movement connected with the Symbolists bore his impress.[3]

The subtlety of Solovyov's mind and the purity of his heart were best expressed in his poetry. Although his poetic work (a single volume of

[3] His influence is also clearly apparent among the Russian intellectuals who have been active in promoting, under the aegis of the Vatican, the Catholicism of the Eastern Rite; many of his followers among Russian *émigrés* after the Revolution became converted to this brand of Catholicism.

collected poems, published after his death) was narrow in scope and subject matter, it exerted a singularly profound influence. He was always devoted to *belles lettres* and was personally acquainted with the leading writers of his time. He was close to Fet, although he reproached the aging poet for his reactionary views, his paganism, and lack of Christian faith, and he was a friend of Dostoevsky, whose attempt to reconcile the Slavophile messianic idea with Western universalism was certainly due to Solovyov's influence. The great novelist and the mystic had gone together to the Monastery of Optina Pustyn to visit Ambrose the Elder, who served as a prototype for the saintly Zossima in *The Brothers Karamazov*.[4] Solovyov also has a definite place in Russian literature as a critic, a translator of ancient and modern poets, and a writer of delightful and witty letters that rival Chekhov's.

At the beginning of the Modernist movement Solovyov laughed at Balmont and Briussov and parodied them in popular jingles (his puns and humorous pieces are lively and amusing). This did not prevent him, however, from contributing to the provocative *World of Art* and from asserting that Symbolism was the very foundation of art. 'Symbols are not an illusion but reality itself,' said Solovyov, and his own poems are highly symbolic. Spiritual eroticism was one of the main themes of his subjective and melodious lyrics, with their enchanting prosody and an ethereal touch that was all his own. A vision of Beauty, which is the symbol of Eternal Womanhood, or of Sophia, the Wisdom of the Scriptures, illuminates these Platonic stanzas, which are full of subtle musicality and eerie allusions. One of his best-known poems, 'The Three Trysts,' tells of Her whose voice spoke to him first when he was nine years old, and again in his youth, when he visited the British Museum, and still later in the Egyptian desert, near Cairo. She made him perceive 'the Shimmer of Divinity, the immortal Purple Crown under the coarse crust of matter.' Playful recitals alternate with lyrical flights, ironical overtones with mystical elation, and the poem ends with a typical Solovyov image: in his vision he affirms the triumph of life over death and snaps the chain of time, drawing near to his Beloved, whose name he dare not utter.

The vision of Truth and Beauty is, to Solovyov, blended with the symbol of Love: the Virgin of the Iridescent Gates, whose eyes gaze into his soul. And, to him, the Eternal Feminine is not Venus Anadyomene, not Aphrodite rising from deceptive sea-foam, but Beauty Eternal, which shines within the center of the universe. He divided all phenomena into the physical ('the deceitful appearance of the world'), the spiritual, and

---

[4] The contention that Dostoevsky used Solovyov as the model for Alyosha Karamazov (as suggested by d'Herbigny in *The Russian Newman*) does not seem well founded.

the mystical — and strove to rise toward the last through ecstasy and exaltation, in which the essence of things was revealed to him in symbols.

The second generation of Symbolists, particularly Blok, felt the charm of these pure and ardent images, and were attracted by Solovyov's 'dry flame.' Symbolism as faith, symbols as signs of ultimate reality, and poetry as intuitive perception of Truth and God: these were the lessons drawn by the young Symbolists from Solovyov's works. They overlooked his initial strictures on the new school and acclaimed him as one of their masters, whose mystical leanings coincided with their own aspirations.

II   A strange mixture of decadence and Christianity is to be found in Vassily Rozanov (1856–1919), one of the most complex and contradictory figures of modern Russian literature. Of middle-class origin, at one time a teacher in provincial schools and later a civil servant, he presented puzzling contrasts in his thought and behavior. Nihilist, cynic, and sinner, he aspired to saintliness and made professions of ardent faith; in his writings, as in his life, he displayed utter sincerity side by side with reptilian hypocrisy. As a journalist, he contributed for many years to the reactionary newspaper *New Times,* in which he defended autocracy, while at the same time he was attacking it in the liberal *Russian Word,* under the pen name of Varvarin. He launched several anti-Semitic campaigns and revived the calumny of the blood-ritual — yet professed his love for Judaism in *The Apocalypse of Our Time*. He was a great admirer of Nietzsche, and claimed to be a disciple of Dostoevsky, whose former mistress, Apollinaria Suslova, Rozanov married for complex sexual and psychological reasons.

Yet despite his moral somersaults and dubious attitudes Rozanov exerted a definite literary influence, and the Decadents as well as the Symbolists admired his strange and ambiguous writings. Joining the new school in the late 'nineties, he formulated its individualistic and anti-social tendency. 'Personal life,' wrote Rozanov, 'is above all things. Nobody has ever stated this; I am the first to do so. One may simply stay home and pick one's nose — or stare at the sunset . . .' 'Each soul is a Phoenix,' he declared later, 'and each soul must burn, and the great bonfire of these burned souls creates the flame of history.' His best writings are highly subjective and amazingly frank: they belong to the genre known as *documents humains* which appeared after World War I, and are kindred to many of the confessions turned out by European writers. 'Every movement of my soul,' he wrote, 'is accompanied by verbal enunciation. I have always written, and I continue to write, in profound anguish — in order to break in some way the circle of loneliness.' He had little respect for literary work and painfully resented the limitations of words as a means of communication. He felt, in general, that all cultural activity was doomed, and he shared Nietzsche's views on the decadence of Christian civilization. His criticism went beyond historical cycles, however, and attacked the heart of the matter: 'It inspires horror to think that each life experience is poured into a gushing, living word — and that is the end of it, the life experience is dead then. Man's temperature, his body temperature, has dropped because of the word.'

In *The Fallen Leaves* (volume I, 1913; volume II, 1915), one of his most remarkable works, he speaks of his own writing: 'I have been hovering around themes, I have never flown at them. This hovering was my life. Themes as if in a dream — one, another, ever so many . . . and I have forgotten them all. I shall not remember them in my grave. In the afterlife I will find myself without themes. The Lord will ask me: "What have you accomplished?" — "Nothing." ' Despite this denial of consistency Rozanov did have recurring themes: under the ashes of sadness, loneliness, and negation the theme of religious anxiety glowed in his book with a true flame. His interest in Western literature and philosophy did not prevent him from being a man of the soil, rooted in the Russian way of life and typically national in his literary style and his manner of thinking. For a time he sympathized with the Slavophiles and fenced with the 'rationalistic spirit' of Europe; next he sang the praises of 'Church, fatherland, and family' as the true foundations and guarantees of Russia's stability; still later he became engrossed in mystical and religious issues. He identified them as the aspects of one and the same enigma: 'Night-Mystery-Religion-Sex.'

Rozanov was instrumental in the move from aestheticism and individualistic aristocratism toward the religious quest, and was one of the most active and influential members of the Religious and Philosophical Society (from which he was expelled in 1913 as an obnoxious anti-Semite, after the infamous Beilis affair). His remarkable book on Dostoevsky's 'Legend of the Grand Inquisitor' (1891, reprinted in 1906) and dozens of other works (among them *Literary Essays,* published in 1899–1900, *In the World of the Obscure and the Uncertain,* 1901, *The Dark Face,* 1911, *Solitaria,* 1912, *Moonlight People,* 1913), some of which were written as confessions in a queer, aphoristic form, reveal his tortuous modes of thinking.

The problem of God was for Rozanov merely another facet of the problem of sex. With an insistence bordering on the neurotic, he asserted that 'the link between sex and God is greater than the bond between mind and God, or even conscience and God.' In his paradoxical book *The Family Problem in Russia* (1903) he contended that the idea of sin and the rejection of sex and earthly pleasures were among the main errors of

Greek Orthodoxy. 'The functions of the flesh are declared sinful, yet they are of the utmost importance. Eating, drinking, making love . . . each is equally important.' The idea that 'man is a natural Christian in sorrow and a natural Pagan in happiness' appalled him. It simply meant that Christianity had turned its back on the world and that the Gospel was 'the book of exhaustions and lassitude.' This he opposed by claiming that 'Christianity ought, at least in part, to become phallic.'

'There is no spiritual friendship without carnal attraction. The body is the beginning of the spirit. The root of the spirit. And the spirit is the smell of the body.' In his efforts to trace the spiritual in the carnal Rozanov indulged in details of bodily functions; some of his pages have a distinct aroma of bedchamber and bathroom. He himself declared: 'My works are blended with neither water nor blood but semen.' His eroticism was, however, not unlike Sologub's, strongly tinged by the idea of death; in fact, when Rozanov speaks of sex and death, he is speaking of God. Little wonder, then, that his ideas were explosive, although in his private life he was considered one of the pillars of the official Church — as was his master Dostoevsky, with whom he had so many traits in common. His last book, *The Apocalypse of Our Times* (1919), contains many passages that are reminiscent of Nietzschean attacks against Christianity: the philosopher's influence on Rozanov is obvious and goes beyond some of the latter's aphorisms, such as 'I am no scoundrel, to be talking about morality.' Rozanov reproaches Christ for his failure to build a decent life on earth — once more the theme of the 'Legend of the Grand Inquisitor' — and alludes to 'an error committed at the Creation — which was a surprise even to the Almighty.' Christianity does not seem capable of repairing the damage wrought by this error, and if it cannot straighten the matter out, it ought to be discarded. 'The sun existed before Christianity, and it is not going to black out even if Christianity should come to an end.' Thus Rozanov, the faithful churchgoer, gnaws at the very foundations of Christianity and hints at the duality of Good and Evil almost in the Manichean sense of a Sologub. He affirmed God in his mature years, yet when he became an old man, he practically accepted the co-existence of God and the Devil.

Rozanov's works were to cast a spell on scores of writers of such various caliber and personality as Hippius and Merezhkovsky, Annensky and Blok, Artzybashev and Remizov. His 'utter nakedness,' as he styled his manner of presenting the bare essentials of concepts and sensations, his extraordinary style, his blending of despair and faith, of mysticism and brute earthiness, of eroticism and awareness of death, all assured him a place of his own in modern Russian literature. Some critics found his writings an outrageous example of moral disintegration, of a putrescent and nihilistic lust for negation, but it would be futile to deny their depth and artistic power. His intimate diaries, his razor-edged literary confessions, which disclose sudden chasms of sensuality, mysticism, or sophistry, belong among the most curious literary documents of the twentieth century — and this despite all the masks under which Rozanov attempted to hide his tormented visage.

III   A religious quest lay behind the varied activities of Dimitry Merezhkovsky (1866–1941), who was poet, novelist, essayist, critic, and moralist. He, too, turned from aestheticism to Christianity, although he was never a Decadent in the strict sense of the term. The son of a nobleman of Ukrainian descent who served in the Czar's private chancellery, Dimitry was influenced, during his student years at the University of St. Petersburg, by Mikhailovsky and Populism; later he turned to Dostoevsky, and finally, discovering a new world in Poe and Baudelaire, he joined the Modernists. As one of their pioneers he began publishing his poetry in 1888 and, in 1892, brought out *Symbols,* a collection of verse.

At the beginning of his career Merezhkovsky laid stress on the 'liberation from life through Beauty,' and on dreams of Hellenic perfection. A man of learning and erudition, he traveled widely in Europe and through the Orient, was profoundly impressed by Greece and Italy, translated Sophocles into Russian, and wrote *Eternal Companions* (1892), a collection of essays on the great figures in world literature. A Westernizer and an aesthete, he was nevertheless perpetually haunted by philosophical and moral problems. By 1900 he had completed the *Christ and Antichrist* trilogy, which brought him fame and in which all his didactic, aesthetic, and religious drives found expression (*Julian the Apostate, or the Death of the Gods,* 1893; *Leonardo da Vinci, or the Gods Resurgent,* 1896; *Peter and Alexis, or the Antichrist,* 1902). These historical novels were so full of material from easily recognizable sources that Minsky called the author the Napoleon of Quotations.

Partly under the influence of Nietzsche and partly driven by his religious zeal, Merezhkovsky presented European history in terms of a struggle between paganism and Christianity, between the flesh and the spirit, between knowledge and faith. His Julian is torn between Christ and Apollo; as a child, clad in somber monastic robes, he ecstatically adores the white nudity of a marble Aphrodite; he seeks the divine brightness of Hellas. But the triumphant new religion destroys the beauty of statues; a mob of Christian fanatics kills Euphorion, the adorable adolescent, and pulls down a pagan temple: the collapse of its columns announces the death of the gods. The Renaissance resurrects the deities of Olympus, who are beyond good and evil, and their magic influence makes artists like Leonardo and Botticelli vacillate between the humility of Christ and the sensuous allurements of classic freedom. Leonardo, who never takes sides, is half Christian, half pagan. He is aware that perfect knowledge means perfect love but is unable to reconcile the contraries. His equivocal art embodies the indecisions and the dichotomy of the Western soul; his disciple Giovanni Boltraffio, a pious Catholic, dies from the embraces of the white She-Devil, who is none other than Aphrodite and, moreover, a succuba. And, finally, Christ and Antichrist join battle in Russia at the turn of the eighteenth century. Peter the Great, depicted as a Leonardo of action, is ruthless and drunk with will to power, even though he is torn by his contradictions. He clashes with his superstitious and narrow-minded son Alexis, who adheres to a rigid faith — and blood, death, and sufferings ensue from this conflict. Christ and Antichrist are contending everywhere, and Christianity is but one phase in the universal struggle toward the ultimate goal — the religion of the Holy Trinity.

Merezhkovsky, bogged down in Hegelian dialectics, sought a solution of the crisis that, in his opinion, was undermining and destroying mankind in the espousal of Christianity with paganism. He spoke of the coming of the Kingdom of the Holy Ghost, when, according to the prophecies of the Apocalypse, 'the Kingdoms of this world . . . become the Kingdoms of our Lord, and of His Christ.' [5] He persisted for many years in playing with and upon contraries, opposing in almost geometrical fashion Christ and Antichrist, God and the devil, 'the precipice above and the precipice below,' the ecstasy of sin and the raptus of saintliness — the 'sacred flesh' and the 'fleshless sacredness.' He used the same method in his essays 'Tolstoy and Dostoevsky' (1901), 'Gogol' (1909), 'Lermontov, Poet of the Superman' (1909), contrasting Tolstoy, as 'seer of the flesh,' with Dostoevsky, as 'seer of the spirit,' or uniting 'the extremes of beauty and ugliness,' or exalting Hermaphrodites as the symbol of a Being who would overcome the limitations of the sexes, and so on and on.

Although the pattern of all these highly sophisticated theories was always the same, Merezhkovsky's religious and political views were in constant flux. At the beginning of the twentieth century he attempted to combine his mystical longings with Orthodox Christianity. As a God-seeker he was active from 1903 to 1907 in editing the magazine *The New Path* and in promoting the Religious and Philosophical Society, in which Symbolists hobnobbed with priests and monks discussed the doctrines of Solovyov with university professors. It was during this period that Merezhkovsky attacked the godless attitude of Russian intellectuals, con-

[5] *Revelation*, XI:15.

demning their radical utilitarianism and advocating the acceptance of the Orthodox Church by the intelligentsia. Dostoevsky and Solovyov were his masters at the time, and he found the idea of a Church-State exceedingly attractive. The revolutionary tide of 1905, however, changed his attitude again. He thundered against autocracy ('that offspring of Antichrist'), berated the state Church ('that stronghold of reaction') for its subservience, and sympathized with the revolutionaries to such an extent that he had to go abroad to escape police reprisals. He maintained that the Russians would never accept any middle-of-the-road solutions: they were more conscious of the imminent collapse of civilization than anyone else was, and were rather pleased about the whole thing. 'They are longing for the beginning of the end,' he asserted. Atonement and apocalyptic visions of universal upheaval became his favorite topics. Was his attitude simply an imitation of Solovyov's, or was it a genuine apprehension of the crisis the Revolution of 1905 seemed to have brought in its wake? At any rate, Merezhkovsky talked as if a mystical illumination had revealed to him the destinies of mankind in general and of Russia in particular.

He remained in France from 1906 to 1912; upon his homecoming security officials at the border seized the manuscript of his play, *Alexander I*. Merezhkovsky was, however, far from a subversive: as a matter of fact he had, as far back as 1906, published *The Coming Ham,* a treatise that depicted collectivism as the reign of philistines, half-wits, and latent criminals not unlike Dostoevsky's Smerdyakov, and pleaded with the revolutionaries to replace socialism with Christianity. After 1909 his writings became foggy; he adopted a high-flown prophetic style often verging on gibberish, and gradually lost his prominence as spokesman for the religious revival. The October Revolution made him an *émigré;* in France he rallied about him a group of intellectuals, old and young, who carried on the St. Petersburg tradition of religious and literary discussions. Merezhkovsky declared himself a mortal foe of the Communists, whom he termed the servants of Antichrist; toward the end of his life he wrote an apology for Mussolini, spoke of fascism in either equivocal or favorable terms, and even welcomed Hitler's invasion of Russia as a 'crusade against the enemies of mankind.' Shortly before his death, however, he seemed to have become disappointed in the Nazis. In exile he continued to be just as industrious as he had been in Russia, and turned out treatises, biographies, essays, and novels — *The Mystery of the Three* (1925), *The Messiah* (1926), *Napoleon* (1929), *Jesus the Unknown* (1932), *Dante* (1939), and so on. But all these books are pale and verbose.

Merezhkovsky's merits and defects as a novelist are most perceptible in the Christ and Antichrist trilogy, which has been translated into many languages and has enjoyed wide popularity in Europe and, to some extent, in America. Merezhkovsky had a remarkable gift for the historical panorama, done in mosaic and purple patches. He utilized original documents, excerpts, and other scholarly tidbits in order to re-create the flavor of a period. All this disparate material was, however, chosen with an eye to proving a thesis. His protagonists are consequently mere abstracts, mere shadowy proponents of concepts. Julian, Leonardo, Alexis, Peter — they all talk like Russian God-seekers and Symbolists of the twentieth century. Outwardly they are historically correct, but hardly ever are they humanly plausible. They all lack life, charm, and spontaneity. While Merezhkovsky's landscapes, portraits, historical details, and still-life are painted with a visual lavishness that accounts for the popularity of his 'restorations' or antiquarian novels, the psychology of his protagonists and the structure of his narrative are cerebral and artificial. His dialectical approach to art was always gelid: Bely compared his books with the Aurora Borealis.

The importance of Merezhkovsky goes beyond his historical novels, which he wrote by manipulating his files much as a librarian compiling a catalogue. He represented a current of thought and a cultural tendency; his essays are therefore of importance mainly in the study of the pre-Revolutionary intelligentsia. Despite their one dimensional philosophy, they aroused new ideas, stirred up controversies, and in general served as a catalyctic agent for the religious revival in Russia at the beginning of this century. Today, however, they are appallingly dated. The modern reader feels very strongly that Merezhkovsky's mysticism is merely verbal, that this expert rhetorician was interested solely in intellectual *escrime*. He knew how to say things brilliantly and how to imply more than he said; he was adept at the mystical *appel* and the metaphysical feint; but his profundity is quite illusory and there is a void, a vacuity, beneath all his esoteric expressions, transcendent hints, pompous symbols, and carefully selected contrasts.

He always talks of the ultimate enigmas — God, Satan, Death, Revolution — but as a literary critic rather than as a philosopher. He proceeds not from the reality of life, not from direct observation, but from some book, some document, some author. He thus becomes merely an echo of all that he has read. His attempts to give the impression of one 'staggered' and 'troubled' could not hide the fact that his mind was always cold and poised. Despite his warm voice — surprisingly strong and sonorous for one of his small frame (he was exceedingly short) — and despite the pretended fervency of his polemics, this encyclopedic mystic never liked human beings, and remained throughout all his activity anemic and lifeless.

IV   Three other philosophers were active in the struggle against 'vulgar positivism' — although operating from entirely different premises. Nicholas Fedorov (1840–1903), librarian of the Moscow Rumiantzev Museum, impressed his friends by his ascetic and saintly life as well as by his doctrine. He maintained that mankind has but one supreme goal — victory over death — and that all forces should be united for this common cause. Only by eliminating death and resurrecting the dead would man solve all the conflicts of his condition and achieve the heights of mystical fulfilment. Although Fedorov's main work, *The Philosophy of the Common Cause* (1906–13), never found a wide response, it was admired by a group of faithful followers.

Nicholas Berdiaev (1874–1948), a nobleman in whom the blood of the Russian gentry was mingled with that of French aristocracy (he was descended, on his mother's side, from the Comtesse de Choiseul), began as a Marxist, was arrested and exiled, but at the turn of the century became a disciple of Solovyov. During and after the Revolution of 1905 he advocated a spiritual interpretation of man and universe and was active in the religious revival. In the Religious and Philosophical Society he, together with Bishop Sergius (who was to become the Patriarch of Moscow), represented a current of progressive orthodoxy. His inner evolution, however, led him away from the Church and he formulated his own system of ideas, in which the recognition of mystical experience and of God as spiritual reality was combined with a growing interest in man's destiny on earth and with a cyclical conception of history. Arrested in 1921 by the Soviet government, he was banished from Russia and became a political *émigré*. He lived in Germany, and finally settled down in Clamart, a suburb of Paris, and won international reputation as one of the most profound exponents of Russian religious thought. In books such as *A New Middle Ages* (1923), *The Destiny of Man* (1931), *The Meaning of History* (1923), *Spirit and Reality* (1937), and *The Origin of Russian Communism* (1937), he analyzed the moral crisis of Western civilization and defended the concept of personality as opposed to the totalitarian absorption of the individual and to the egotistical, narrow assertion of self. Christianity to Berdiaev was identical with humanism, and he felt that the idea of social justice was inherent in the religion that was born from the sacrifice of the Son of God for the regeneration of mankind. According to his interpretation, a deep religiosity and universalism had permeated the whole development of Russian intelligentsia, including the Communists. The metaphysical and the social were but two aspects of the same quest for truth; despite all their short-comings and crimes, Socialists and Maximalists strove unconsciously for a harmony between the human and the divine. This conception determined Berdiaev's position as a 'left-wing' philosopher: he attempted to spiritualize modern social and political aspirations toward a better society while assuming a strong anti-capitalist attitude and defending the ideal of freedom. Like Dostoevsky he had faith in the Russian idea as religious universality, and he followed Solovyov in the latter's concepts of salvation through collectivity and of the supreme metaphysical value of humanity.

Berdiaev, the Christian philosopher, was the last survivor of the trend that began with Chaadaiev and Khomiakov [6] and continued with Dostoevsky and Solovyov, and his connection with the Slavophiles and also with Hegelian philosophy was apparent. Leo Shestov (the pen name of Leo Schwartzmann, 1866–1938) represented a completely different intellectual climate. His God was irrational and beyond good and evil; although Shestov identified religious quest as one of mankind's central ideas, he attacked from the positions of relativism and skepticism the traditional concepts of radical intelligentsia. A solitary thinker, he followed Nietzsche in the 'revaluation' of all accepted formulas and dogmas. The Symbolists liked his essays on Shakespeare, his books on *Good in the Teachings of Tolstoy and Nietzsche* (1900) and *Dostoevsky and Nietzsche* (1901), as well as his articles on writers and philosophers (from Ibsen and Chekhov to Husserl and Kirkegaard), in which he sharply criticized rationalism in art and philosophy. Shestov questioned the very foundations of logic, metaphysics, and culture, and shattered the orderly outlines of many philosophical systems. In general he distrusted reason and spoke with scorn about futile attempts of logical minds who would like to imprison reality within rationalistic blueprints.

Shestov's bold challenge went beyond the expectations of the Symbolists. In a brilliant paradoxical manner this Russian interpreter of Kirkegaard and the predecessor of the existentialists hailed simplicity and truthfulness and the scarcity of rhetorical ornament as the main virtues of Russian literature. He also claimed that the lack of cultural fetters led the Russians to a bizarre freedom of thought: they never ceased quarreling with the universe and re-examining most of the basic values. 'We left all that is limited to the European bourgeoisie.' The Russian feels he can do anything — a sort of provincial courage — and therefore is afraid of nothing. Not systems of ideas but contradictions of ideas, not affirmations but questions, not logical concepts but anarchical outbursts,

[6] See Slonim, op. cit. ch. 7.

not structure but fantasy — these are the highest achievements of the explosive Russian mind. And its quest is beyond truth and falsehood — which are both rational concepts; it is an exploration of the free and unimaginable regions of Supreme Irrationality we call God.

The son of a wealthy Jewish merchant, this nihilistically minded writer, whose words had a peculiar corrosive quality, had to leave Russia after 1917 as a 'scion of the bourgeois class,' about which he had written such derogatory things. He lived in Berlin and Paris, dying in the latter as a political *émigré*. His most significant books published in exile were *Dostoevsky — Tolstoy* (1923), *The Borders of Life* (1927), *The Shackled Parmenides* (1930), and *Kirkegaard and Existential Philosophy* (1936).

v   Merezhkovsky, as well as the entire religious movement in Russia, had reverted to these very problems, to the same didactic, moralistic attitude, that they had rejected so completely during the Decadent period. The circle had closed, and the former aesthetes and individualists talked of God-in-mankind and the Christian State. Solovyov's collective salvation, Rozanov's criticism of the Church's neglect of the flesh, Merezhkovsky's search for the Third Reign as a solution to the historical crisis were all inspired by the same quest for a better world that had been the basis for the socialism of the Populists and Marxists; in Russia religion and art were expected to solve moral and political problems. Despite the differences of their doctrines, neo-mystics and revolutionaries, neo-Christians and atheistic radicals had something in common: they were bound to find a meeting ground and even to collaborate.

The evolution of the rebels of yesterday corresponded to the changes throughout Russian society: the reaction and the oppressive atmosphere of the 'eighties and the early 'nineties were giving place to a new upsurge of national activity. While the Decadents were experimenting with new rhythms and the mystics were discussing the Supreme Good and the Second Advent, social and economic conditions were undergoing a transformation. The famine of 1891 and the death of Alexander III in 1894 marked the end of moral and political stagnation, although it is true that the autocratic regime did not show any signs of progress or good will. When the *Zemstvo* of Tver, acting as a mouthpiece for the enlightened aristocracy, addressed a petition of reforms to Nicholas II (1894–1918), the new Czar saw their liberal aspirations as 'senseless dreams and dangerous fantasies.' He intended to continue the policies of his father, whom he had both respected and feared. As a man and as a ruler, however, Nicholas II was inferior to his sturdy predecessor. The last of the Czars was a mediocre person without any vision or knowledge, unable to grasp all the complexities of the problems he had to face. Everything about him was drab, dull, insignificant: he might have made a passable officer in some provincial garrison but he was utterly out of place as the absolute sovereign of a gigantic state. His reign was ill-omened from the start: during the coronation festivities in Moscow, a panic swept over the crowd assembled on Khodynka, a suburban meadow surrounded by ravines, and thousands were trampled and injured, many killed. The incompetence of the police made things worse, rescue work and first aid were inefficient — and Khodynka remained in popular memory as a calamity of blood and horror.[7]

In order to preserve and maintain the autocracy, Nicholas II turned to such reactionary bureaucrats as Ivan L. Goremykin (1839–1917), who became his Minister of the Interior, and General Dmitry ('Don't spare the cartridges!') Trepov (1855–1906), whom he appointed Governor-General of St. Petersburg. One thousand per cent Russianism, persecutions of Poles, Finns, Ukrainians, Caucasians, and Asiatic peoples, pogroms of Jews (that in Kishinev, in 1903, was the most horrible), restrictive measures against education and culture — these were the main features of domestic policy. Reactionary officials who relied on the repressive measures of Alexander III were not long in discovering, however, that the situation was becoming far different from that of the 'eighties. Despite all the obstacles of the administration the country was developing industrially. The output of manufactured goods increased: production of cotton, steel, and coal doubled and tripled within one decade. Skilled workers, of whom there had been but 720,000 under Alexander III, numbered at least two million by 1900. Despite the economic crises of 1899 and 1902, caused by the slump in wheat prices, foreign capital had invested more than one billion gold rubles in Russian enterprises and had come to own over a third of the national industry. Her grain trade had won for Russia a leading position in the international market; technical progress had encouraged the growth of railroads and towns. This rapid industrialization was handicapped, however, by the precarious state of Russian finances: Serghei Witte (1849–1915), the Czar's most influential minister, attempted to bolster the economy through foreign loans (by 1905 Witte had doubled Russia's foreign debt to three billion gold rubles, and the treasury was paying out 130 million rubles yearly in interest). The unsolved agrarian problem also precluded a healthy economic development: the 85 million peasants had only 41 per cent of the arable land, as against the 22 per cent belonging to the big landowners, the 34.7 per cent held by the treasury and members of the Im-

[7] For a description masterly in both detail and background, see chs. XVII and XVIII of Gorky's *The Bystander*, translated by B. G. Guerney (New York, 1930).

perial family, and the 2.3 per cent of the Church. Statistics show that by 1914 eleven million peasants had no land, while the land of six million others was absolutely insufficient for their survival.

These factors explain the character of the liberal and Socialist movements at the beginning of the twentieth century. The expansion of capitalism and the consequent increase of the proletariat extended the popularity of Marxism, while the worsening of the agrarian crisis and the mounting discontent of the peasants favored the return of Populism. Between these two extremes of the Socialist intelligentsia the liberals also increased in numbers and influence; they found support in the educated bourgeoisie of the towns and the economically declining aristocracy of the countryside. The liberal opposition to the regime included mild monarchists, former Slavophiles, and erstwhile Westernizers, all of whom were striving to achieve reforms through pacific means and who placed their 'all-national platform' in opposition to the 'class egoism' of the Socialists. The Union of Liberation, formed in 1903 by the ex-Marxists Peter Struve and Catherine Kuskova-Prokopovich and by such active workers in the *zemstvos* as T. I. Rodichev, Ivan I. Petrunkevich, and others, became in 1905 the basis of the Constitutional Democratic party,[8] or the Party of the People's Freedom — the most important organization of the liberal bourgeoisie, led by Paul N. Miliukov, Vladimir D. Nabokov, Prince Paul A. Dolgorukov, Vassily A. Maklakov, M. M. Vinaver, and other representatives of the intelligentsia and the liberal professions. The party organ, *Liberation,* was published abroad, but its leaders controlled many other publications, such as the Moscow daily *Russian Gazette,* from 1906 to 1917, another daily, *Speech,* published in St. Petersburg; the important monthly *The Messenger of Europe,* as well as many provincial dailies. The Constitutional Democrats had a strong following in academic circles; they also had many adherents in literature and the arts, for the most part among the disciples of firmly established schools. Since most of the members of this party were well-educated aristocrats, lawyers, physicians, university professors, officials, and scions of the wealthy bourgeoisie, they as a rule disliked 'Decadent trash and mystical nonsense,' and this attitude determined the policies of several important publishing houses under their control; their sons and daughters, however, were for the most part modernists and socialists.

The bridge between the liberals and Socialists was formed mainly by a group of intellectuals who were in sympathy with the Populists and who came back in 1901 to start the clandestine Social Revolutionist party.[9] Its founders, Catherine Breshko-Breshkovskaya (1844–1924), Gregory

---

[8] The Constitutional Democrats shortly were nicknamed Cadets, from *ka, de,* the initial letters.

[9] Or the Essars, as the Social Revolutionists came to be known. Its platform and bylaws were formally adopted at the party's first convention in 1905.

Guershuni (1870–1908), Michael Gotz (1866–1906), Victor Chernov (1873–1952) a sociological theoretician and editor of *Revolutionary Russia* (a review, the first issue of which was published in 1901 in Finland), all considered themselves the heirs of and successors to the Party of the People's Will. Although closer to Marxism than their predecessors of the 'seventies had been, the Essars never failed to point out all the differences between them and the Marxists. Their individualistic socialism was based on moral grounds rather than on the concept of economic necessity. Faithful to the ideal of man's harmonious and full development, the Social Revolutionist party insisted on the role of the individual in history. On this score they were backed by the Russian sociological school, represented mainly by the historian Nicholas Kareyev (1850–1931) and the liberal scholar Maxim Kovalevsky (1851–1916).

The leaders of the new party also opposed to the Marxian economic monism the pluralistic theory of multiple historical factors. They attached great importance to the popular desire for independence, and demanded autonomy for all the peoples of Russia within the framework of a vast republican federation. The study of Russian history and economics led the Social Revolutionists to an affirmation of the peculiarities in the country's social structure. Russia was an agricultural land; the peasants played a dominant role in its life; the progress of capitalism within the country was bound to take a different course from that it had followed in the West; the political struggle for liberation was led by intellectuals, peasants, and workmen rather than by the bourgeoisie, as had almost always been the case in Europe. These premises determined the program and the tactics of the Essars. They believed that the collapse of Czarism would come as a result of a joint attack by the working masses, with the peasants predominating, and under the leadership of a revolutionary intelligentsia. Consequently they rejected the idea of a dictatorship of the proletariat, and insisted that the agrarian problem would form the crux of the revolutionary transformation. The revolution in Russia would bring about all the freedoms, plus a Constituent Assembly to form a democratic federative republic, but at the same time it would abolish private ownership of land and carry out its socialization, its partition among the peasants. Naturally this agrarian revolution would also deliver the death-blow to capitalism in Russia and act as a springboard for further socialistic developments. Thus the Russian revolution, without being either a true bourgeois or a true socialist one, would assume its own specific character.

As in the 'seventies, the most heterogenous elements — ranging from intellectuals and 'folk-intelligentsia' to representatives of the middle-class peasantry — rallied round this doctrine of neo-Populism, the ideas of which were widely disseminated through clandestine literature as well as in legal magazines such as *The Wealth of Russia,* edited by Korolenko,

Mikhailovsky, and Nicholas Annensky (brother of the poet). A score or so of young writers, some of them hailing from villages or provincial towns, revived in these periodicals the tradition of the Writers of the Soil. Side by side with this realistic trend there was, however, a strong modernistic one among the neo-Populists. Their doctrines, and particularly their terroristic practices, had a strong flavor of romanticism, which always attracted the Modernists. Some future historian will undoubtedly find the correlation between the Romantic revival and the terroristic romanticism of the Social Revolutionists. At any rate it is a fact that the Essars were in sympathy with new currents in art and literature, while at the same time such modern poets and novelists as Blok, Bely, Essenin, Andreyev, and many others were often associated with Essar circles.

The resumption of the terroristic tactics of the Party of the People's Will by the Social Revolutionists was, undoubtedly, one of the main reasons for their increasing prestige. The Essar combat sections — which acted in the name of the oppressed people — recruited their members from all walks of society, including university students, army officers, school teachers, farmers, and workmen, and covered the country with a network of underground organizations. In 1901 Peter Karpovich, an Essar, assassinated the Minister of Public Instruction, Nicholas P. Bogolepov, who was held responsible for drafting students into the army as a repressive measure against the academic and political agitation in the universities. This was followed by other terroristic acts, such as those against Minister of the Interior Dmitry S. Sipiaghin, assassinated in 1902 by Stepan Balmashev. The assassination in 1904, by Egor Sazonov, of Minister of the Interior V. von Plehve, and that in 1905, by Ivan Kalyaev, of Grand Duke Serghei, Governor General of Moscow, both considered pillars of reaction, were the most sensational exploits of the combat division of the party, which had revived the heroic traditions of the past. Yet all these self-sacrificing young men and women could not suspect that Evno Azef, the greatest agent provocateur of all time, was among the leaders of the terrorist movement.

The mounting popularity of the Essars and the romantic aura that surrounded their activities were watched with hostility by their Marxist rivals. Lenin accused the Social Revolutionists of being the party of the petty bourgeoisie, and attacked them in particular for regarding the peasantry as an undifferentiated whole and for not paying enough attention to the social distinctions between the *kulaks,* or well-to-do peasants, and the lack-land ones. In general, Lenin identified the 'peasant' mentality of the neo-Populists with the narrow-mindedness and nationalism of the middle class, while he rejected the terroristic tactics as 'anti-historical,' and called the Essars 'the party of revolutionary adventurers.'

The disputations between the Social Democrats and the Social Revolutionists had the same intensity and acrimoniousness as the polemics between the Slavophiles and the Westernizers had had half a century before. But now it was the Social Revolutionists who were pointing out the national features of the Russian revolution while the Marxists argued as followers of the West. In his book *On the Development of the Monistic Concept of History* (1895), Plekhanov (under the pen name of Beltov) interpreted the struggle between the Populists and Marxists as the continuation of the old battle between the adherents of national isolationism or self-containment and the partisans of Western progress. In his opinion the Social Democrats were representatives of European civilization who opposed the anarchical tendencies of national isolation. He appealed to the liberal bourgeoisie to lend its support to the Marxists in their fight against 'Populist barbarism.' Some of the Marxists, it may be pointed out, had extended their Western leanings to art and literature, and favored the early Decadents as agents of European culture.

At the turn of the century, when Marxism had attained the peak of its popularity, many intellectuals (young teachers and professors, for the most part) rallied around the *New Word* monthly and called themselves Legal Marxists. One of their leaders, Peter Struve (1870–1944), the author of *Critical Notes on the Economic Development of Russia,* welcomed capitalism as a guarantee of Westernization and cultural growth. A number of other leaders of this group, as trained economists, published the *Labor's Cause* organ; they denied any necessity of political struggle, insisted that the change in regime ought to be carried out by the bourgeoisie, and recommended that the workers should concentrate on purely economic claims. In 1900 quite a few Legal Marxists veered toward religiousness and idealism — Nicholas Berdiaev, Prince Eugene N. Trubetskoy (1862–1920), Semion Frank (1874–1950), Serghei Bulgakov (1871–1944) — while Struve, a man of wide culture, a brilliant journalist, went through a variegated career that finally turned him into a monarchist and a conservative nationalist.

While Plekhanov's writings reinforced the theoretical foundations of revolutionary Marxism, Lenin fought in his polemical works against such 'deviations of Marxism as economism,' as well as against the Populists. Vladimir Ilyich Ulianov (1870–1924), who came to be known as Nicholas Lenin, was the son of a school director; he was born in Simbirsk, on the Volga. His brother Alexander was hanged in 1887 for revolutionary activities and Vladimir, then a student at the University of Kazan, was compelled to abandon his studies and return home. In 1893 he went to St. Petersburg, where he soon became prominent in Marxist circles and proved his mettle as a polemicist. His attacks against the Populists, and particularly against 'liberal' Populists, were later collected under the title of *Who the 'Friends of the People' Are, and How They Fight against Social Democrats.* Arrested in 1895, he was sent to Siberia in 1897, and while in exile he wrote, under the pen name of Ilyin, another of his important works, *The Development of Capitalism in Russia* (1899). In his *Materials for the Study of Economic Conditions in Russia* (for which he used the pen name of Tulin) he criticized those who, because of their lack of confidence in the strength of the proletariat, were recommending an alliance with the bourgeoisie.

After the expiration of his Siberian exile in 1900 Lenin went abroad and became co-editor, with Plekhanov, of *The Spark,* a review that had for its slogan 'From the spark will spring the flame!' — a quotation from the answer of the exiled Decembrists to Pushkin's *Epistle*.[10] *The Spark,* published by *émigrés,* became a potent weapon in Lenin's struggle against 'opportunists, revisionists, Populists,' and other 'enemies of the proletarian movement.' It also helped to disseminate his ideas about the necessity of forging a strong disciplined party of revolutionary Marxists. The Social Democratic party of Russia (the 'Essdecks') was founded in the late 'nineties and had its first clandestine convention at Minsk in 1898. A second convention took place in London in 1903, and had a momentous impact. Two factions clashed at the convention: that led by Lenin, Plekhanov, and Paul B. Axelrod (1850–1928) finally won the majority and adopted the name of Bolsheviki (from the Russian word for majority, *bolshinstvo — bolshevik* originally meaning one belonging to the majority), while the group led by Yuly Martov-Zederbaum (1873–1923) and Leon Trotzky (Leo Bronstein, born 1879, assassinated 1940) took the name of Mensheviki (from *menshinstvo,* minority). The Bolsheviks had faith in the sweep and might of the imminent revolution and wanted to assure 'political hegemony of the proletariat in the national struggle for liberation.' They criticized the Mensheviks, who were prepared to form an alliance with the liberal bourgeoisie for the supreme assault on absolutism. The Bolsheviks also advised the peasants to accept the leadership of the proletariat as the chief revolutionary force, and proclaimed the necessity of organizing the party as a fighting unit and the vanguard of the working class, with centralized leadership, a precise platform and ideology, and a corps of professional revolutionists. Consequently the struggle over the opening paragraph of the party's constitution was of the utmost importance: Lenin did not agree that the acceptance of the party's program and the payment of dues (Martov's proposal) were sufficient. He demanded 'personal activity in one of the party's organizations' as a prerequisite for membership, and succeeded in winning the majority.

Thus, as far back as 1903, Lenin and his followers had outlined a

[10] Cf. Slonim, op. cit. p. 103.

party structure based on ideological dictatorship, strict discipline, and a carefully planned organization. The Bolsheviks and the Mensheviks continued their struggle for leadership within the Social Democratic party until 1906, when Plekhanov joined the Mensheviks and the split between the two factions became complete. A large group of writers, mainly of the realistic school, rallied around the Marxists and contributed to their clandestine press, as well as to Marxist magazines and monthlies published legally in Russia. Gorky, Smidovich-Veressaev, Serafimovich, Stepan G. Petrov (well known by the pen name of Skitaletz — the Wanderer), Vladimir H. Tan ('Bogoraz-Tan,' recognized as poet, novelist, and ethnographer), and a score or so of young novelists and playwrights of minor importance, as well as such critics as Peter Kogan (1872–1932), Anatoly Lunacharsky (1875–1933), and, to some extent, Dmitry N. Ovsianiko-Kulikovsky (1853–1920), all contributed to *The Beginning, Life, God's World, Contemporary World,* and other Marxist periodicals. Most of these writers were hostile toward the prevalent Decadent and Symbolist movements, and their criticism of contemporaneous art and literature frequently became as heated as political debates.

The beginning of the twentieth century was, on the whole, an exciting period in Russia, filled with stir and hope. The intellectuals were discussing aesthetic, religious, and social problems; the Modernists were battling with the realists; the God-seekers were attacking the positivists; the liberals were gathering their forces; the Marxists and the Populists were contending for ideological leadership, while the masses — and this was the most significant fact — were deliberately coming to the fore: the workers struck and demonstrated on May Day in various cities, particularly in Batum, Rostov, and Sormovo (as described by Gorky in *Mother*); the peasants rose up in the Ukraine and the Caucasus; the university students clashed with the police in the streets. Anti-governmental organizations were mushrooming throughout the empire, the whole fabric of absolutism was straining, and the explosions of bombs heralded the coming of an imminent eruption. It was as if a menacing wind, stirring up the dust and the dead leaves, splintering the trees, and shattering the houses, was sweeping over the country.

It was clear that Russia, following the alternate rhythm of reaction and reform that had hitherto determined the cyclic development of her history, was now entering a new period of upheaval and transformation.

7

GORKY

TWENTIETH-CENTURY RUSSIA has produced several novelists and storytellers whose talent and craftsmanship were not only equal but in some instances superior to those of Maxim Gorky. Nevertheless he was the most popular of all his contemporaries and remained a central figure throughout the most turbulent and tragic years in his country's history. His name never ceased to provoke curses or praise, his works were never received with indifference; whatever eclipses he may have experienced were brief and partial, and after each, which some critics regarded as total, he managed to reappear in greater glory than ever. Toward the end of his life he was proclaimed the foster father and guide of Soviet literature; eight hundred thousand people, headed by Stalin and all the leaders of state, attended his funeral at the Red Square in Moscow in 1936. After his death (for which, according to the Communist party, criminal machinations of political enemies were responsible) [1] he attained virtual canonization. Everything in the Soviet Union attests to his extraordinary reputation: Nizhni Novgorod, his native town, has been renamed Gorky, the Moscow Art Theater and a score of other institutions bear his name, his works have reached (between 1917 and 1947) a circulation of 45 million copies — setting a record above that of *any* Russian classic — while his artistry is presented to the new generation as a lofty model for admiration and emulation.

This remarkable status was not due merely to Gorky's literary merits. His life and personality, his political and cultural activities, the part he

---

[1] During the Moscow Trials of 1937–8 Yagoda, the former Chief of Secret Police, made a 'confession' in which he stated that he had 'ordered' Gorky's physicians to poison Gorky and his son Maxim; the trial documents mention camphor as the drug used. In connection with this mysterious affair, Dr. Samuel Levin was executed and Professor Dimitri Pletnev was sent to Siberia.

had played in the revolutionary movement — all these combined to assure him an exceptional place in the history of his times.

Gorky was inordinately proud of showing his pre-Revolutionary passport, which, in addition to giving his real name, Alexis Maximovich Peshkov, stated his trade: Journeyman of the Dyers' Guild. His father had been a worker in a paperhanging and upholstery establishment; his mother, nee Varvara Kashirina, was the daughter of a former Volga barge-hauler who had made some money and become the owner of several dyeing establishments. Alexis was born in 1868 in Nizhni Novgorod, on the Volga. His father died when he was five, and his mother when he was nine. Brought up in his grandparents' house, he found himself in the crass and cruel world of the provincial lower middle class; his initiation to life was hard, painful, and at times horrible. It included severe beatings, scenes of violence, savage greed, and sheer brutality. His grandfather went bankrupt and almost went mad. The youngster had to help his grandmother, who had become a ragpicker. After five months of primary schooling — this was the only formal education he ever received — the orphan, at the age of eight, was compelled to earn his own living. There began for him a long stretch of physical and moral bondage, and a succession of ordeals and humiliations. He was by turns a servant, a cobbler's apprentice, a scullion in a ship's galley, an errand boy for an icon-maker, and worked at a dozen other odd jobs along the Volga docks.

Reading was his sole refuge from hardships and peonage. The chief cook of a Volga steamer had instilled in him a veritable passion for the printed word, and the boy voraciously read anything and everything — dream-books, cloak-and-dagger romances (for the most part from the French), Pushkin's poetry, the lives of the saints. This love of reading often got him into trouble: once he became so engrossed in an adventure tale that he forgot to put water into a heated samovar, with the result that it became unsoldered. His employer whipped him with pine boughs so ferociously that he had to be taken to a hospital, where forty-two slivers were extracted from his swollen back.

At the age of fifteen the gawky adolescent, whose almost morose face was but seldom illuminated by the smile of his kind blue eyes, felt sharply the discrepancy between the realities of his life and the dreams and visions inspired by his reading. Beauty, happiness, and justice had nothing to do with his coarse and grimy surroundings. Despite all his experiences of poverty and violence, he loved men — even though he distrusted them and knew the full measure of their vices. 'I gave myself a solemn pledge that when I grew up I would help people and serve them honestly.' This pledge he never broke, and the idea of serving humanity, of social and moral duty, was deeply rooted in both Gorky the writer and Gorky the man. His rebellion against misery and brutality was natural and intuitive, and in rationalizing his emotional reactions, he aspired to deeds that would transform the world of cruelty, poverty, and ignorance he had to face daily.

In his poverty-stricken youth, however, this aspiration could not be realized. When young Peshkov went to Kazan, it had been with the secret ambition of going to school, even to a university; instead he was compelled to do manual labor. Between the ages of sixteen and twenty he had been a servant, a gardener, a night watchman, a docker, a baker. The most important aspect of his Kazan period was his contact with socialistic intellectuals; he mixed with liberals, Populists, and a few Marxists, and read their underground literature. Although he shared the antigovernment mood of his new friends, he felt himself a stranger among them; their sentimental prattle about the People (with a capital P) irritated him, and he was shocked by the vagueness of their idealism as well as by their lack of practical sense and moral fortitude. He was, nevertheless, thankful to a group of university students and political exiles who helped him in his self-education; he dealt with this period in one of his autobiographical books, bearing the ironic title *My Universities*.

He had an astonishing memory, and his reading, despite all its haphazardness, laid solid foundations for his intellectual growth. Of course, only an individual with Gorky's heroic endurance and his passion for learning could contrive to read and study after putting in a fourteen-hour day in a bakery, where he was earning all of three rubles a month. The physical strain, however, was not as dangerous as the moral anxiety. The contradictions between new ideas and his senseless existence, the dissatisfaction with himself and with his surroundings, the fear of not finding any escape from his wage-slavery, and the oppressive atmosphere of the 'eighties, with their reigning tedium and reaction — all these drove him almost insane. With his last coppers he bought a second-hand revolver and tried to commit suicide. The bullet perforated one of his lungs, and he had to lie for weeks in a hospital. After his release he resumed his struggle and his wanderings. He worked with milk-and-water Populists in futile attempts at peaceful propaganda in the villages, and came under the eyes of the police; he joined the crew of a fishing boat, worked for a railroad and in a bottling factory — and read and wrote in every spare moment.

He showed his first literary attempts (most of them in verse) only to his best friends: Nicholas Lanin, a lawyer, who had offered Gorky a place as a clerk in his office, and the writer Vladimir Korolenko, who helped him with literary advice and urged him to utilize the vast amount of material he had accumulated.

In 1889, after new difficulties with the police, he became a hobo. Three years were spent in crossing on foot the Ukraine, the Don region, the Crimea, and the Caucasus; he visited monasteries, worked as a farm hand, earned a meager pittance as an artisan, had hundreds of adventures, and met literally thousands of men and women.

In 1892, filled with the spirit of protest and restlessness, he found himself in Tbilisi (Tiflis), capital of Georgia, where he met Alexander Kaluzhny, a former member of the Party of the People's Will, who impressed him very much; he also came in contact with a workers' revolutionary group. It was Kaluzhny who, after hearing the young man tell of his wanderings, shut him up in a room and made him write down one of the incidents. A few days later it appeared in *The Caucasus,* a local daily, under the title of 'Makar Chudra' and was signed with the pen name Maxim Gorky (literally Maxim the Bitter) which was to become so famous. From then on (it was in September 1892) a new life began for the twenty-four-year-old hobo.

Upon his return to Nizhni Novgorod in 1893, Lanin and Korolenko had secured for him a position on the staff of a local newspaper. He also worked for publications in Samara and Nizhni Novgorod, and wrote sketches, poems, articles, and editorial pieces. This journalistic apprenticeship lasted five years; it brought him financial security for the first time in his life, and also gave him the opportunity of acquiring skill and craftsmanship in his writing.

In 1895 he married Catherine Volzhskaya, who had been proofreader on a daily to which he was a contributor; in the same year his 'Chelkash' was published in the influential Populist monthly *The Wealth of Russia.* This marked his real debut in the metropolitan press: from then on he contributed to the leading periodicals in Moscow and St. Petersburg; he had won recognition and his popularity was growing. The only drawback was his health: in 1896 he suffered an attack of pulmonary tuberculosis, which was to afflict him all his life.

When the tales Maxim Gorky had first published in various monthlies and dailies were collected and brought out in two volumes in 1898, they enjoyed a great success, their circulation reaching 100,000 in a short time — a figure previously attained only by Tolstoy. Gorky became famous almost overnight, and he achieved a place unique in the history of modern Russian letters, which are lacking in 'literary sensations.' By the turn of the century he was the hero of the day, whose life served as material for a legend. Crowds gathered in Odessa at the gallery where a portrait of him was exhibited; in the streets of big cities beggars claimed to be Gorky's brother-hoboes and thus prospered in their panhandling; young men by the thousands imitated Gorky's sartorial idiosyncracies by sporting black, buttoned-at-the-neck blouses, by wearing boots and carry-ing knobby sticks, longer but otherwise not unlike shillelaghs. When, in 1901, Gorky moved to St. Petersburg, his appearance in the streets caused traffic jams and police had to rescue him from overenthusiastic admirers. His plays *The Petty Bourgeois* and, particularly, *The Lower Depths,* staged by the Moscow Art Theater in 1902, were smash hits. The latter play was promptly translated for stages throughout the world; it ran for 200 performances in Berlin alone. These foreign versions made Gorky very popular abroad, particularly in Germany, Italy, and France.

Gorky's prominence as the spokesman for the revolutionary move-ment paralleled his literary fame. In 1901, after the brutal police meas-ures against university students who had organized a political demon-stration in St. Petersburg, Gorky wrote his poem, 'The Stormy Petrel,' which hailed the petrel as the herald of the tempest. Nobody missed the obvious symbolism of the poem, and it was construed throughout Rus-sia as a welcome to the coming revolutionary storm. The magazine in which it had appeared was suspended by governmental orders and Gorky, whose close association with the Social Democrats was an open secret, was arrested. As his tuberculosis grew worse again in prison, he was released and allowed to go to the Crimea, where he met Tolstoy and Chekhov. Both impressed him greatly and became his lifelong friends. In 1902 another incident brought him to the fore: his election to the Academy of Science and Letters was rescinded because of the Czar's disapproval; Chekhov and Korolenko were the only ones who resigned from the Academy in protest against this administrative abuse.

The general public was not alone in seeing Gorky as one of the lead-ers of the opposition — the Czarist authorities were equally perceptive. The success of his plays was as much political as literary. At the dress rehearsal of *The Petty Bourgeois* the gendarmes and constabulary swarmed around the theater, and plainclothesmen doubled as ushers in the house. 'It looked much more like a preparation for a battle than for a dress rehearsal,' Stanislavsky wrote in his memoirs. *The Lower Depths* was received with enthusiasm because of the appeals for freedom the audience heard in the lines of Satin and other protagonists. There were nineteen calls for the author on opening night. When the Moscow Art Theater went on tour it had to give *The Lower Depths* for fifty con-secutive nights in St. Petersburg, but the play was thereafter banned in the provinces by orders of the police.

Gorky was the idol of the liberal intelligentsia, but his own attitude toward his admirers contained the seeds of future dissensions. The plebe-ian and revolutionary who advocated upheaval and struggle looked with suspicion at the 'weaklings' — the 'progressively minded' noblemen and parlor-pinks. In *Summer Residents* (which, like most of his plays, shows Chekhov's influence) he represented intellectuals and mild liberals as wishy-washy chatterboxes, unable to make a sacrifice or put up a fight. 'We are mere transients and summer residents in our own country,' says the heroine of the play. 'We live on this earth as strangers, and we aren't the sort of useful creatures life really needs . . . it seems to me that soon — tomorrow perhaps — other men, strong and bold, will arrive and mop us up as so much muck.' Upon the publication of the play in 1904 these statements provoked mixed reactions. In other works as well he displayed the same harsh attitude toward the moderate wing of the progressive movement. The events deepened the conflict between the old intelligentsia sprung from the privileged classes and this writer who sided with the proletarian revolution and did not mince words in accusing the intellectuals of passivity and lack of courage. His break with them was not long in coming.

Gorky's revolutionary activity reached its peak during the Moscow armed rebellion of December 1905, when all Russia was ablaze. At the beginning of the next year he was arrested, became ill, began spitting blood, and was released from his cell in the fortress of SS. Peter and Paul through the pressure of public opinion throughout Europe — petitions for his liberation addressed to the Czarist government had been signed by thousands of prominent men such as Briand, Jaurès, Rodin, and others. Nevertheless he was far from safe and had to go abroad. Leonid Krassin, who eventually became financial adviser to the Bolsheviks, suggested that Gorky visit the United States to collect money for the revolutionary movement, as well as to protest against the loans the Czarist government was soliciting there, in France, and elsewhere. The contention of Russian socialists was that such loans would help to crush completely the already subsiding revolutionary agitation.

Gorky arrived in New York in April 1906. After a brilliant reception at the pier and front-page publicity in all the newspapers, which headlined 'the great writer' and the 'ambassador of the Russian people,' both press and public suddenly turned against him on moral grounds when it became known that his traveling companion, the beautiful and talented actress Maria Andreyeva, was not his legal but his common-law wife. The banquets in his honor were canceled; such literary figures as Mark Twain and William Dean Howells turned their backs on the Russian, who was thrown out in the middle of the night from a prominent New York hotel and had to take refuge in the house of an American admirer on Staten Island. This scandal, which the Czar's embassy in Washington helped to foment, as well as Gorky's open support of American strikers and left-wing labor organizations, completely discredited his mission: he collected no more than ten thousand dollars and withdrew to the Adirondacks, where he wrote his revolutionary novel, *Mother,* and a series of angry articles against American capitalism and the City of the Yellow Devil (or Mammon), as he called New York. Incidentally, Gorky's American impressions, as well as his violent diatribes against France ('I spit at you a spittoonful of bile and blood,' he wrote in his pamphlet, 'La Belle France'), were not at all well received in Russia: most critics disliked their hasty generalities and their polemical tone and found them dangerously anti-Western.

Upon his return to Europe Gorky settled as a political *émigré* in Italy, and his villa on the Island of Capri became the meeting place of Bolsheviks, Mensheviks, Populists, expatriates of all kinds, and visitors from Russia — writers both young and old, artists, and intellectuals. Gorky's popularity was, however, on the decline in Russia. The publication of *Mother* in 1907 was acclaimed by workers and socialists in all countries (it had been quickly translated into two dozen languages), and Lenin hailed it as a courageous affirmation of socialist ideals, but it was hardly to the liking of Russian intellectuals; it seemed so much of an anachronism in the then prevailing atmosphere of defeat and triumphant governmental reaction. Those very people who had adored the author of 'The Stormy Petrel' as the symbol of the movement of liberation now berated him for clinging to a lost cause. Dispirited fellow-travelers, intellectuals hagridden by pessimism, and a peace-at-any-price bourgeoisie were all irritated by Gorky's refusal to admit the failure of the Revolution. He seemed to them stubborn, gauche, out of date, and silly. It was not hard to point out all the aesthetic shortcomings of *Mother,* as well as the verbosity of his formless and didactic plays (*The Enemies, The Barbarians, The Children of the Sun*). The critics rolled up their sleeves and went to work on Gorky and his popularity. Aikhenwald wrote that all the tragedy of Gorky's heroes lay in their impecuniousness. Philosophov, the friend and collaborator of Merejkovsky and Hippius, stated that 'two things have ruined Gorky: success and a mad infatuation with Socialism . . . Gorky, as a writer, ceased to exist when he became involved with the Revolution.'

Gorky's finish, Gorky's death, Gorky's downfall — these and similar refrains sounded throughout 1907–09 the mounting hostility of a considerable segment of public opinion against the writer who at the beginning of the century had been worshipped by ecstatic multitudes. Yet it was precisely during these years and the years following this literary lynching that Gorky wrote his best works: *A Confession, Summer, The Small Town of Okurov, The Life of Matthew Kozhemyakin, All through Russia, Childhood,* and he was also working during this period on the sequels to *Childhood* — *Out in the World* and *My Universities* — and on his *Reminiscences.*

In 1913 an amnesty was granted to certain political offenders on the occasion of the tricentenary of the Romanov dynasty, and Gorky was able to return home after seven years of productive exile. He soon found that the bourgeois intellectuals were still eyeing him askance; his articles in the Bolshevik press and his editorship of *Annals,* the Marxian monthly (1915–19), did not help in closing the gap between him and all those who frowned at his 'Social-Democratic art.'

He had quite a large following among the democratic intellectuals, however, and among general readers; he also had a number of literary disciples, some of them of proletarian origin. These adherents of the Gorky school all considered themselves stark realists and were opposed to the refinements and the formalistic research of the Symbolists and Decadents. Together with their master they formed a group of 'left-wingers,' strongly tinged with Marxian ideas. Gorky's further attitudes toward literature and revolution during and after 1917 were therefore a logical development of this position.

II   'Men do not know how to live,' says the old gypsy who is the narrator of Gorky's first tale, 'Makar Chudra' (1892); they work and die like slaves, and in this they do not resemble the proud men of his own tribe. The hero, Loyko Zobar, had fallen in love with the beautiful and willful Rodda, and wound up by killing her, since she wanted to dominate him and he refused to surrender his freedom — even to love. Izerghil, whose brave lovers defied law and convention, tells legends about men of might: the Son of the Eagle, free but solitary and incapable of loving, and Danko, the hero, who, in order to save his own people lost in a dark forest, tore the heart out of his breast and held it aloft as a torch to light the road to salvation ('Izerghil the Crone,' 1895). A khan and his son both loved the same captive girl, yet each refused to renounce her, and therefore together they cast the object of their rivalry into the sea ('The Khan and His Son'). The wounded falcon tells the grass snake that he has fought bravely and enjoyed the height of the sky in his bold flights — and in a supreme effort to fly again he is crushed against the rocks. The grass snake laughs at this useless death inasmuch as those who are born to crawl know nothing of flight, but the poet hails 'the wisdom of life in the madness of the brave,' which fills their hearts with yearning for freedom and light ('The Song of the Falcon,' 1895). Love is also a sacred madness: a young girl intoxicated by her first passion, holds a tremendous power — she makes

Death itself retreat before the might of her sincere, simple love ('The Maiden and Death').[2]

When young Gorky passed from romantic gypsies, Promethean Dankos, and heroic falcons to more ordinary folk, he endowed his new heroes and heroines — tramps and prostitutes — with the same pride, strength, and love of freedom he had celebrated in his first legends. Chelkash (in the story of the same name), a wharf rat and a drunkard, despises the weakness and the bourgeois dreams of the peasant lad Gavrila, with whom he has temporarily joined forces; he has utter contempt for money and squanders it right and left whenever he manages to get any; he is ready to commit crime and robbery, since he accepts the laws of the human jungle: the merciless struggle for existence and the survival of the fittest. Malva, a Carmen of the Black Sea, maintains freedom in all her love affairs and always acts as an independent, strong-willed creature. In general, the strong men and women who maintain their individuality are Gorky's favorite heroes and heroines. He respects strength of character wherever he finds it — and this explains the note of admiration with which in his later works he portrayed not only rebels and revolutionaries but also those extremely predatory representatives of capitalism of whom he could hardly approve according to his political convictions. Silan Petrov, the boss in 'On the Rafts,' one of Gorky's early stories, an old slave driver who is tireless in work and in love-making, is the prototype of Ilya Artamonov in the novel *The Artamonov Business* and is akin to old Bulychev in the play *Egor Bulychev and Others*. Vitality, pulsing life, the manifestation of primitive impulses — both moral and physical — appealed to Gorky, and in his first period he was the poet of what has come to be known as rugged individualism.

This was one of the reasons for the immediate success of his romantic and somewhat Nietzschean stories. Their impressionistic style was hardly a novelty in the late 'nineties, when various deviations from classical realism were prevalent. Their spirit, however, was something unexpected and novel, and it delighted readers who had become tired of the drab and bleak literary palette. The newcomer's picturesque brigands, romantic tramps, and legendary gypsies — all these magnificent specimens of manhood who vociferously proclaimed 'Life is narrow but my heart is wide' — created a startling eruption amid the depressing atmosphere of the period.

Educated society, which felt itself devitalized by the autocratic re-

---

[2] This poem, written in 1892, after 'Makar Chudra,' was not published until 1917. When Gorky read it in 1931 to Voroshilov and Stalin, the latter wrote on the manuscript: 'This is more powerful than Goethe's "love triumphs over death," in *Faust*.'

gime, simply loved the lust for life and the yearning for action of the Gorkian hoboes, the barefooted ones. Similar characters had, of course, appeared in Russian fiction before; but even though historians of literature could point to such writers as Narezhny, Karonin, Levitov, and Uspensky as Gorky's predecessors, these tramps of Gorky's came as a revelation to the average reader. They belonged to a relatively new social group. The impoverishment of the villages had led to unemployment and thousands upon thousands were tramping the countryside in search of work; the mode of life, the sufferings and discontent of these hordes of the lumpen proletariat presented a challenge to the regime in general and to the growth of capitalism in particular.

Unlike the Populists, who did pastels of the patience and saintliness of the traditional peasantry, Gorky portrayed the denizens of the slums, of the ports and lodging houses, as turbulent, violent, and seething with conscious and instinctive protest against the inhuman conditions in which they were compelled to exist. Yet poverty, crime, and despair could not kill the sparks of love and creativeness within them.

Still, it was not solely this affirmation of common humanity that made Gorky so popular. When Gorky was highly praised for having shown these qualities in his heroes, Tolstoy shrugged his shoulders and made a caustic remark: 'I knew long before Gorky that tramps have souls.' Much more significant was the refusal of his hoboes to be passive or to become resigned to their fate. They were wrathful, forceful human beings, ready to challenge the very order of things that turned them into thieves, drunkards, and derelicts. They symbolized the revolt of the downtrodden individual against the political and social machine that continued to exploit and crush them. This was the true message readers received from Gorky's stories and it found a response amid the general mood of the turn of the century, with its awakening of the masses and the increasing political activities of educated society.

The romantic tendency and the spirit of protest in Gorky's short stories between 1894 and 1898 ran parallel to the trend of critical realism: he concentrated more and more on the depiction of poverty, ignorance, and the sufferings of the lower classes. The directness and even the brutality of these pictures led some critics to speak of Gorky's naturalism. If this term is applied as it was in connection with Zola, it becomes quite obvious that Gorky never aimed at the documentary objectivity of the French school: his tales always have warm lyrical overtones that are definitely lacking in the novels of the French master. Gorky painted the dregs of humanity with the passion and compassion of a romantic and a revolutionary. Certain defects of these works are due precisely to their emotional overflow: the pity, indignation, or anger of the author is all too vocal, and he uses almost melodramatic devices to score direct hits on the sympathy of his readers. Two *leit-motifs* are predominant in Gorky's work: realistic and crude representation of misery and violence, and a dream of humaneness and beauty that emphasizes the dreariness of reality, yet also builds up a sense of revolt.

In these respects Gorky was a faithful follower of Russian literary tradition. Thus we have the starving youth whom a miserable streetwalker shields with her body against the cold of a November night ('Once in Autumn'); the tramp who is set to kill but abandons his criminal intentions because a girl about to commit suicide needs help ('Emelyan Pilyai'); the migratory workers who steal the silver clasps from a Bible, but give them back to the old woman who values the book so highly ('The Affair of the Clasps'); the poor cook Arina, who is so jeered at and persecuted by her coarse companions that she hangs herself ('Boredom') — these and many others of his stories carried on the trend started by Gogol and Dostoevsky. Although often marred by sentimentality these tales fitted into that great category of works about the 'wronged and the humiliated' which played such a prominent part in Russian letters. They revealed the same concern for the underdog, the same love for the 'little man' which has been so often considered the most characteristic trait of nineteenth-century Russian novelists. Their difference lay in that besides compassion and humanitarian sentimentalism Gorky displayed in his sketches other significant features. His realism was harsh, crude, pitiless; easy tears and sentimental situations did not hide the feelings of hatred and rebellion, which were completely lacking in Gogol, and were sublimated into preachments of Christian slave-morality in Dostoevsky. Although in many instances — particularly in his morbid interest in human suffering — Gorky has been linked to the latter, he is as far from the spirit of Christian quietism as was another writer who had influenced him — Saltykov-Shchedrin.

For Gorky evil is not a metaphysical problem as it is for the author of *The Brothers Karamazov,* or a result of the discrepancy between the truth of religion and the wrongs of civilization, as it is for Tolstoy: it is mainly a question of the ways of life, of its faulty organization, of material conditions and social wrongs. Man's sufferings are, for Gorky, caused by political despotism, class division, and social injustice. There is nothing vague about his criticism: like his predecessors of the 'forties and the 'sixties he is strongly attached to the earth. He was often reproached for his lack of depth, for his avoidance of the fundamental issues of human nature. But Gorky believed that the so-called metaphysical or philosophical approach to life which disregards the particular for imaginary generalities is hypocritical and obnoxious. A truthful and fearless observer, he scarcely saw anything beyond the concreteness of life as it is actually lived. Almost from the beginning of his literary career he evinced this tendency toward realism. He concentrated on the sordid details, primarily those of a physical nature: hunger, drunkenness, pain, filth, the lack of all physical essentials. With the exception of Dostoevsky, there is no other Russian writer of the nineteenth century who dealt as much as Gorky did with physical violence and murder. Whatever the psychological explanation may be in terms of Gorky's personality, it would be next to impossible to detect any grin of sadistic pleasure in his gruesome descriptions of wives mangled by their husbands, of vagabonds beaten up by police. From his early childhood he had been deeply affected by all the excesses of violence around him: the fury of blows, the floggings, the madness of drunken brawls. He had become aware of physical violence as a main feature of Russian life, and its exposé remained one of his principal objectives; he denounced it not only as an Asiatic heritage, a survival of the Tartar yoke, but also as a result of ignorance and oppression: the cruelty of the common people was bred by their misery and was a release as well as a compensation for their slavery.[3]

During the years of his literary apprenticeship Gorky had come under the influence of various writers, from Chekhov ('Boredom,' a story about a merchant who cannot get rid of an oppressive feeling of futility, is definitely Chekhovian) to Dostoevsky, whom Gorky hated and rejected on ideological grounds. Most of the sketches and tales he wrote between 1892 and 1895 are weak and imitative, yet even in these attempts of the young writer, as well as in his more successful and occasionally brilliant stories of later years (1895–8 are the best of this period), there is a core of constant elements. The themes of violence, brutality, and despair appear even in *Paul the Unfortunate* (*Orphan Paul* in the English version), his first novel, which he refused — quite wisely — to include in his collected works, but the revision of which he began toward the end of his life. Paul, an ugly and unhappy shoemaker's apprentice, falls in love with a prostitute and, finding it impossible to make her 'go straight,' kills her. In the story 'Conclusion' the public whipping of an unfaithful wife is described in gruesome detail (Gorky had witnessed the scene in an Ukrainian village, had interceded for the victim, and, in his turn, was so brutally attacked by the infuriated peasants that he had to be taken to a hospital). In 'Bukoemov' the incidents of violence are so frequent that the hero says, 'How can I feel pity when I'm always seeing

---

[3] Gorky himself had an amazing capacity for enduring physical pain; since he detested narcotics, none was administered when he was on the operating table or in a dentist's chair.

people getting beaten up?' In 'Ex-Humans' there is an unbroken succession of fist fights and set-tos, and Kwalda, an ex-officer, rules his lodging house by brute force.

In 'The Red Devil' Vasska, the janitor of a bordello, is expert at flogging and whips the girls soundly for any breach of discipline. In *Three of Them,* a novel that describes the sad experiences of adolescents from the lower middle class, a blacksmith kills his wife, a barkeeper gives his son such a thrashing that the poor fellow winds up in a hospital, while Ilya, the hero of the novel, murders a rich merchant, lives with the woman his victim had been keeping, and finally, in a frenzy, threatens everybody with a knife and takes his own life. In *Foma Gordeyev,* a novel dealing with Volga capitalists, scenes of violence are quite as frequent as in any other work of Gorky's; *The Lower Depths* culminates in a murder.

Police tortures are fully described in *Mother.* In 1908 Gorky reverted to the themes of cruelty and brutality in his autobiographical trilogy, *Childhood, Out in the World,* and *My Universities,* as well as in *The Small Town of Okurov* and *The Life of Matthew Kozhemyakin* — beatings, clubbings, and general mayhem crowd the pages of all these works.

In Gorky's early writings this theme of man's inhumanity to man runs parallel to two other powerful themes: humanity amid beastliness and man's yearning for liberation. The bakers in 'Twenty-six Men and a Girl,' one of Gorky's best stories, lead the joyless existence of slaves, but they idealize Tania, a girl who personifies for them beauty and love. But when she fails to live up to this exalted idealization and succumbs to a soldier, they compensate for their frustration by vile oaths and atrocious behavior against their fallen idol. All of Gorky's unhappy heroes are forever seeking true love and freedom.

All these aspirations in man are best summarized in *The Lower Depths,* which is Gorky's best play. The milieu is a lodging house run by the avaricious, cruel Kostylev, who leeches on to his unfortunate lodgers. His wife, Vassilissa, instigates her lover, the thief Pepel, to kill her husband, but when Pepel proves unfaithful to her she turns him over to the police. The ex-humans of the doss house range from the Baron, who at one time owned houses and race horses but who has degenerated because of his own laziness and lack of will power, to the illiterate Tartar and Pepel (the name means ashes), the son of a gallowsbird and an expert thief in his own right. The keysmith Kleshch, the prostitute Nastia, the alcoholic Actor — all are victims of a poverty as incurable as leprosy. Their 'mortal fate' derives directly from that lack of freedom, of human rights and dignity, to which the masses were condemned in Czarist Russia. Their only consolation consists of lies and dreams — and Luka, the little old pilgrim, fosters their illusions. He is a folk-philosopher, one of those innumerable religious tramps who traipsed all over Russia, visiting monasteries, telling more or less edifying stories to the peasants, and feeding consoling pap to the wretched in drawling monologues interspersed with puns and proverbs. He rekindles the lodgers' hopes for a better life and brings back to them some measure of self-confidence. 'It don't make no difference to me,' says Luka, 'I respect everybody, even crooks, too. To my way of thinking there ain't a flea to be found that's bad all around.' 'Listen, old timer: is there a God?' asks Pepel, and Luka replies in a low voice: 'If you believe, there is, if you don't there ain't. Whatever you believe in, that thing is.' He repeats the same nebulous yet consoling reasoning to Nastia, whose notions of romantic love are derived from translations of French yellow-backs, and to the Actor, who dreams of some sanatorium with a miraculous cure for alcoholics. Luka is an incarnation of compassion and hope.

Subsequently, however, Gorky became dubious of his own creation and wondered whether Luka was at all benignant, whether he was actually pernicious. He wrote, in 1932, that *The Lower Depths* was 'dated and even harmful, while the image of Luka is false.' Luka's Tolstoyan nonresistance to evil, his resignation, his superficial treatment of all ills by vague yet solacing dicta — these traits belonged to the tradition of Holy Mother Russia, to Dostoevsky's 'humble souls,' to his Christlike Prince Myshkin in *The Idiot,* or to Alësha Karamazov — in short, to that Christian trend in life and literature which Gorky ended by rejecting completely as 'paregoric for the unhappy.' This very play, however, is not without a character in opposition to Luka: the cynical Satin, who comprehends that all roads are barred to the barefooted ones and who pits his concept of resistance against Luka's concept of compassion. 'For him who is his own master, who is independent and doesn't devour that which is not his own — what need has he of the lie? Truth is the God of the free man!'

Satin makes other affirmations that have a strange sound in the stifling den where men crushed by degradation and fear are huddling in cold and hunger: 'Man — there's your truth! . . . M-a-n! That's magnificent. That sounds grand. M-a-n! You must respect man. Not pity him — not degrade him through pity. You must respect him!'

This imperishable longing for the 'right' kind of life, for justice and truth, which Gorky emphasized in all his ex-humans and which he found in all Russians was the core of his own faith. He believed in man despite man's inhumanity and beastliness, and he had a passion for mankind. Typical of this is 'The Birth of a Man,' in which he describes a young peasant woman, a migratory worker, who, while on the road, gives birth to a son. The great mystery of nativity takes place in the steppe on the shore of the Black Sea, and the mother, helped by the tramp who is the narrator, is alone with her child in the wilderness of the plain. The blending of tenderness, naturalistic detail, and exaltation in this short story conveys the full character of Gorky's robust humaneness.

III   Gorky's artistry during the first period (1882–1902) was uneven. The tales that made him famous then have lost most of their charm for the reader of today. They are certainly colorful, dramatic, and vigorous, and already show that power of characterization which later was Gorky's principal asset as a writer. Their defects, however, are also patent: their primitive construction, a sentimentality so naïve as to border on bad taste, picturesque language, and lusty details lapsing into rhetoric and bathos. And the author is over-exuberant and high-pitched, using too many words of indignation and wrath or of tenderness and sympathy. He is, in general, inclined toward exaggeration and employs only blacks and whites. His philosophy is too obvious and his desire to put over a message and to convince the reader makes him obtrusive and didactic. The dramatic element is the dynamic force within his plots, yet he lacks the sense of structure. This is particularly evident in his first novels, such as *Three of Them* — an almost formless sequence of incidents, of isolated scenes and repulsive details; despite the intensity and rich texture of the narrative, it never acquires an organic unity.

The same may be said of *Foma Gordeyev* (1899), a novel that marked an important milestone in Gorky's literary development. It represents the Masters of Life, the rising capitalist class — a subject that fascinated Gorky and to which he was to return in later works. Foma's father, Ignat, a strong, lustful man who veers from frantic activity and wild debauchery to remorse and atonement, is an incarnation of the driving force of the rising class, its urge for accumulation and acquisition. But Foma, who has inherited Ignat's fortune, becomes alienated from his environment. He is a seeker after the meaning of life; he wants to find a useful outlet for his strong passions and vague longings, and falls victim to those who have 'narrowed life down, made it a prison, chained the soul.' In the course of his struggle against the Masters he is ruined, is stripped of all his possessions, and turns into a drunkard, an ex-human.

The story of his downfall is unfolded in a series of scenes, and although the main characters are masterfully drawn, with that abundance of vivid details so typical of Gorky's style, the novel leaves the impression that the author lacks control of his material — that he is, in fact, somewhat overwhelmed by it.

The looseness of construction is compensated for, however, by forceful descriptions of provincial life, and particularly by the 'national flavor' of the Volga merchants. This makes Gorky akin to the Regionalists and the Writers of the Soil. In general, Gorky's whole manner — his broad canvasses, colorful bold strokes, folkloristic reminiscences, popular expressions, and heroes who have not severed their ties with ancient customs and traditions — puts him close to Pisemsky, Ostrovsky, Melnikov, Mamin-Sibiriak, and the Populists. What made him different from writers with Slavophile overtones, however, was his decidedly Western and socialist orientation. He wanted to change the life he portrayed in his tales and novels, and he was convinced he had to contribute to that end not only by his writings but by direct activity as well. This determined his work at the beginning of the twentieth century. Bugrov, a rich shipowner, had once told him: 'You ought to spin yarns and not bother with untying the knots,' but Gorky was never satisfied with the yarn alone.

The period after the *Lower Depths* (from 1902 on) — which includes 'The Stormy Petrel' and his polemical plays, *Vassa Zheleznova* (1904), *Summer Residents* (1905), *The Barbarians, The Enemies* (1906) — culminated in *Mother,* the novel in which Gorky attempted to portray the revolutionary, the New Hero of his time. He had already outlined this type in some of his plays. Nil, the railroad mechanic in *The Petty Bourgeois,* proclaims: 'He who toils is the master,' 'Rights are not granted — they are taken,' 'Every train schedule is subject to change.' Sinzov, the professional revolutionist in *The Enemies,* is another precursor of this New Hero. As material for *Mother,* Gorky utilized the strike and the political demonstrations that actually had taken place in 1902 in the industrial town of Sormovo, and the workman Peter Zalomov and his mother served as prototypes for the hero and his mother. Paul, a young worker, joins the revolutionaries, carries the red banner in a mass demonstration, and is thrown into jail. Nilovna, his mother, a simple-minded, illiterate woman of forty, is worried about her son and is afraid of his association with the Reds. Yet when she gets to know his companions better and realizes their integrity and spirit of sacrifice, she feels that they are the salt of the earth, the seekers after truth, the true disciples of Christ, and little by little she comes to side with them. She begins by rendering them small services, helps them more and more, and finally becomes converted to their faith because she senses 'the truth that is bound to triumph.' The aesthetic drawbacks of this work are obvious. Some of the minor characters are well drawn, but Paul and his comrades, as well as Nilovna herself, are done as smudged romantic stencils. The whole canvas utilizes but two colors: unrelieved black for officers, policemen, and other representatives of the ruling classes, and a poetic pastel pink for their opponents. The revolutionaries are so idealized that they become as sweet and unreal as angels in children's picture books. They all talk a great deal, as if they were reciting propaganda leaflets, and even Nilovna makes a speech after her arrest — a scene of brutality and martyrdom bringing the novel to a close. The rhetorical eloquence throughout makes the book's message too shrill and often distorts the contours of characters. From the first pages the reader can easily guess what is coming next, and the story follows an obvious pattern, with no surprises. The characters, except for Nilovna, are static and uniform, and the manner of description is two-dimensional and never conveys any feeling of depth. But the most exasperating thing about *Mother* is that while Russian revolutionaries have very often been men and women of extraordinary moral rectitude who lived and died like saints, when Gorky tried to portray them that way, the result was flat and false. The similarity of his heroes to actual persons has nothing to do with their artistic reality: they do not ring true and are not aesthetically convincing.

There were, and still are, however, certain literary and extra-literary reasons that made *Mother* significant and explain why millions of copies of the novel were avidly read not only in Russia but abroad in dozens of translations. It was the first panoramic and frank picture in fiction of the Russian Socialist movement and of the ideological changes within the working class. Up to this time, there had been in Russian literature only a few indirect and somewhat subdued representations of revolutionary activity (except for the anti-revolutionary novels of the 'seventies). This had been due partly to the censorship: such liberal writers as Turgenev in *Virgin Soil,* were deliberately vague about their revolutionary heroes, while the radicals, such as Chernyshevsky in *What Is To Be Done?,* limited themselves to allusions and hints. All such novels had dealt exclusively with intellectuals. Dostoevsky in *The Possessed* and Tolstoy in *Resurrection* portrayed the revolutionists either critically or incidentally, fitting such figures into a whole that had to do with general moral and religious concepts. Gorky's was a one-way novel, with a singleness of purpose that determined its limitations but also endowed it with definite forcefulness. It was a book on the revolutionary awakening of the Russian people, and its heroes were representatives of the new class. Their portraits may have been schematic and flat and lacking in the usual literary color of the author — yet they reflected the psychology of those determined men and women who were ready to immolate themselves on the altar of their cause. Paul and his friends were proclaiming the Communist mentality. Ten years later people like those portrayed by Gorky seized power in Russia and built and promoted the Bolshevik party, which demanded their complete self-sacrifice and devotion. No wonder, then, that *Mother* has become a classic in the USSR: many Soviet writers have felt its impact, especially Dimitry Furmanov, Alexander Malyshkin, and Nicholas Ostrovsky — *The Tempering of the Steel,* by Ostrovsky, follows Gorky's pattern in many points.

As a proletarian and revolutionary novel *Mother* naturally established a literary pattern to be followed by many imitators. The style of the novel, maintained on a high pitch from first to last, is that of an adept of a new religion — the ecstatic, emotional, occasionally wrathful tone of a zealot. And it is this style that gives unity to *Mother,* despite all its stilted sentimentalism and symbolic schematism.

IV   The new period in Gorky's literary development, immediately following the publication of *Mother,* produced his most mature works. Between the thwarted Revolution of 1905 and the triumphant Revolution of 1917 he maintained all the good qualities of his early work and succeeded in overcoming many of his defects. While the intelligentsia fell prey to morbid disillusionment and escapism, Gorky continued to profess his faith in the inner goodness of man and kept his socialistic convictions, which were for him a logical corollary of his humaneness and his hatred of the iniquities and inequalities of Russian life. *Confession* and *Summer,* the two novels he wrote in 1908 and 1909 at Capri, were strongly optimistic. Matthew, the hero of *Confession,* is a God-seeker, one of those Russian peasants who wandered through the country in search of true faith; he finally comes to the conclusion that humanity is God and that people, as a collective force, may truly work miracles. Egor Trofimov, the leading character in *Summer,* who was at one time a military clerk, propagandizes revolution among the peasants with a thoroughly Gorkian feeling of the saintliness of the cause, and the book ends on a symbolic, almost religious, note.

While *Confession* reflected the interest Russian intellectuals displayed after 1905 in religious problems, *Summer* was more in the traditional socialistic vein; both novels, however, were not without Populist overtones. They also had a strong folkloristic flavor — as a matter of fact, in his Italian exile Gorky spent a great deal of time studying folklore. Both novels are supposedly stories told by men whose style maintains all the inflections and peculiarities of popular idiom. Stylization, rhythmic divisions of sentences, inversions, and Biblical images prevail in *Confession* and make it highly lyrical and a trifle artificial. *Summer* is written in a simpler vein, although its hero also uses idiomatic expressions and occasionally talks like a village preacher. These two transitional works bear the stigmata of sentimentalism and of splashed primary colors, but they do reveal Gorky's intensified concern with his craftsmanship. In the years to come he retained his new manner of using folkloristic devices and poetic language, but with more discernment and a greater sense of proportion. In general, he became more sensitive to formal problems and consciously bridled his natural inclinations toward a profusion of language and a plethora of detail. He turned deliberately to realistic descriptions of Old Russia, and his later novels, drawn from his personal experience, remain his highest achievements.

It would be fair to say that he had little inventive imagination, that the structure of his novels was faulty, and that, in general, he belonged to that large group of Russian realists who never wanted to produce and never could produce 'well-made' novels (the Turgenev-Chekhov school, of course, does not fall into this category, and Dostoevsky and Tolstoy, who also dismissed traditional well-turned works of art, had created their own great forms). *The Small Town of Okurov* (1910), *The Life of Matthew Kozhemyakin* (1911), the three autobiographical novels, *Childhood* (1913), *In the World* (1915), and *My Universities* (1923), as well as a succession of short stories such as 'Mordovka,' 'A Useless Life,' 'A Tale of Unrequited Love,' and his *Reminiscences,* all belong to the huge body of Gorkian memoirs.

Most of these works unfold a panorama of poverty, boredom, and cruelty. Horribly true as a genre picture of provincial life is the small town of Okurov, where even debauchery is dismal (even though the local brothel is called Little Paradise), where the drinking is joyless and the beatings are a matter of routine. Sima Devushkin, the humble town poet, declares in his halting lines: 'The woods are before us and the swamps are behind: we, God forgive us, do not care for life.' Another character seconds him: 'This burg is like a graveyard — there's a grave yawning for all things.' The inhabitants of Okurov still cling to old customs and fight the Europeanization of the country; their seventeenth-century way of life is a strange mixture of Asiatic nonchalance and Byzantine rigidity. They are ignorant, callous, and cruel; bigotry, chauvinism, and brutality make their hatred and envy dangerous. As in small towns the world over they enjoy torturing people and animals. Young men are killed or crippled in free-for-alls, amid the general delight of the onlookers.

The children in *The Life of Matthew Kozhemyakin* tie buckets to dogs' tails, throw sand in the eyes of beggars to find out if they are really blind, spill grease on the wooden sidewalks to make the passers-by fall, while their fathers kill one another for a bottle of vodka, ruin trees out of sheer love of destruction, and indulge in all sorts of brute mischief. Their everyday existence is blurred by monotony and aimlessness.

In *Childhood* Gorky also hit out at the prejudices and backwardness of the lower middle class, at the brutality, depravity, and animalism of the vast population of the Volga region he knew so well. The picture of the country one gets from this series of novels is the most depressing ever done by any writer since Gogol in *Dead Souls*. Gorky is, it is true, inclined to exaggeration and to the accumulation of striking and repulsive details in order to put across his critical exposé. Nevertheless his Okurov has become almost as much of a symbol in Russia as Sinclair Lewis' *Main Street* has in the United States. Gorky never hides his feelings about Asia-in-Russia, as he put it. His position was that of a Westernizer and of a rationalist, and he desired intelligent action to dispel the passive attitudes of dormant Russia. 'Do you know what Rasseya [4] is?' asks Pushkarev, the soldier in *The Life of Matthew Kozhemyakin*. 'There's no end to her; she has lots of ravines, swamps, steppes, stretches of sand — and all these must be put in order. There's work for two hundred years ahead in Russia. Well, let's do something about it, let's work and put her in order.' 'I'll tell you from all my heart,' says Tiunov in *The Small Town of Okurov,* 'this Russian people is a good people on this earth, a gifted, solid folk.'

'God sent man on this earth for good deeds,' proclaims Kozhemyakin, 'and to embellish life through joy — and what have we done with that life?' This longing for beauty and kindness often expresses itself in love. Throughout his writings Gorky points out that ignorant and bestial men see women only as objects of pleasure, and talk only of their feminine quirks, lies, and wiles, of their devious minds and predatory carnality. But they are wrong: 'Man's most intelligent achievement is his capacity or art of loving women, of worshipping their beauty; everything beautiful in the world owes its origin to love of women.' This romantic attitude does not preclude the author's wholesome acceptance of the flesh: 'A full and profound feminine caress makes the body flame and helps the soul to glow brightly and joyously.' ('Mordovka,' a short story, illustrates this attitude.)

The most attractive figures in Gorky's description of his own childhood are women, with the possible exception of his mother. Frustrated in his need for maternal affection, Gorky transferred his love to his grandmother. She told him fairy tales, saved him from beatings with her own body, and kept up a hearty optimism through all catastrophes and misfortunes. While the God of his grandfather was a remote, wrathful, and vengeful Master, his grandmother's God was human and kind, like herself. This unforgettable characterization of his grandmother is one of Gorky's masterpieces; it is quite possible that he wanted to show in Nilovna (*Mother*) what his grandmother would have become under other circumstances.

[4] A form of popular speech for 'Russia.'

In the three autobiographical novels, of which *Childhood* is undoubtedly the best, Gorky presented a whole gallery of character sketches, ranging from merchants and small shopkeepers to tramps, criminals, policemen, artisans, peasants, and intellectuals. Only in *Childhood* did he register his own violent reactions against the squalor of his early surroundings and speak at some length about himself. In *Out in the World* and *My Universities* he is simply the eye that sees and the ear that hears. With that marvelous visual and auditory memory which made him such an extraordinary storyteller in his conversation, he described in full the oppressed lower classes, their struggle for a crust of bread, and their desperate attempts to maintain some level of human dignity amid noisome surroundings and exhausting manual labor in the jungle of ferocious competition. He revealed how coarseness and ignorance were bolstered by the inhuman administration of corrupt police and by the whole system of class discrimination. What makes the autobiographical trilogy (and particularly *Childhood*) so attractive is that this realistic exposé, despite its tragic character, is permeated with a joyful sense of life. Vigor and affirmation emanate from these pages, and Gorky's virile attitude toward life is expressed in a message of faith and hope.

Gorky himself answered his critics when, at the end of Chapter XII in *Childhood,* he wrote: 'When I recall the leaden abominations of savage life in Russia, I sometimes ask myself: Is it worth while talking about them? And, with renewed conviction I answer myself: Yes, because they are the most tenacious, most vile reality of our life, and they have not yet abated. One must know them thoroughly to be able to root them out of man's memory and soul . . . There is another, more positive reason which compels me to paint these abominations. Although they are revolting and weigh upon us and crush to death many beautiful souls, the Russians are so wholesome and young in spirit that they can overcome them — and they will succeed in overcoming them. Our life is startling not because it consists of a self-perpetuating and greasy layer of beastly refuse, but because out of this layer bright, creative, wholesome, and good sprouts do come up, despite everything, and they arouse an indestructible hope of our resurgence into a luminous human life.'

This faith forms the background of an extraordinary variety of characterization: all of Gorky's novels between 1908 and 1923 are devoid of sustained plots; they are a series of realistic scenes, but they swarm with a host of figures who have an amazing vitality and completeness. The same art of characterization is displayed in *Reminiscences:* wonderful portraits of Tolstoy, Chekhov, Korolenko, Karonin, and others make this book one of the most remarkable in modern Russian literature. Gorky's memoirs of Lenin, although strongly marred by political considerations, belong in the same category. After the Revolution of 1917 Gorky continued his memoirs and also produced some new works dealing with Russia's past. The most important of these was *The Artamanov Business,* in which he returned to the theme he had explored in *Foma Gordeyev.* But instead of portraying an individual he now gave the history of three generations of Russian capitalists. The best pages of this novel, which becomes overcrowded and somewhat confused, are devoted to Ilya, founder of the Artamonov dynasty, a powerful and insatiable peasant whose strength and vitality reveal the usual Gorkian admiration for strong men, be they capitalists or tramps. By showing how the business took hold of Ilya's children and molded their lives, depriving them of any real happiness, Gorky wanted to symbolize the process of dehumanization inherent in capitalist accumulation. Some of his characterizations, such as those of Peter and of his wife Natalia, of Nikita, a hunchback obsessed by sex and the dream of a saintly life, and the scenes describing the third generation of shallow men and women who perish during the revolutionary upheaval are extremely vivid. Nevertheless it is difficult to accept *The Artamanov Business* as a completely successful artistic achievement. The same may be said of two of his plays, *Egor Bulychev and Others* and *Dostigaev and Others,* both written in 1932–3. The latter is too sketchy and seems incomplete, but the first has some gripping passages and dramatic situations. It is the drama of a tycoon who toward the end of his life (an end that coincides with the beginning of the Revolution) realizes the futility of all his work. Faced with death, Bulychev questions all the values he has lived for and his monologues acquire an emotional and symbolic meaning.

All the later works by Gorky were, in a way, an attempt to give a social analysis of the downfall of Russian capitalism, and were hailed as such by Soviet critics. His last was a tetralogical chronicle, *Klim Samghin;* its final scenes, including the arrival of Lenin in Petrograd in 1917 and the violent death of the hero, exist only in rough drafts. The author's aim was to give a chronological account of Russian life between 1870 and 1917, encompassing all the ideological battles among the intellectuals. The biography of Klim Samghin, a shallow and self-centered philistine who at one time had been a fellow-traveler of the liberal movement, serves as a vehicle for the story. In a way Klim incarnates all those shortcomings of the intelligentsia to which Gorky objected throughout his life; this footling hero is offset by Kutuzov, a Bolshevik who is as outspoken and full of life as Klim is hypocritical and morbid. Although the novel contains a considerable number of descriptive passages of value, the narrative is formless, lengthy, and the whole work is dull and flat. It might be used as a fictional illustration of the history of pre-Revolutionary Russia, but it does not hold any significant place in Russian letters.

v   From the time Gorky had left Nizhni Novgorod for St. Petersburg he had been constantly associated with the Social Democrats, and particularly with the Bolshevik faction. Writers who sympathized with Marxism rallied round him and contributed to the literary annuals *Znanye* (Knowledge), which Gorky began editing in 1902. *Znanye* favored writers of peasant and proletarian origin, although it must be said in all fairness that it also welcomed non-socialist authors from the aristocracy. Gorky had always helped the Bolsheviks; he contributed to their press, gave Lenin five thousand rubles toward the costs of *The Spark,* and secured considerable financial backing for him from the millionaire Savva Morozov, the Maecenas of the Moscow Art Theater. It must be pointed out that between 1900 and 1906 rich merchants contributed huge sums to the treasuries of socialist parties.

At the end of 1906, upon his return from America, Gorky went to the London conference of the Social Democratic party and observed the conflict between Lenin and Plekhanov, as well as the struggle between various groups of Mensheviks and Bolsheviks. His own position was somewhat ambiguous. On the one hand he had strong personal attachment for the Bolsheviks, and Lenin valued his friendship highly. Yet he had never been a regular member of the party, and as a 'sympathizer' was not subject to any formal discipline. His *Mother* had won him the unanimous approval of socialist leaders, but no sooner had he settled on the Island of Capri than he was surrounded by Lunacharsky, Bogdanov, and other 'heretics.' They all belonged to the group of 'God-builders,' who strove to reconcile Marxism and religion or, like Bogdanov and Paul Yushkevich, attempted to replace dialectical materialism by empirio-criticism, the fashionable philosophy of Ernest Mach and Richard Avenarius. The religious spirit of Gorky's *Confession* provoked a sharp rebuke from Lenin, who saw in the novel the reflection of a dangerous ideological deviation. When, in 1909, Gorky organized at Capri a school for training Russian workmen in socialism, he invited among others such lecturers as Trotsky and Kautsky, of whom Lenin could not approve. Gorky also contributed to Alexander V. Amphitheatrov's politically unstable *Contemporary* and, among other Populist publications, to *Legacies;* the visit paid to Capri by Victor Chernov, the leader of the Social Revolutionaries, also provoked many rumors. The correspondence (of which only excerpts are available) between Gorky and Lenin (who came to Capri in 1910) shows that the Bolshevik leader made desperate but not very successful efforts to keep the writer in line. In 1912 Gorky published articles in the St. Petersburg newspaper *Pravda* and in other Bolshevik periodicals, but the note of God-seeking in them fretted and displeased Lenin.

During World War I Gorky had taken an anti-militarist stand and had formed a connection with the Internationalists, a Marxist group. At the outbreak of the 1917 Revolution he and some of his friends founded *The New Life,* a daily designed to defend the positions of independent left-wing socialism. The newspaper criticized Kerensky's government as well as Lenin's 'Communist hysteria.' When the Bolsheviks seized power in November 1917, Gorky assumed a position that caused Trotsky to dub him Culture's Psalmodist. Gorky sharply criticized the first steps of the Communist regime; he represented a group of socialist intellectuals who were afraid of the corrupting influence of power on ideological leaders, and were shocked by the bloodshed and horrors of the Revolution. They tried desperately to save cultural and moral values from being swamped in the stormy sea of hatred and internecine war. Lenin's organ called Gorky's group (which included Kamenev, Zinoviev, and Martov) 'petty bourgeois chatterers' and the famous writer, whose fiftieth birthday anniversary had been forgotten in the tumult of the momentous events, replied with bitterness: 'For seventeen years I have considered myself a Socialist-Democrat . . . but I regard myself as a heretic in every group and party.' His position was a difficult one: the new government was made up of his old friends, yet he was attacking them because he was deeply disturbed about their terroristic methods and was pleading for freedom of expression: 'No matter in whose hands the government be, I support the human right to regard it critically.' He spoke of the 'despotism of yesterday's slaves,' and even went so far as to declare in one of his articles: 'Lenin and Trotzky have become infected by the bacillus of power; they show a disgraceful attitude toward the freedoms of speech and of person and toward all democratic rights.' He accused Lenin of having a merciless, aristocratic attitude toward the masses of the people. Even in the heat of the polemics, however, he paid his respect to the personality of his former friend, whom he had not seen since 1913: 'Lenin, this man of exceptional force, one of the biggest and most radiant figures in international social democracy, experiments and works like a chemist in his laboratory.'

The Bolshevik press responded with insults and rebuttals to Gorky's journalistic activity in 1918 — *Pravda* accused him of betrayal and wrote that he had 'sold out to the Constitutional Democracy and was fawning after the bourgeoisie.'

The moderate liberals and the conservatives, on the other hand, hated Gorky because of his equivocal position between the opponents of the regime and the regime itself, since he supported the idea of the proletarian revolution. This hatred became vicious in the following years (1919–21) when, under the influence of the civil war and the intervention of foreign powers, Gorky decided to give his support to the government for the defense of the Revolution. In 1919 he published his appeal *Follow Us,* pleading with the intellectuals to forget their scruples and to form a common front against reactionary generals and the Western powers. In many instances he continued to be critical of the Communist leaders, yet he felt that the preservation of cultural values was a much more fitting task for him than political journalism. His frequent meetings with Lenin, who helped him in protecting literature and the arts, which were so seriously threatened by the political struggle, famine, and general misery, sealed his reconciliation with the government in power.

Lenin and the other Bolshevik leaders spared no effort to have the great writer on their side; Gorky knew this and utilized his unique position to help the intellectuals. Future historians of the period of military Communism will determine fully the great debt Russian culture owes to Gorky. He saved hundreds of artists, writers, and scholars from starvation, humiliation, and death. He intervened on behalf of grand dukes and poets, of former bourgeois and professors sentenced to death. His was a gigantic task: he was trying to preserve the intelligentsia, whom he styled the 'only draft-horse harnessed to the ponderous wagon of Russian history.' To provide them with work and bread Gorky organized International Literature, a huge publishing enterprise supported by the state, which employed hundreds of writers and scholars as translators, researchers, and editors; he also founded The House of Art and The House of the Scholar, which gave shelter to hundreds of intellectuals in Petrograd.

In 1920 his friends used to say that Gorky was not a man but an institution. His activity was not limited to material help only — he brought together old writers and discovered new talents, offering the latter not only counsel but aid. 'Like a Pied Piper, he piped the song of reunion, and people in great numbers took courage and emerged from their caves,' wrote K. Fedin. Many of the young writers saw in him their literary godfather, and his role in the formation of Soviet literature, as well as his beneficial influence on the government's policy toward art in 1919–21, are undeniable.

In 1921 his varied activities and the poor living conditions undermined his health; the official version of the story is that Lenin urged him to go abroad. This, however, does not fully explain his prolonged absence from home. Why should Gorky have stayed in Capo di Sorrento, in Fascist Italy, rather than in Communist Crimea — especially during the period of 1921–8, the momentous years of the consolidation of the regime that hailed him as its greatest moral supporter? All those who, like the present writer, have had the opportunity of meeting Gorky in Europe know perfectly well that his departure was not entirely for reasons of health. Gorky had found the whole political atmosphere in Russia too oppressive. He often expressed his concern about the lack of freedom at home and never concealed his aversion to censorship. It was common knowledge that many things in his native land irritated him. At the beginning he hoped to accomplish in Europe what he could not do in Russia. He started a monthly, *Besseda* (Colloquy), the aim of which was to reunite Soviet writers with the most liberal of the *émigré* literati; he also promoted a publishing house in Berlin, whose purpose was to print and export Russian books to the USSR. But after a short period of activity in Germany and Czechoslovakia he retired to Capo di Sorrento.

By this time he had become appalled by the short-sightedness and inflexibility of the *émigrés:* their press never failed to vilify and slander him, and Zinaida Hippius called him the Gentle Hottentot, to the delight of her readers.

In Italy he devoted himself to writing and to correspondence with his friends in Russia. *My Universities, The Artamonov Business,* several short stories, and the first volume of *Klim Samghin* were written during this period. He received and answered hundreds of letters from Russian readers and writers, some of whom came on pilgrimages to see him, and these contacts strengthened his ties with the new generation. The cultural progress in the USSR and, particularly, the liquidation of illiteracy and the education of the masses outbalanced, in his opinion, all the shortcomings of the regime, and by 1927 he had become definitely reconciled to the new order. At the same time, the Kremlin was exerting a gentle but constant pressure for his return. When he finally yielded and came to Moscow for his sixtieth birthday, he was received with honors not usually conferred even upon heads of states.

From then on, both in his speeches and in his writings, Gorky gave unconditional support to the Soviet leaders. Whatever his objections to the rigors of the party line may have been, he felt it his duty to contribute to the building of the USSR, and he told his friends that all socialistically inclined intellectuals should refrain from any public criticism of the Soviet Union for the sake of its future achievements. The spread of Fascism in Europe also played a considerable part in shaping his convictions. Just as in 1918, he became an institution — the Pontiff of Russian literature, as he called himself with a grin. His influence, bolstered by his personal ties with Stalin, was vast: he built up or tore down literary reputations, he intervened in the Kremlin whenever the lid of repression was clamped down too tightly on things cultural. He was exceedingly active in some reforms and in the liberalization of the party's literary policy in 1932. His speeches in favor of literary craftsmanship and against red tape in the arts were of the utmost importance and of indubitable effectiveness. On the other hand, the position he held compelled him to carry out various functions for which he was not fitted. He was, for instance, asked to give his authoritative opinion on all sorts of current events, and he did this clumsily or naïvely by writing sentimental or irate articles in a popular, journalistic style. On many occasions he was forced to defend most inhuman and tyrannical actions of Soviet government. The party used him very much as some ecclesiastical groups use holy relics.

His new works — the two plays and *Klim Samghin* — were hardly additions to the main body of his writings. He felt that he ought to limit himself to the representation of the past and, while all the Soviet critics thundered against novelists who did not 'reflect their own times,' Gorky made no attempt whatsoever to deal with contemporary life and did not write on Communist Russia. It was odd and somewhat paradoxical that the man admired as the leader of Soviet literature and the dean of proletarian writers belonged, because of his subject matter, completely to the pre-Revolutionary period. His almost religious dreams of freedom and justice, his realistic exposés of Russian life, his social and national feelings likewise followed the nineteenth-century tradition, and he stood out as one of the last representatives of the old culture.

Yet, after his death, certain additional aspects became apparent and gave the clue to a better understanding of Gorky's role in Russian life and letters. Although in his humaneness and realism he carried on the trends of the past, his work had also opened new vistas. His heroes were not the noblemen of Turgenev, the aristocrats of Tolstoy, the frenzied youths of Dostoevsky, or the despondent intellectuals of Chekhov — they were workers, dockers, hoboes, lower-middle-class artisans, merchants sprung from the peasantry, or *déclassés* burghers. He proclaimed — by his own life, by the themes of his novels, and by his literary methods — the advent of an art created by the lower classes and devoted to them, an art devoid of refinement, almost crude in its naturalism, yet full of virility, of generous ideas, and of exuberant, somewhat primitive vitality. Soviet readers, most of whom had been but recently introduced to the arts, responded enthusiastically to the writer who had come from the same milieu as they had and whose combination of tenderness and toughness, faith in reason, concreteness, didacticism, and popular language appealed so much to their minds and hearts.

Gorky regarded his profession as 'an important and responsible public service' and insisted that a writer should be politically active: he was therefore in full agreement with the basic principles of Communist aesthetics. Moreover, as a proletarian, the author of *Mother,* a socialist, and a revolutionary, he seemed the ideal embodiment of these very principles, and his blending of romanticism with realistic observation, his belief in man, and his optimistic rationalism were proclaimed the essentials of the theory that was given the name Socialist Realism. This explains Gorky's dual position: as the guardian of the national cultural heritage and the teacher of the new generation, he forms the bridge between the literature of Imperial Russia and that of the Soviet Union.

8

1905 AND ITS AFTERMATH

I   THE MOVEMENT FOR LIBERATION, which by 1904 stirred all strata of Russian society, was due to the awakening of the masses resulting from economic and social changes at the turn of the century, to liberal opposition, and to the underground activity of the socialist parties. Various factors contributed to bringing this movement to its peak, and the Russo-Japanese War was one of the most decisive. It began in January 1904 with a treacherous attack on the Russian fleet at Port Arthur, and developed into a succession of reverses and disasters for the Imperial armed forces. Although Russian soldiers and sailors demonstrated their usual stamina and courage, their hearts were not in this campaign, which was fought for obscure reasons on foreign soil, thousands of miles from home. The war was also unpopular among the educated groups, who accused the government of having unleashed the conflict with the ulterior motive of creating a diversion.

At the same time this war, not unlike the Crimean Campaign of the 'fifties, revealed the unpreparedness and corruption of the Czarist regime. Many of those in high command cared more for their comfort and their drinking parties than for strategic moves. Instead of badly needed ordnance and shells carloads of holy images were sent to the front. No subversive propaganda could undermine autocracy more than this picture of incompetence, venality, and debauchery which recruits saw in Manchuria.

The surrender of Port Arthur (in rather suspicious circumstances) after a siege of eleven months, the defeat at Mukden (where, out of an army of 300,000, the Russians lost 120,000 men killed, wounded, and captured), and the naval disaster at Tsushima sealed the defeat of the Russian Empire. The hasty peace concluded at Portsmouth, New Hampshire, in August 1905, could hardly stop the repercussions of this unhappy war: the Far Eastern campaign led to an increase in the cost of living and to deterioration of conditions in agriculture and industry; it stimulated general discontent, gave a tremendous advantage to the opposition, and represented a great loss of prestige for the regime. The labor movement, which had been steadily growing since the beginning of the century, now assumed a political character. Strikes and mass demonstrations led to clashes with the police, some of which turned into pitched battles. The peasants were restless because of the precarious land situation and the recruiting of the younger men, while the blows dealt by the terrorists against the most hated representatives of bureaucratic reaction kept the intelligentsia and the middle class in a state of nervous suspense. By the end of 1904, when the government made some vague promises of constitutional reforms, Russia had its first 'political spring' since 1861. The progressive elements were seized with feverish activity; at banquets held in common by aristocrats, burghers, and democratic intellectuals, speakers and toast-masters hailed Freedom and the Constitution. Hundreds of petitions demanded the transformation of autocracy into a parliamentary monarchy. Scientific reunions, professional conventions, and all sorts of meetings were voting political resolutions. At public readings of the stories of Gorky or Korolenko, or the poems of Nekrassov, every liberal allusion provoked thunderous applause. Auditoriums became scenes of political demonstrations, while 'La Marseillaise,' the revolutionary anthem banned by Russian police, resounded in academic halls.

An innocent traveler visiting Russia at this time heard the slogan 'Down with autocracy' so often that he decided it was the favorite Russian saying. The momentum of the Movement for Liberation was increasing daily. And while the liberal bourgeoisie, and particularly the Constitutional Democrats, maintained their confidence in legal or semilegal pressure against the government, the Social Revolutionaries and the Bolsheviks advocated armed rebellion and had visions of a democratic republic. The liberal and revolutionary agitation as well as the labor and peasant movements spread throughout the Empire: in Poland, in the Baltic provinces, in the Ukraine, in White Russia and various parts of the Caucasus, the demands for reforms were proclaimed together with claims for national autonomy or outright independence, and national liberal or socialist parties were as active as their Russian comrades.

On Sunday, 9 January (22, New Style) 1905, some 150,000 workmen in St. Petersburg marched to the Winter Palace in order to present their petitions to the Czar. Their columns, carrying holy banners and portraits of Nicholas II, were met by the fire of police guns. More than a thousand demonstrators, including women and children, were killed, and twice that number were wounded.

This Bloody Sunday had a tremendous effect. Protest strikes and anti-government demonstrations swept the country. The indignation of liberals and socialists rose to unprecedented heights. There were hundreds of appeals for an 'attack against Czarism,' and street disorders became more violent than ever. Lenin, who was in Geneva at the time, entitled one of his articles in the clandestine press 'The Beginning of the Revolution in Russia' — and he was absolutely correct. The march to the Winter Palace served as an introduction to events of greater and more threatening magnitude. In the next few months Russia was shattered by explosions of bombs, by peasant uprisings, and by an uninterrupted series of clashes between the defenders of the regime and its growing opposition. Some 14,000 strikes, of which 10,000 were coupled with political demands, involved several million workers in 1905. The agitation also spread to civil servants, administration employees, students, reservists, and demobilized soldiers. The mutiny on board the warship *Potemkin,* which carried the red flag in the Black Sea waters and shelled the port of Odessa, proved that even the Army and the Navy — the traditional pillars of the regime — could not be relied upon.

The peace with Japan and the timorous discussion of reforms in governmental committees failed to appease public opinion, and by the end of 1905 the whole country was ablaze. In October the general strike of railroads, mail, telegraph, schools, mills, the press, public utilities, and private enterprises practically paralyzed the nation. Mass demonstrations and much barricading of streets in scores of towns took place during this strike. Unable to cope with the situation by brute force, the government, although reluctant, sought a compromise. On 17 October (30, New Style) 1905, a manifesto by the Czar promised the convocation of a State Duma, an elected legislative body, as well as freedom of speech, of the press, and of assembly.

These concessions, which at first caused great rejoicing among the liberals, were, however, immediately offset by pogroms of Jews and intellectuals, organized by the Czarist authorities in order to show that 'the true Russians did not want any reforms; it is only the Jews and the students who are stirring up trouble.' The socialists accused the government of foul play and double dealing. The Bolsheviks and the Essars, whose ranks had been swelled by *émigrés* returned from their European exile (such as Lenin, Trotzky, Martov, Chernov, Avxentiev, and many others), advocated an armed uprising that would 'storm and demolish the citadel of Czarism.' At this moment of utter confusion (or the Days of Freedom, as they were called later), the authority of the government was badly shaken. For the first time, political parties began to operate in the open; their literature was distributed in the streets or at public meetings, and newspapers and hastily organized publishing houses, taking advantage of a momentary abolition of censorship, printed millions of copies of works hitherto banned. Books by Herzen, Lavrov, Chernyshevsky, the Decembrists, and all clandestine literature in general suddenly became available to the masses. Newspapers and the numerous newly established weeklies discarded their cryptic Aesopic language and enjoyed full freedom of expression for the first time in the history of Russia. Dozens of satirical sheets made vitriolic fun of the regime and the Romanov dynasty. It looked as if the downfall of autocracy was a matter of just a few months.

These expectations were, however, grossly miscalculated. The Cadets (Constitutional Democrats), the liberal bourgeoisie, the progressive landowners, and a part of the middle class, as well as some of the enlightened Monarchists (for the most part former Slavophiles who had rallied round the conservative party of 17 October), were all frightened by the violence of the revolutionary outburst and the sweep of the popular movement: peasants were burning old manors, soldiers were rebeling and killing officers, workmen were stoning police patrols, terrorists were throwing bombs, holding up branches of the State Bank, erecting barricades, and arming their 'combat detachments.' The rebellions in the Caucasus or in the Baltic provinces, where the farmers were murdering the barons, and the sudden demands for civil rights and autonomy by various ethnic stocks and nationalities in the Empire threatened the very foundation of the State. A large united front of the bourgeoisie, ranging from mild liberals to the Octobrists, wanted to restore order, to use legal methods, to consolidate the positions already won. A considerable proportion of the intelligentsia was even prepared to lend a helping hand to the government in its struggle against the menace of anarchy, and this was the beginning of their rift with the radicals. The unity of the Movement for Liberation was definitely broken.

The socialists, who denounced the 'betrayal' of the liberals and regarded the government's policy of reforms and appeasements as merely attempts to gain time, lacked unity and overestimated the awakening of the masses, at the same time underestimating the strength of the bureaucratic administration. The Mensheviks, now led by Plekhanov, saw the revolution as a stage of the inevitable capitalistic development: its aim was the establishment of a bourgeois democratic regime within which the forces of labor could begin their struggle for power. The Bolsheviks, on the other hand, claimed that the bourgeoisie had manifested its anti-revolutionary tendencies and that only the dictatorship of the working masses could guarantee the victory and facilitate the passage from autocracy to socialistic transformations. And while the Bolsheviks hoped to overthrow the regime by armed force, the majority of the Mensheviks preferred more pacific means.

This difference of opinions did not prevent both factions from detesting the Essars, whom they accused of being 'adventurers' and the 'scions of petty bourgeoisie'; they also condemned the method of individual terror, so extensively practiced by the Socialist Revolutionists. The Essars, in their turn, reproached the Mensheviks with lack of courage and with philistinism, and sneered at the inability of the Bolsheviks to offer any solution of the land problem. The Essars, moreover, also had their factions, ranging from 'maximalists,' who rejected any legal methods, to dissenters who had formed in 1906 the Party of Popular Labor: the latter rallied the moderate Populists round a program of democratic socialism and rejected terror and armed rebellion.

By December 1905, the spectacular armed mutinies in the navy at Cronstadt and Sebastopol, and the celebrated uprising of workmen in Moscow, where pitched battles had been fought in the streets for several days, with an extensive use of artillery, had been crushed by the government. All the efforts of the St. Petersburg Soviet Council of delegates from various unions and socialist parties, in which Trotzky played the leading role, to help the rebels had failed to produce any important result. This was the turning point: although scattered revolts, street demonstrations, and acts of terrorism continued to flare up (sometimes extensively, stirring up whole regions) in 1906 and, to some extent in 1907, the revolutionary movement was losing momentum; the forces of the government, on the contrary, were steadily gaining vigor in their successful counteroffensive. By 1907 it became obvious that the regime had won the battle: it had the whole country under control again and was resorting to every sort of repressive measure to extinguish the smoldering remnants of the great fire.

In 1905–6 the masses had for the first time taken part in the revolutionary movement, which had been initiated by isolated groups of the intelligentsia, but their rebellion had been chaotic and lacking in organization and singleness of purpose. The enormous territory of the empire had also been one of the obstacles in the unity and timing of the revolution, while its leaders, because of the splitting up of parties and factions, had failed to channel and to synchronize all the sporadic and scattered outbreaks of popular discontent. The peasants, especially, had not been ripe for a systematic and sustained attack against the regime; the majority of them still had some illusions about the Czar or remained passive. The army, despite isolated uprisings, was strictly regimented and obedient to their commanders — the cavalry in particular had remained faithful to the authorities. The bureaucratic apparatus, the police force, the various special corps of security troops had been untouched by subversive propaganda, and the government, after the first shock, had used them adroitly. The revolutionaries also had underestimated the number of conservatives and reactionaries, including the Black Hundreds: aggressive bands of hoodlums and unemployed who were organized by the police and utilized by the government at the last moment.

Nevertheless, although autocracy had not been overthrown, it had been compelled to make concessions and to establish at least a semblance of a parliamentary regime. It is true that this experiment was by no means conclusive: it lasted only twelve years. No one can tell whether its development and consolidation would have altered the fate of Russia. The events of 1905 showed that there was an enormous amount of explosive material within the people; they also emphasized a trend that was historically inevitable, although only a few realized its full significance at that time: the masses had entered the battle under the leadership of extremists; the direction of the popular movement always remained in the hands of the socialist parties, and ideas of radical social and economic transformation found an enthusiastic response among the workers and greatly appealed to the peasants and the lower middle class. Today it is apparent that 1905 served as a dress rehearsal for the final Revolution of 1917, and the study of events during 1905 and after offers a key for the understanding of Communist successes in Russia following the collapse of Czarism.

The reaction that set in after the subsiding of the revolutionary wave was brutal and merciless. In punitive expeditions, led by such generals as Min, Rieman, Rennenkampf, and Admirals Chukhnin and Dubassov (subsequently shot by revolutionaries), tens of thousands were tortured, flogged, and jailed and thousands of others were executed without trial. In one year several thousand persons were court-martialed and twenty thousand sentenced to hard labor in Siberia. The inmates of prisons could be counted by hundreds of thousands. In 1908 there were 1959 death sentences for political offenses, and in 1909, 1435.

In 1907 Tolstoy published 'I Cannot Remain Silent,' his protest against capital punishment, and Korolenko protested in 1910 with his 'Everyday Happening.' Many contemporary writers described the executions in their tales and novels (see Andreyev's 'The Seven Who Were Hanged,' Sergheiev-Tsensky's 'Lieutenant Babaev,' and Serafimovich's 'Moscow Uprising'). Many of these works were confiscated after the restoration of censorship: in 1908–9 more than a thousand newspapers and magazines were forced to suspend publication. Some statistical data of that period sound exceedingly odd: 40 works of Tolstoy confiscated, 600 pogroms staged, and 7000 gallows put up.

The first and the second Dumas were dissolved, since many of the deputies were leftists and demanded constitutional guarantees and a land reform. In June 1907, Peter Stolypin (1862–1911), the strong man of the regime, who had been given almost dictatorial powers, introduced a new electoral law enabling a group of 230 landowners to send as many delegates to an electoral college as 1000 city dwellers or 60,000 peasants could send. The population of Central Asia had no right to vote, Poland could elect only 12 deputies, while the 'remote regions' sent only 39 representatives to the Duma. In the third Duma, called Stolypin's Duma, the landowners had 202 deputies, or 46 per cent of the legislative body.

Faithful to his slogan, 'order first, reforms afterward,' Stolypin next initiated his agrarian reform, through which the peasants were forced to abandon the *mir* in order to become individual farmers. This policy aimed at the destruction of the collective ownership and cultivation of the land that formed the basis of Populist and socialist hopes. Stolypin wanted to create a peasant middle class on which the monarchy and the 'elements of order' could rely in the future. At the same time he tried to alleviate the misery of the peasants by adopting extensive measures of migration: in 1906–10 more than two and a half million farmers moved to Siberia and Central Asia. Although Stolypin's reform could not change the fact that almost 150 million hectares of the best arable land belonged to privileged groups, it did start a transformation of the Russian village: two million peasant households on an area of 18 million hectares left the *mir* and became private landowners.

At the same time Stolypin, who certainly was the most talented representative of Russian conservatism, adopted protective measures for the promotion of capitalism: between 1908 and 1914 the construction of railroads, factories, housing, and roads made big strides; financial and industrial capital had increased rapidly, and the growth of banking was surprising. Together with these economic developments, skilled labor increased in number (2,588,000 in 1913 as against 1,765,000 in 1908), and industrial production had by 1916 gone up to 8 billion rubles. The Europeanization of the country had also made rapid strides: by 1916 Russia was no longer the one great village she had been throughout the nineteenth century: the rise of towns and the expansion of big cities made the upper middle class and the bourgeoisie more active and added to their financial and social weight.

Although the revolutionary period did bring about a slight liberalization of the regime, including improvements in labor conditions, more freedom for the press, some expansion of education, and the founding

of the Duma — a distorted parliament but an elected legislative body
nevertheless — the oppression and poverty of the masses, the administrative abuses, the rigidity and irresponsibility of autocracy, and its
contempt for human rights remained unchanged: the foundations of the
autocratic regime, although battered and shaken, had withstood the
revolutionary upheaval, and the timid constitutional practices, patterned
after the Western democracies, were constantly drowned in the high
seas of authoritarian dictatorship. This situation lasted to the very end of
the Empire.

II   The blossoming of intellectual and
artistic life that had begun in the 'nineties continued throughout the years
of intense political activity. The two decades before the fall of Czarism
have often been called the Silver Age of Russian culture, as compared
with the Golden Age of the mid-nineteenth century. It did not produce
such gigantic figures as the classic era initiated by Pushkin and Gogol, but
it had a larger diffusion and range. The progress was rapid and intense
in all the fields of science — the physiologists led by Ilya Mechnikov
(1845–1916) and Ivan Pavlov (1849–1936), the botanists by Konstantin Timiriazev (1843–1920) and Ivan Michurin (1855–1935);
physics were represented by Alexander Popov (1859–1905), one of the
pioneers in wireless telegraphy, the geologists Alexander Karpinsky
(1847–1936) and Vassily Williams (1863–1939), the geochemist Vladimir Vernadsky (1863–1945), the aerodynamicist Nicholas Zhukovsky
(1847–1921), and many other scientists who brought research to unprecedented heights. In the humanities historians such as Vassily Kliu-
chevsky (1841–1911) and Serghei Platonov (1860–1933) and literary
critics such as Alexander Vesselovsky (1838–1906), Semion Vengerov
(1855–1920), Razumnik Ivanov-Razumnik (1878–1945), Michael
Gershenzon (1869–1925), Yuly Aikhenwald (1872–1928) all produced works of the highest value.

The universities attained a high level of scholarship and were true
centers of research and culture. Their political role as promoters of the
liberal movement was also great: students and professors alike took
active part in protests against abuse and in the struggle for academic freedom and for student organizations. All Russian universities belonged to
the State and were controlled by the government. By 1912 the eleven
State universities had enrollments of 137,000 students; private institutions of higher learning, particularly women's colleges and art schools,
were also increasing in number. Scientific and cultural societies, together
with a network of private university extension courses (called People's
Universities), were to be found everywhere in Russia. While the gov-

ernment still controlled the majority of secondary educational institutions (the *gymnasias*) and the military and technical academies, the *zemstvos* (autonomous rural bodies), as well as the municipalities, made great headway in elementary education. In 1914, the *zemstvos* spent 106 million rubles ($53,000,000) for schools and controlled 13,000 public libraries.

In painting, besides the *World of Art* group of V. Serov, M. Vrubel, A. Benois, M. Dobuzhinsky, N. Roerich, N. Somov, and many others, there were the realistic school led by Ilya Repin and the religious painters, such as Victor Vasnetzov (1848–1926) and Michael Nesterov (1862–1942). The theater was in flower with the Moscow Art Theater, the Bolshoi (Great) Theater of Moscow, the Maly (Little) and Alexandrinsky theaters in St. Petersburg, and a score of other new ventures. The ballet, subsidized by the government, had developed brilliantly. In music, of the Mighty Five group, originally consisting of Mussorgsky, Borodin, Kuy, Rimsky-Korsakov, and Balakirev, only the last three were still alive and carrying on the classic tradition together with Serghei Taneyev (1850–1918), Alexander Glazunov (1865–1936), Anton Arensky (1861–1906), Michael Ippolitov-Ivanov (1859–1935), Rheinhold Glière (1875–1950), and Alexander Grechaninov (1864–1955). The new mystical trend was represented by Alexander Scriabine (1871–1915), with his universally renowned tone poems *Ecstasy, Prometheus,* and other works for the piano and orchestra. Serghei Rachmaninov (1873–1943), Serghei Prokofiev (1891–1953), and Nicholas Medtner (1880–1953) — the new generation of young composers — were already at work, as was one of their most brilliant contemporaries — Igor Stravinsky (born in 1882; his *Petrushka* ballet was first performed in 1911).

What made the beginning of the twentieth century so fruitful and exciting was the general atmosphere of eagerness and expectation among the intellectuals, whose ranks were constantly gaining adherents among the scions of the middle and lower classes. The publication of a book, the production of a new play, the opening of an exhibition was a memorable event in Russia's large cities: it was a source of enjoyment, of discussions, and of inspiration. Intellectual interests expanded and grew, and the intelligentsia found itself much more important numerically than ever before. The growth of the daily press and of publishing in general had been steady since the end of the 'nineties; it became feverish about 1905, when the circulation of periodicals, pamphlets, and books reached figures hitherto unheard of in Russia, and even after the curtailment imposed by the reaction of 1907–8 there was a steady development of the publishing business. In 1901 only 11,000 titles of books were published in Russia; by 1913 the number had risen to 34,000.

The daily papers reflected all shades of public opinion — ranging from labor organs edited by Bolsheviks and Mensheviks to the liberally academic *Moscow Gazette,* the St. Petersburg *Speech,* and the conservative *New Times.* Some informative dailies, such as the *Russian Word,* reached a circulation of over a million, and a number of provincial dailies in Kiev, Odessa, Rostov, and so on had a very wide public. A new feature, which seemed a sign of the times, was the appearance of cheap dailies for the half-educated masses. In the book trade such publishing ventures as *The Don Word* (controlled by the radical intelligentsia) and *The Intermediary* (directed by the disciples of Tolstoy) launched whole series of pamphlet-size books, selling from a kopeck up, which found a hitherto untapped group of readers. Another salient feature was the tremendous number of translations from all foreign languages. In no other country were great European and American authors read as eagerly as in Russia. Whether this was due to the increased process of Europeanization or to other causes, the fact remains that dozens of publishing houses made a specialty of bringing to the Russians the most renowned works of French, German, English, Italian, American, Scandinavian, and other literatures.

In general, the upsurge of national energy was most patent in the domain of belles-lettres. The literary revival initiated by the Modernists of the 'nineties brought forth at the beginning of the twentieth century a new group of poets, novelists, and essayists. This artistic renaissance continued throughout the two decades preceding the 1917 Revolution and overlapped the first years of the Soviet era.

At the beginning of the century the atmosphere had been a hopeful one; expectation of great events filled the plays of Chekhov and the tales of Gorky; a number of minor realistic writers also mirrored this mood — as did the Decadents and the Symbolists: in 1901 Gorky wrote 'The Stormy Petrel,' but Briussov, Sologub, Balmont, and their friends also published an array of revolutionary poems. The group of writers who had rallied round Gorky and his *Znanye* publishing house was especially typical of the Days of Freedom and Revolt. Some of them were of proletarian and peasant origin, as in the case of Semion Podiachev (1866–1947) and Ivan Volnov (1885–1931), whose crude and almost photographic stories dealing with factories and village life had a pointed social message. Others, such as Nicholas Teleshov (1867–1947), who achieved a higher degree of literary craft, and Ivan Nazhivin (1874–1940), a prolific author of far too many novels, were distinctly Tolstoyan in their moral preaching. Stepan Petrov (1868–1934), who wrote under the pen name of Skitaletz (Wanderer) in his sketches about tramps, and Serghei Gusev-Orenburgsky (1867), the chronicler of provincial clergy, followed Gorky's manner. The same can be said about one of the most important members of the group, Alexander Serafimovich (Popov) (1863–1949), the son of a Cossack officer, who joined the revolutionists and underwent arrest and exile. His expressive and vivid stories of the lower middle class enjoyed some success. After 1921 he became the head censor of the Soviets, and *The Iron Stream* (1924), his novel of the Russian civil war, gained wide popularity in the USSR. Another Social Democrat, Vikenty Smidovich-Veressaev (1867–1946), the son of a nobleman of Polish descent (both father and son were physicians), registered in his short novels the political and ideological changes in the intelligentsia; his *Notes of a Physician* (1901) was a best seller. Like Serafimovich, he reached the peak of his popularity under the Soviets; he, too, published a novel on the civil war, *The Deadlock* (1922), and was highly praised for his lively montage-biographies of Pushkin and other Russian classics, as well as for his translations from the Greek. Eugene Chirikov (1864–1937), also of noble descent, was the author of social plays and light, sentimental novels about youth; he emigrated after 1917 and died in exile in Prague. Semion Yushkevich (1868–1927) devoted himself to the portrayal of lusty and vulgar Jewish 'acquirers' as opposed to humble and kind-hearted poor Jews; his sentimental novels and plays were popular in 1910–12. All these writers, as well as dozens of others whose names are not mentioned here because they have slight historical significance, expressed the hopes and elation of their time; their works were animated by the spirit of rebellion, of social protest, and of political optimism.

After the decline of the Movement for Liberation, however, the literary scene changed rapidly. Pessimism and moral lassitude became prevalent between 1906 and 1912. While the Decadents and the Symbolists offered an escape into fantasy, exoticism, sex, and mysticism, the realistic writers simply mirrored the gloom and disillusionment of the intelligentsia. The failure of 1905 shattered the faith of the intellectuals in themselves and in the masses. In the years of moral disintegration and psychological complexes that followed the defeat, the most cherished ideals and illusions of the radical intelligentsia were drowned in the turbid welter of reaction. The atmosphere seemed foul and unwholesome. In 1908 it became public knowledge that Evno Azef, one of the leaders of the terrorist organization of the Social Revolutionaries, was a paid agent of the Secret Police — just as proved to be the case with Malinovsky, the Bolshevik deputy to the Duma and a friend of Lenin. These revelations brought a wave of suicides in their wake.

Former terrorists such as Victor Savinkov (Ropshin) (1879–1925), published autobiographical novels (*The Pale Horse,* 1909, and *That*

Which Never Happened, 1912) in which, under the thin disguise of fiction, they presented their revolutionary experiences in a Modernistic style, with a great deal of morbidity and repentance. Revisionists were active everywhere: in the Social Democratic party they wanted to liquidate the tactics of the past. The 'heresy' of God-builders, who looked for a religious bolstering of socialism, became, together with other philosophical deviations, the target of Lenin's virulent attacks.

Some of the Populists criticized the terroristic tactics of the Social Revolutionists, while others advocated reformism, and a dwindling handful of Bolsheviks and die-hards showed an inclination for the anarchists. Certain groups were attracted by Syndicalism; others bitterly reproved the intellectuals and advised the workers to break with the effete and corrupt intelligentsia. The Liberal Revisionists tried to revaluate the principles that had always been considered sacred in radical circles — their attempts were the most spectacular. This group published *Milestones* (1909), a collection of articles that made a frontal attack against 'socialistic and revolutionary illusions.' Peter Struve, one of the leaders, hailed the European middle class as the paragon of wisdom and stability, and denounced the anti-bourgeois spirit of the intelligentsia as romantic nonsense; he expressed his gratitude to the government that had put an end to the upsurge of the anarchical, bloodthirsty, and ignorant masses. Other contributors to *Milestones* claimed that revolutionary and socialistic activities had drained all the forces of the intelligentsia and deranged its thinking. They asserted that the intellectuals, spellbound by their fatal infatuation, had forgotten the supreme values: God, nation, individual. A return to religion, to idealistic philosophy, to contemplation and individual perfection, as well as to sound nationalism, was recommended as the only possible cure.

The way numerous groups of the educated society followed this advice did not meet fully the expectations of the *Milestones* group. Individualism and 'healthy nationalism' turned into egotistical gratification of appetites or bombastic chauvinism. The reaction against the ascetic morality of the revolutionaries easily degenerated into debauchery or outright hedonism. Sexual pleasure and aesthetic enjoyment were proclaimed far superior to the antiquated ideas of public service or political activity. Erotic literature attained a sudden and tremendous vogue. All European authors who dealt with problems of sex — Strindberg, Wedekind, Weininger, and a score of French novelists, from Mirbeau to Rémy de Gourmont — were speedily translated and avidly read. Publishing ventures such as *The Facts of Life, The Mysteries of Sex,* and the like flourished next to openly pornographic publications. Native writers such as Anatole Kamensky (b. 1877), with his stories of virile males and wicked females (*Woman, Leda,* 1910), or Nicholas Oliger (1882–1919) glorified physical love and the pleasures of the senses. Their writings were responsible for the formation of numerous Leagues of Free Love and clandestine clubs, where young people showed their daring by organizing Athenian Nights. It was typical of Russian intellectuals that they were not satisfied with merely gratifying their desires: they sought to prove that in doing so they were asserting their moral superiority and were accomplishing an act of liberation. Literature of pseudo-Nietzschean character flooded the book market, and the somber, snobbish heroes and beautiful, enigma-ridden heroines of Anastasia Verbitzkaia (1861–1928), who explored the intricacies of sex, free love, and 'intensified living,' were tremendously popular (particularly her best seller, *The Keys to Happiness,* 1909–13, a pretentious, pompous, and melodramatic novel in five volumes). Verbitzkaia was followed by a score or so of minor writers, who mingled suggestive scenes with challenging statements about the Emancipation of the Senses and the right to pleasure — E. Nagrodskaia [1] (1866–1939), *The Wrath of Dionysus* (1910); and Vladimir Vinnichenko (1880–1951), *Self Honesty* (1911).

The younger generation also avidly read the Decadents and raved about the Intensification of Desires and the Sharpening of Sensations as the supreme goals of life. The vogue of the Modernists was matched by a predilection for demonism and black magic: side by side with groups devoted to free love there were suicide clubs, Satanists, and so on. This search for morbidity, perversion, and strangeness explains why the writers of the late 'nineties met with such success after 1905: in the atmosphere of decay and social reaction a large portion of the educated society looked for spice and excitement in the works of Valery Briussov, Konstantin Balmont, and Theodore Sologub, while the popularity of Andreyev had its roots in the same psycho-social environment.

One of the most significant novels of this period was undoubtedly *Sanin* (1907), the work of Michael Artzybashev (1878–1927). In his first stories, which he began publishing in 1901, Artzybashev was under the double influence of Tolstoy and Dostoevsky. The hero of his 'Lande's Death' (1904), in reality a popular version of Prince Myshkin (*The Idiot*), is a non-resister to evil and rejects physical love. Later, however, Artzybashev concentrated precisely on the portrayal of sex and violence: his story of the high-school student who murders his headmaster ('Pasha Tumanov,' 1905) and particularly his tales of the revolutionary period depicting punitive expeditions, mass executions, bloodshed, and death throes are not devoid of a certain gruesome power. They all imply that man is by nature a scoundrel, that life has no meaning, while culture is

[1] Daughter of Panaeva-Golovacheva; see *The Epic of Russian Literature,* p. 232.

merely a blind for unspeakable instincts. Sanin, the hero of Artzybashev's most important novel, repeats these statements and also expresses his contempt for any code of morality. His philosophy is quite simple: 'I do what I want to do and can do'; man should be as free as a bird; he has the right to enjoy love-making without fear or scruples — and the liberation of his body is one of the great tasks of modern times. As a novel of 'sexual emancipation' *Sanin* fits into the general anti-puritanical and erotic trend of twentieth-century European literature, but its hero belongs to a Russian environment. His theory and practice of sexual freedom, which are described with naturalistic details, are offered to the reader as an answer to all questions concerning life.

Just as half a century before Chernyshevsky had portrayed Rachmetov (in *What Is To Be Done*) as a model man of his generation, so Artzybashev presented Sanin. Those who saw in the much discussed novel only suggestive scenes, shocking their morality or titillating their senses, were mistaken: it was, as is usual in Russia, a book with a message, and Sanin slept with all his mistresses to prove a thesis rather than to obey a natural urge. Artzybashev preached physiological gratification as a credo, and the influence of his novel was amazingly extensive and completely disproportionate to its limited intrinsic value. It expressed the mentality of bourgeois youth who sought to forget the unpleasant experiences of an abortive revolution and needed new idols to worship; it also challenged the customary restraint of Russian writers in matters of sex. The realistic school of the nineteenth century had avoided any direct description of physical passion. This tradition was broken by the Decadents and Symbolists, and Artzybashev reflected the new spirit.

Liberation through the assertion of the flesh, however, did not make Sanin very happy. The kind of love he advocated brought but momentary relief: *amor furor brevis*. Artzybashev's eroticism, like that of most of his contemporaries, had pessimistic overtones and seemed more like an outlet than like self-affirmation. The heroes of his next novel, *At the Brink* (1911–12), oscillate between sexual desire and the death instinct, and seven of them commit suicide; this lengthy, utterly gloomy work of decay and annihilation goes on and on in endless conversations and stops only because most of its protagonists are dead. Artzybashev's plays were also despondent and negativistic (*The Law of the Savage, Jealousy, War*). On the whole, Artzybashev's characters were schematic and artificial; they did not live but presented evidence and made declarations of faith or disbelief. Although, as a writer, Artzybashev had some dramatic qualities and knew how to build suspense in a thrilling plot, his success was not due to any enduring literary assets. His naturalism was crude, and his ideas imitative or superficial. He emigrated in 1923 and died four years later in Poland. By that time it had become obvious that the work of this second-rate writer offered merely historical interest: he represented and reflected the era of reaction on the eve of World War I.

III   Next to the *Zeitgeist,* the spirit of the times which is to be felt directly or indirectly in all the works of this period, there existed not only many creative personalities but also a diversity of stylistic tendencies. Aesthetic attitudes and literary schools ranged from innovators to traditionalists, from religious symbolists to social realists, while in the background there were the actions and counteractions of such extensive movements as Populism and nationalism on the one hand and, on the other, Westernization and imitativeness of Europe.

Since the turn of the century the Decadents and Symbolists had been rapidly gaining control in poetry and exerting strong pressure in the theater, where, next to Chekhov, the places of honor were occupied by Ibsen, Maeterlinck, and a number of minor European playwrights. In prose, however, realism was deeply rooted, although the Symbolists were instrumental in its renewal and transformation. Certainly Chekhov and Gorky had introduced stylistic changes that made their work different from the classics; this was true even more of Bunin, Kuprin, and Andreyev (in his early period). Yet continuation rather than innovation was typical of the realists' comeback in the first decade of this century. In all of their works, nevertheless, the social and didactic tendencies were considerably toned down after 1905.

The most traditional of the new writers was assuredly Ivan Bunin (1870–1953). The son of an impoverished nobleman, a native of that region of Central Russia where almost all of the great classics were born, Bunin never received a formal education. After holding various white-collar jobs, he devoted himself to writing, having fallen under the strong influence of Tolstoy. At first he won recognition by his polished Parnassian poems, which ignored Modernistic aspirations, and by his excellent translations (among which those of Byron and that of Longfellow's *Hiawatha,* were the best). His first collection of short stories was published in 1892 — the year in which the name of Maxim Gorky appeared in print for the first time.

In 1895 Bunin settled in St. Petersburg, later associating himself with the *Znanye* group and becoming a contributor to liberal monthlies — without, however, sharing their radical opinions. In 1909 he was elected to the Russian Academy. Although his works never reached a large circulation, he was considered an accomplished stylist. *The Village* (1909) and *Sukhodol* (Dry Valley, 1911) were followed by colorful travelogues (he traveled widely, for the most part in the Orient) and a succession of excellent short stories published between 1912 and 1916: 'The Chalice of Life,' 'On the Road,' 'The Dreams of Chang,' 'Brethren'; 'The Gentleman from San Francisco,' the story for which he is best known, was first published in 1915. In 1920 he left Russia as a resolute opponent of the Soviets and made France his home. The works he published as an *émigré* — short stories and such novels as *Mitya's Love* (1925), *The Life of Arseniev* (1930), its sequel *Lika* (1939) — belong among the best of twentieth-century Russian prose. In 1933 he was awarded the Nobel prize for literature — the first Russian writer to win this honor.

His first long tale, *The Village,* was in the vein of critical realism. It depicted the backwardness of the countryside the soil of which is rich yet does not prevent the recurring scourge of famine: as one of his heroes puts it, although the region trades in grain only a hundred people have bread enough. The peasants live in filth and drunkenness, they are cruel and violent, and one of them exclaims: 'There's nobody as savage as our people!' Balashkin, the *esprit fort* of taverns and market places, goes further and indicts the whole country: 'Heavens, what a land! Pushkin and Lermontov were killed; Pisarev drowned, Ryleyev was hanged, Polezhaev was broken as a private, Shevchenko got a ten-year stretch in jail, Dostoevsky was sent to the scaffold, Gogol went out of his mind. And what about Koltzov, Nikitin, Rechetnikov, Pomialovsky, Levitov? All these died from poverty, privation, and alcoholism. Is there any other such country in the whole world, may it be thrice accursed!' The life of the rich peasant Tikhon, so bent on acquisition of property that he never finds the time to visit a near-by grove of birches, is as senseless as that of his shiftless brother Kuzma; everybody is unhappy and coarse, surrounded by laziness, bestiality, and impotence. This nightmarish novel, which surpasses the gloominess of Chekhov's 'Muzhiks' and reminds one of Gorky's naturalism, is not, however, relieved either by Chekhovian melancholic tolerance or by Gorky's social optimism. On the contrary, Bunin was inclined to challenge any complacency, or any faith in man. According to his writings (see also 'A Night Conversation,' 1911, and 'Ivan the Weeper,' 1913), all Populist and humanitarian ideas are mere illusions: the typical Russian is neither Platon Karataev (in *War and Peace*), nor Alësha Karamazov, but old Karamazov himself, or Khlestakov (the braggart hero of Gogol's *Inspector General*), or any one of the ruthless, greedy merchants of Saltykov — a Kolupaev or a Razuvaev, or that eighteenth-century monster, Saltychikha, who tortured her serfs. This poor opinion of his own people corresponds to Bunin's general attitude toward his heroes: he does not sympathize with them and never fails to show his contempt for the human animal.

The critics received *The Village* with mixed feelings: it struck the pessimistic notes that were current in the era of disillusionment and 'revision of values,' but Bunin's insistence on the sordid and brutal side of country life seemed 'reactionary and exaggerated.' On the other hand, not even Bunin's foes could deny the pictorial qualities of his novel, in which men and things were portrayed with sensual forcefulness and plastic precision in exact, dramatic, and crisp language. Bunin affirmed and expanded these stylistic features in *Dry Valley,* a sad picture of the poverty and insanity that accompany the decay of the landed gentry. He resumed this theme twenty years later in *The Life of Arseniev.* In *Dry Valley* the stylistic and poetic elements again come to the fore. Bunin's sentences have the rhythmic structure of Turgenev's and Chekhov's, but his language is utterly simple and colloquial. He uses a colorful and frequently brilliant vocabulary, strewn with folk expressions as well as with poetic and highly literary figures of speech; his verbal texture is rich, abundant, expressive, and his occasionally long periods are masterfully constructed. *The Village* and, to a lesser extent, *Dry Valley* were the only large works in which Bunin paid tribute to the tradition of critical realism; subsequently he departed further and further from any social implications, and this determined his place in Russian letters. Although he rejected the Decadents and the Symbolists, his contempt for humanity, his reluctance to deliver moral judgments, his whole approach to life and people revealed a predominantly aesthetic attitude. A realist-aesthete with a generally pessimistic outlook: this is how Bunin appeared in his works before and after 1917.

The plots of his short stories are usually very simple. A dog watches his master, a destitute ship captain, drinking himself to death to forget his unfaithful wife ('The Dreams of Chang'). A rickshaw boy in Colombo dies from exhaustion under the indifferent eyes of white culture-bearers ('Brethren'). A rich American dies of a stroke at Capri during a pleasure cruise; his body is returned to the States aboard the same steamer on which he had started out; dancing and flirting go on as usual, while 'at the bottom of the black hold stood a tarred coffin, in close proximity to the somber and sultry depths of the ship which was toilsomely overcoming the darkness, the ocean, the snowstorm' ('The Gentleman from San Francisco'). As an *émigré,* Bunin added a nostalgic note to his stories. He became the poet of recollections, the seeker after things past and gone, and he compared his writings to the rose of Jericho — a dry withered plant that blossoms anew when put into water. 'I sink the roots and stems of my past into the living waters of my heart, into the pure moisture of love, grief, and tenderness — and my cherished plant wonderfully comes to life again.'

His tales evoked the Russia of fields and noble manors ('The Grammar of Love'), the charm of fragrant gardens and native landscapes, and the youthful love of squires, noble young ladies, and peasant girls ('The Star of Love') — the beautiful sunset of a perishing social class. Bunin, the typical Russian squire, who resented his exile and was homesick, embodies the nostalgia and melancholic longings of his fellow expatriates. His novelette, *Mitya's Love,* not unrelated to Chekhov's 'Volodya,' describes the sexual awakening of an adolescent against the background of a nobleman's estate, and the dichotomy between platonic love and the degrading experience of physical initiation which impels the hero to suicide. Remembrances of things past form the plot of *The Life of Arseniev,* which abounds in lyrical descriptions of decaying manors and scenes of death; *Lika,* a love story, has its own intensity of wonder and sorrow, its own poetic dimension of desire, longing, jealousy, and amorous elation.

In general love (or, to be more precise, remembrance of love) was one of Bunin's main themes, particularly in his later years. All his love stories are sad and invariably have a tragic ending: Mitya kills himself; the mistress of the writer (in 'Henry') is murdered by her former lover when she is on the threshold of a new and happy life; the old *émigré* whose lonely existence is finally illuminated by love and tenderness suddenly dies in the Metro from a heart attack ('In Paris'); the beautiful Nathalie passes away just when her tormented love finds fulfilment ('Nathalie'); Elaghin kills the woman whose love was for him supreme joy and unendurable anguish ('The Elaghin Affair'); the poor young girl who decides to become a prostitute and falls in love with the first man she sleeps with dies from tuberculosis ('Three Rubles'). All these endings may seem surprising and brusque, as if the author did not know what to do with his characters and hence sentenced them to premature deaths. But these endings are perfectly consistent with Bunin's romantic conception of love, which he combines with a cynical awareness of its coarse physical reality — and he resorts to the same method Turgenev used.

Love is an illuminating inspiration, a brief and tense moment, as Blok put it — and therefore it cannot endure. It is like dawn or lightning. Men aspire to a durable happiness for which they are not born. We want it for life — and we get it for a night, like the hero of 'Sunstroke,' who spent a few hours with a woman he met aboard a ship, and suddenly realized after her departure that he loved her passionately, yet had failed to learn her name and address. Whenever we attempt to make love permanent, it either turns into the boredom of habit or takes its vengeance by bringing about catastrophes. Bunin's lovers remember only moments of tension, the intoxication, the blissful dizziness, the pungent bite of passion. Like the Romantics, Bunin believes that only fleeting moments are beautiful, and cherishes only what is fated to die soon.

The themes of love and death disclose the essence of Bunin's art. Like Turgenev he sees in love a supreme revelation of the enchantment of life, to which he is extremely sensitive.

The remarkable acuteness and the hard brilliancy of his style correspond to his sensorial and sensual precision. He is, above all, the writer of visual details, of forms, lines, and colors, and he renders with pagan joy all earthy, bodily traits, all concrete signs of nature and men. His exactness and completeness remind one of Tolstoy's manner; there is, however, neither Devil nor God in Bunin's world. Everything is external and concrete, and everything is devoid of meaning, subject to evanescence and decay, even though the sky may be sapphire, the sun shine triumphantly, flowers smell enchantingly, and women be adorable. This may seem too simple and naïve a description, yet it is Bunin's attitude. He is allured by the loveliness of nature and appalled by its aloofness; he is bewitched and frightened by the splendor of the world. He emphasizes both the magnificence of the universe and the insignificance of man. This contrast underlies all his philosophy — if such a term may be applied to a writer of his kind. In 'The Star of Love' the hero kisses the neck of his horse, 'to sense the coarse smell, to feel the earthly flesh — without which it would be too frightening to exist in this world.' The feeling that flesh represents life with all its fascination, beauty, and madness is counterbalanced in Bunin by an oceanic or cosmic feeling. The night and the sea and the stars make him sense Nature, the Great Mother, who absorbs and dissolves everything and from whom all things are reborn. This is the way of all flesh, the wheel of life — and only the stupid children of man try to resist it, grow rebellious, and refuse to accept the truth ('Mara' and, above all, 'Cicadas').

This almost Hindu outlook (he stressed it in his biography of Tolstoy, as well as in his books on the Near East) is, nevertheless, contradictory to his fear of death. Its shadow is always cast over his stories, and the horror of the nothingness to which all who live are sentenced envelops Bunin's work in a shroud of anxiety and gloom. Nothing is worth concern or attachment, for everything will turn to dust; chance is the only law of life; there is no value or meaning to labor, politics, or knowledge — the highest aspirations, the loftiest hopes are shadows and fade like flowers, or are as futile as butterflies.

Poet of sensations, instinctual drives, and recollections, Bunin seldom enters into psychological analysis or portrait-painting; in general, he wants to present rather than to explain. He produces characteristics rather than characters, and all his heroes are sketchy, almost without form. One can read a dozen of Bunin's tales without once getting a complete picture of a type, of a character. Yet at the same time the bodily features of each individual, his sensations, his fluctuating emotions are depicted with surprising accuracy — and we remember the way the young lover rode on horseback on a starry night in spring, or how the herbs smelled in the manor garden when the beloved sat on the bench, or how her father drank his tea from a tumbler in a silver glass holder. The concrete traits of this visible, measurable world are described in plastic relief and with delight. This delight in sounds, colors, volume, feelings, sensations is matched by a poignant feeling of decay — and therein lies the peculiarity of Bunin's manner. The flux of sensations and desires, all the illusions and dreams of man, which are in constant change, are projected against a static setting of nature. This prose also possesses a finality: whatever he describes is caught and imprisoned in a plastic, almost sculptural image; his prose is precise and solid in its contours. This is why his art evokes so frequently the similes of chiseling, of cameos and carved gems, and why, in a poem that gives his artistic credo, he speaks of inscribing a sonnet with a steel dagger on the glacier of a mountain peak.

His craftsmanship, his verbal perfection, has a slightly chilly quality. Bunin lacks compassion or immediate interest in human beings: a purely aesthetic fascination of recollection and an icy awareness of death prevail in all his work. He never departs from a haughty, aristocratic contempt for all the trivialities of existence, all struggle or endeavor, which he rejects as utterly futile. Both in his memoirs and in his essays on contemporary topics (including Communism) he displays such a spiteful attitude toward his contemporaries, such an urge to point out the defects and foibles of his former friends, that these irate, malevolent pages stand out as particularly destructive. In general, the great formal beauty of Bunin's writings is not matched by any corresponding moral or intellectual greatness — he is not attached to ideas or human beings — and this marks his work with the tarnish of coldness. This scarcity of human warmth also sets limitations to his role in Russian letters: he can be considered only as an epigone of the great masters.

Marxian critics interpret his pessimism, his nostalgia, and almost nihilistic coldness as manifestations of the gloom caused by the disappearance of the social group to which he belonged. A poet in the aristocratic tradition, linked to the patrician writers and poets of the 'sixties, this lyrical storyteller depicts the final disintegration of the nests of the gentlefolk, and seeks refuge in external perfection or vague mysticism because he can find no place in life. Although the Communist press has always stressed the 'reactionary substance' of Bunin's work, it has had to acknowledge that this leading *émigré* writer is a superb stylist and the most brilliant representative of the schools of Turgenev and Chekhov in contemporary Russian letters.

IV   Alexander Kuprin (1870 – 1938), although artistically less important than Bunin, appealed more to the average reader because of the spontaneity and human qualities of his talent. He had none of Bunin's aristocratic refinement and was often handicapped by his lack of culture and lapses of taste. If in some instances he did reveal a certain wisdom, it was all intuitive and did not bear any trace of intellectual depth or ideological vision. What made Kuprin an attractive and popular writer was his zest for life and a wholesome realism; his vitality was akin to Gorky's, but it was a natural instinctual life-force, without Gorky's moralizing and social tendencies. Tolstoy said that Kuprin wrote with truth and sincerity, and this was high praise indeed from so severe a critic.

Upon graduation from a military school in Moscow, Kuprin served in the army as a commissioned officer; after his resignation he held dozens of jobs: he was a newspaperman, an actor, a surveyor, a singer, a carpenter, and he enjoyed this rolling-stone existence. He loved the company of strong healthy people who were good trenchermen and knew how to use their bodies skillfully, and this accounts for the picaresque streak in some of his tales, such as 'My Days as an Actor' or 'The Laestrygonians,' a delightful series of sketches dealing with the Greek fishermen on the Crimean littoral. His first novelette, 'Moloch' (1896), described a steel mill as a monster devouring human lives. This anti-capitalistic tale was none too original, but it showed the author's gift for observation and for creating an illusion of reality.

Kuprin became widely known after the success of *The Duel* (1905), a novel in which he depicted the empty and senseless life of a provincial garrison. Romashov, its hero, an idealistically inclined young officer, feels frustrated by army routine and monotony, as well as by his love affairs, and dies a stupid death as the victim of vile intrigue, frivolous women, and unscrupulous men. *The Duel* was published during the Russo-Japanese War, and its picture of officers, soldiers, and army life had much verisimilitude; its anti-militaristic spirit also held a great appeal for the radical intelligentsia. The tales and novels Kuprin published between 1905 and 1917 made him a favorite with the reading public. The curiosity and interest the writer displayed in people and environments gave an amazing variety to his subject matter, in contrast with Bunin's uniformity. Kuprin is much more down to earth, and while

Bunin concentrates on the individual detail, Kuprin is attracted by an assemblage of traits that depicts a milieu, a way of life. He therefore likes to describe a social group as well as its members: an army garrison (*The Duel*), a house of ill repute and a red-light district (*Yama the Pit*), a cheap hotel ('The River of Life'), a provincial theatrical company on the road, a circus, a fishing village. 'I throw out a big net,' he once told the present writer, 'and I haul in all sorts of fish — great and small.'

A motley crew struts through his pages: a primitive peasant girl, daughter of the local witch, who falls in love with a young hunter in the wild forests of White Russia ('Olessia'); the adroit criminals of Odessa, who send a delegation of expert light-fingered practitioners to protest against the slur that they had anything to do with a pogrom ('The Affront'); a Japanese spy acting as a Russian officer, who maintains his masquerade successfully until he shouts 'Banzai!' while asleep in the arms of a prostitute ('Captain Rybnikov'); clowns, acrobats, and lion tamers watching with awe the sudden death of a fellow performer, the wrestler Arbusov ('At the Circus'); an office drudge who falls in love with a princess, sends her a bracelet of garnets, and then calmly, deliberately, takes his own life, since all its meaning lay in his hopeless love ('The Bracelet of Garnets'); the wise King Solomon, who cherishes above all things the swarthy young girl he met in a vineyard ('Sulamith'); the girls of a brothel in a red-light district of southern Russia and their friends, clients, pimps, and masters, who love and suffer and are sucked into the quagmire of vice and despair (*Yama the Pit*); an industrialist who is bewitched by the silvery voice of a governess ('In the Darkness'); the Jewish fiddler Sasha, who entertains sailors and dockers in an Odessa beer hall and, after breaking his violin on the head of a stool pigeon, loses the use of his left hand through the ministration of the secret police, but reappears before his rough and sentimental audience as a virtuoso on the ocarina — for 'you can cripple a man, but art will endure all things and will all things conquer!' ('Gambrinus'). And what a colorful gallery of minor characters these are in the writings of Kuprin — the novelist Shchavinsky (in 'Captain Rybnikov'), who collects 'rare and strange human specimens,' or the white-slave trader Semion Horizon, or the old general who visits the princess of 'The Bracelet of Garnets,' or the bit of human driftwood who delivers his life-monologue in 'Off the Street' and calls all men 'lodgers of the Lord.'

Kuprin is equally stirred by those who live in the best apartments and by those who can never pay their rent but are always stirring up trouble. There is little moralistic discrimination in his work. He is simply absorbed by people, their talk, their adventures, their good and bad luck, their love affairs. It is revealing that he depicted children as well as adults, and that he paid no less attention to animals than to human beings; he has excellent sketches and stories of dogs, cats, lions, and elephants, while his 'Emerald,' the story of a race horse, is as much of a minor masterpiece as Tolstoy's 'Yardstick.' Sometimes Kuprin tries to generalize or to deliver dicta, such as the concluding sentence of 'Gambrinus,' cited above, or to philosophize, as in 'Sulamith,' or to criticize poverty, as in *Yama the Pit:* 'As long as there is property there will be poverty; prostitution will always co-exist with marriage.' All these attempts should not, however, be taken too seriously; actually Kuprin does not care much for philosophy, for social advances, for problems and ideas — but he is delighted when he can describe a port tavern ('The Old City of Marseilles'), a brothel, a beer hall, and tell a good yarn about men with red blood in their veins. He loves strength, physical prowess, professional skill, and takes real pleasure in fishing, hunting, gargantuan repasts, and Pantagruelian drinking bouts; he is at his best with artisans, jockeys, and acrobats. This is why he fails when he wants to put over some social or moral idea. For instance, in the amorphous *Yama the Pit,* which created such a sensation in Russia and abroad because of its subject matter, the conversations of his mouthpiece, Platonov, who 'investigates life,' are dull and false, although the girls themselves and their sordid surroundings are vividly depicted.

Kuprin, like so many simple-minded, elemental people, idealized love and often presented it with old-fashioned and naïve sentimentalism. The naturalistic detail of the affair of a seasick woman and her brutal lover aboard a steamer ('Seasickness') is not typical of Kuprin: in this tale he simply paid tribute to the vogue of a reactionary period, when it was customary to treat sex crudely. More in line with his attitude is Nazansky, one of the characters in *The Duel,* who is disgusted that love has been made the topic of smutty stories, pornographic postcards, and dubious musical comedies. Men, say Nazansky, are ashamed to speak well of women lest they lose their pose of superiority. Real love, however, is the highest and the most beautiful thing in the world — and only a fortunate few, a select number out of unhappy millions, understand what it means. 'Sulamith' and 'The Bracelet of Garnets' are hymns of boundless, intense love: 'All things will pass away, but the love of a poor girl from a vineyard and of the great king will never fade or be forgotten, for love is strong as death and each woman who loves is a queen, and love is magnificent.'

It is true that the Biblical stylization in 'Sulamith' does not quite come off, and that the pathetic sweetness of 'The Bracelet of Garnets' is somewhat cheap and overemphasized; yet Kuprin's good faith and sincerity make the average reader overlook these obvious defects. Then, too, he is an expert storyteller: the unfolding of the plot in 'The Bracelet of Garnets' is carried out with such skill and completeness that the whole stands out as an excellent story. Although Kuprin's forthright, simple, and colloquial style does not possess the perfection and brittleness of Bunin's rhythmic sentences, and his lyrical passages often sound flat, yet his narrative moves along at a good pace and has dramatic quality. In these respects he is akin to Western storytellers. He greatly admired Kipling and Jack London, and wrote an excellent essay on the latter, which contributed to London's wide popularity in Russia.

In 1923 Kuprin joined the *émigrés* in Paris. Unlike Bunin, who had continued to turn out brilliant works in his self-imposed exile, Kuprin was badly affected by being uprooted from his native soil. In his autobiographical novels (*The Cadets, The Turning Point*) and in a few short stories produced in Paris, only isolated passages remind one of the old Kuprin, of the exultant lover of life, the dynamic observer, the poet of romantic love, the friend of bohemians and animals. Whoever met him in the 1930's in Paris had the painful impression that this heavy-set, sad-looking, ailing, and often intoxicated man was spent and broken. The Soviet government allowed him to come home in 1937, where he died a year later.

Although both Bunin and Kuprin were called traditional realists, they followed the trend of critical realism only at the beginning of their literary careers. Bunin departed from it after *The Village* and deliberately narrowed down his subject matter to sensations, love, and death, projected against the recollections of old Russia in evanescence. Kuprin, who in his youth had felt strongly the impact of Tolstoy's methods and later was attracted by Western writers, was more attentive than Bunin to the painting of backgrounds. Nevertheless Kuprin remained aloof to moral and social issues; he used power of his realistic observation to build dynamic plots enhanced by romantic overtones and thrilling narrative qualities. In his work one would seek even more vainly than in that of Bunin for those psychological depths, inner anxieties, and contentions with God and man that make the works of the great realists so meaningful and exciting. Do these missing qualities indicate a weakening (or indeed the decline) of the classical tradition? Are the attitudes of these two writers, so different in their temperaments and styles, due simply to their personalities, to that irreducible x which determines any creative art? Or do these men reflect — perhaps unconsciously — the crisis among the intellectuals?

After the debacle of 1905 a considerable part of Russian society no longer felt attracted by the ideals of the nineteenth century; they broke their allegiance not only to radicalism but to the didactic tendencies of critical realism as well. Bunin and Kuprin, although only ten years younger than Chekhov, belonged to this new generation. They shrank from any 'messages' and this was the chief reason for their hostility toward Gorky. The writers who were still concerned with great issues were either socially inspired, like Gorky and his group, or had gone in for religion, like the Symbolists. Those who maintained an intermediate position — between realistic tradition and Symbolistic innovation — fell victims of their own duality, as was the case with Leonid Andreyev, the morbid explorer of metaphysical mysteries on the crossroad of two schools.

v   In 1900 Gorky had brought to a literary meeting a young, remarkably handsome lawyer, Leonid Andreyev, who read aloud a short story of his, entitled 'Silence.' It was highly praised as distinctly original and soon appeared in *Everybody's Journal,* which welcomed new talents. A year later Andreyev's first collection of short stories was brought out by Gorky's publishing organization, *Znanye,* and met with general acceptance: 47,000 copies of the book were sold within two months. From that point on Andreyev enjoyed the widest popularity, equal to that of Chekhov or Gorky, and his new works never failed to provoke outbursts of enthusiastic or angry comment. No other Russian writer, with the exception of Gorky, has been so highly praised and so viciously denigrated as Andreyev: Korney Chukovsky, the critic, compiled a veritable 'Schimpfs lexicon,' or dictionary of abuse, from the epithets aimed at this writer, who was singled out as a butt by the press. To his admirers he was nothing less than a genius; to his foes he was a frog who had puffed himself up into an ox; he was a poseur, a pseudo-mystic; to the public he was a best-selling author, and his book the hit of each season. This unusual literary fortune proved to be very unstable: today Andreyev is seldom read; he is forgotten in Russia, as well as abroad, where his celebrity verged on notoriety. His fame was pyrotechnical: despite its momentary brilliance it has left scarcely a trace.

The son of a land surveyor, Leonid Andreyev (1871–1919) studied law at the University of St. Petersburg and had a hard struggle against poverty and loneliness. His work as a portrait-painter brought him only coppers, and he had to undergo actual privations. A neurotic, subject to fits of depression and to a persecution mania, he made three unsuccessful attempts at suicide. His law practice was limited to one court case — which he lost; he next tried his hand as a newspaper reporter and funnyman, if sardonicism can be regarded as humor. His first stories, written in the customary vein of realistic narrative, were either depressing or paradoxical. A man kills his beloved because she was lying to him, and rejoices because 'the demon of falsehood and doubt which had sucked his blood no longer dwelt in her immobile pupils'; but after the murder he grows as restless 'as a panther in a cage, for falsehood itself had not been killed' ('The Lie'). A man who at last makes a grand slam with no trumps dies at the card table without ever knowing that there was an ace in the draw ('The Grand Slam'). The inmates of a leprosarium vainly attempt to climb over the wall separating them from the world of the living ('The Wall'). Paul, a young student, contracts syphilis, kills the prostitute who had infected him, and takes his own life ('In the Fog'). An idealistic student and a gentle young girl are attacked in a suburban forest by a gang of hooligans; the girl is raped and the student is slugged, but when he comes to and looks at his female companion, he becomes as bestial as any of the hoodlums who had run away ('The Abyss'). Kerzhentsev, an intellectual physician, kills the husband of the woman who did not respond to his love and simulates madness; but in the institution where he is placed for observation, pretense insidiously transforms itself into reality: he comes to doubt his own sanity, his logical thought betrays him, he can no longer discern between hallucinations and the functions of the reason and loses his mind ('Thought').

This theme of madness is recurrent in much of Andreyev's work. The hero of 'The Ghosts' is a madman who finally lands in an asylum. In 'The Life of Father Fiveisky' (1903), the accumulation of nightmares reaches a maddening peak. Vassily is an Orthodox priest; his wife is an alcoholic and becomes insane; her first son dies, her second is an idiot, half-child and half-beast. Cripples, lunatics, and perverts come to confession, and Father Vassily has to listen to a beggar who has raped a little girl, whom he paid three kopecks and then strangled. When Vassily's wife perishes in a fire, the priest rebels against a God who permits all such horrors to happen, and in his rage and mad despair he begins to blaspheme.

Among the other fixations of Andreyev were the idea of death and a morbid, neurotic predilection for ugliness and distortion. A comparison between his work and Goya's has been made by B. G. Guerney, but it would be far more apt to compare Andreyev with Hieronymos Bosch, whose 'Torments of St. Anthony,' 'The Seven Cardinal Sins,' and other canvasses breathe the same spirit of baroque and monstrous art.

While depicting the monstrosity, ugliness, and dull triviality of life, Andreyev insisted upon two main negations: the omnipotence of death and the failure of reason. There is no harmony between intellect and instinct; the mind is a Satanic jest, a cheat, and man cannot rely on reason, which is deceptive and hostile; we are, therefore, lost amid gloom and solitude.

This condemnation of all rational and moral values and a voluptuous surrender to chaotic destructive drives arising from the pit of primordial elements were bolstered by social and anarchistic overtones during the years of revolutionary agitation. In 1905 Andreyev described the war in Manchuria in a tale of horror ('Red Laughter'), which is as anti-militaristic as Garshin's 'Four Days,' whence it drew its inspiration. In 'The Governor-General' he presented an old official who had given orders to shoot at political demonstrators and is responsible for the killing of thirty-five men, nine women, and three children; he knows perfectly well that the revolutionaries are going to take vengeance, and awaits his death with sad resignation. The best work of this period is undoubtedly 'Seven Who Were Hanged' (1908) — a forceful portrayal of seven revolutionaries awaiting, each in solitary confinement, their inevitable executions. The poignancy of this grim tale of death is enhanced by the obvious sympathy with which the author paints the revolutionaries.

A friend of radicals and socialists (for the most part of the Social Revolutionaries), Andreyev professed strong anti-bourgeois feelings. In his ironic tale, 'Christians,' a prostitute refuses to take an oath in court lest she offend God, and the magistrates, greatly annoyed by her scruples, try to hush up the whole incident: 'It is cheerful and comfortable in the courtroom, with its electric lights. But, beyond the windows, darkness reigns.' In the symbolic play, *King Hunger* (1907), the anonymous masses march to seize the dwellings of the rich and threaten to raze the city (18,000 copies of the play were sold on the day of its publication).

These social notes in Andreyev's stories and allegories, all clothed in symbolic imagery, had definite anarchical and pessimistic tones. The latter became loud, almost shrill, during the years of reaction, when the writer's acute disappointment in the liberal movement was aggravated by his personal feeling of emptiness and futility after the death of his first wife. His tales and plays between 1907 and 1912 were received by thousands of readers as an expression of their own despondency. 'There is neither God nor Devil,' says the bartender Tiukha in the play *Savva* (1906). 'The only thing that exists are vile faces. Plenty of vile faces. Very funny.' Everything is illusion: love, purity, freedom. A prisoner becomes so used to his cell and bars that he does not want to get free; liberation scares him to death; prison alone is safe, confinement alone is protective — and he sings their praises ('My Diary'). A revolutionary who is hiding in a bordello and is boasting of his merits to a prostitute is startled by her question: 'How do you dare to be good when I am bad?' He suddenly realizes the futility of merit and heroism in a world of evil, the moral impossibility of being good, and stays on with her; he plunges into the night of self-abasement because all rational thinking is a lie, and only the appeal of hidden instincts is real and can bring man closer to the primordial chaos ('Darkness,' 1907).

What, in general, is the difference between right and wrong? Nobody understands anything, and knowledge is as fatal as death, according to Andreyev. Lazarus was brought back to life after being dead for three days and three nights, and the work of death was suspended — but it was not abolished. Lazarus had glimpsed the forbidden region beyond life — and now his gaze turns the joy of lovers into distress, upsets the thinking of the wise, and makes the work of the laborer futile and his bread bitter; the Emperor who orders Lazarus' eyes to be seared with a hot iron is right ('Lazarus,' 1906). Judas loves Jesus dearly but hates mankind and distrusts men. Yet he is willing to put them to a supreme test: he will betray Christ and then see whether His followers will have enough courage to fight for Him and save Him. But men let Jesus die: Judas' last hopes are crushed and he hangs himself ('Judas Iscariot,' 1907).

The futility of all mortal desires is illustrated in *The Life of Man* (1906), a morality play in which the protagonists are designated by generic appellations: The Man, His Wife, Their Son. At one side of the stage, near the wings, Someone in Gray reads aloud by the light of a candle the chronicle of Man's life. He comments and explains while the scenes unfold before the audience: the Man and his young Wife are haunted by poverty and dream of imaginary feasts (this is the best part of the play); later the dreams come true but materialization is less thrilling than expectation; when Man becomes rich and famous, misfortunes assail him: his Son dies, he is broken and lonely, he falls ill and becomes impotent; drunkards and harpies watch his agony — and then Someone in Gray blows out the candle.

By 1908 Andreyev reached the zenith of his career. His books were avidly read, and his plays drew enthusiastic audiences throughout Russia. He was acclaimed as 'the most profound' contemporary storyteller and the most 'original' playwright. This nihilist and pessimist who pronounced the word *death* with the same lust with which an old debauchee utters the name of *woman,* and who felt so keenly the limitations of the human mind and the futility of human endeavor, reveled in publicity and in being in the public eye. He had a sense of the inanity of all things; like Poe, he felt deeply the Universal Night, yet all his sensitivity to the tragic and the horrible did not prevent him from being vain, frivolous, theatrical, and in a state of continual excitement. He made a great deal of money with his writings and spent it all; he loved a fast way of life, lavish receptions, and sumptuous, pretentious decors — witness his villa in Finland with its bizarre furnishings. With his mane of black hair, the burning eyes in a pale, handsome face, and a proud, mobile mouth, he looked like a Dark Hero; there was something precious in his elegant gait and gestures; he wore velvet jackets and page-caps, and posed as a Renaissance painter. His friend Ilya Repin, the great artist, called him Lorenzo the Magnificent.

But what came naturally to a Medici was a pose in Andreyev. He loved to attract attention, to be admired, and to play a part. His own heroes were masks which he changed often, one after another, in that tremendous theatrical enterprise which all his work actually was for him. He was always the same, in his life and in his writings: turbulent, hyperbolic, loud, spectacular — and utterly unhappy, unable to cope with his inner emptiness. All his great energy was spent on turning the mill of thought and the wheels of words — with the same result attained by Sysiphus. Work was for him an escape; he considered it a narcotic and was absorbed by this 'second reality' with the morbid passion of a drug addict. The idol of the public lived as if he were in a desert — a lone individual who did not belong anywhere, to any groups or schools. He dropped his old friend Gorky; he refused to join the Symbolists, although he used their devices; after a personal association with the Social Revolutionaries he turned against the revolution in general, and in 1917–18 declared himself a sworn enemy of the Bolsheviks. His mind was undisciplined, he did not care for knowledge, and Gorky reproached him for his indolence and lack of curiosity and learning; Andreyev counterbalanced these shortcomings, however, by the feverish activity of his imagination and intellect. Although very intense, this activity was limited in range, and it did not save him from the pitfalls of bad taste and exaggeration.

It is certain that his feeling for death, his attraction toward the metaphysical (though on a fairly simple plane) and the horrible, his interest in mysteries rather than in ways of existence were all perfectly genuine. But next to this basic sincerity there was also his love of stage effects, of spectacular poses, of pseudo-emotional tricks. He loved to frighten his readers ('He tries to scare me,' said Tolstoy, 'but I don't get scared') or to puzzle and shock them — and he used coarse, cheap devices and histrionic techniques. The style of most of his tales and of a good many of his plays is high-pitched, rhetorical, grandiloquent, full of promposity and turgid metaphors: 'Freedom is perishing; the poor bride is wreathed with white flowers which faded at the hour of nuptial celebrations.' The following is typical of his heavy-paced, solemnly intoned prose: 'As if he were cursed by an unknown curse, he has been laden, since his youth, with the heavy burden of grief, disease, and distress, and the bleeding wounds of his heart were never healed; he remained solitary among men, even as a planet amidst other planets, and it seemed that a peculiar aura, fatal and destructive, surrounded him like a transparent, invisible cloud.'

Andreyev always dealt with God, Death, Fate, with the ultimate problems of being; but artificiality and pretense made his voice sound hollow and strained; he tried to appear metaphysically profound but failed to be convincing, and the depth of his profundity is questionable. A contemporary remarked that Andreyev, in his wrestling with the mysteries of the world, beat his head against the wall — yet that wall seemed to be part of a comfortable drawing room. He pounded the drum so hard to ballyhoo his tragedies, he piled up such an agglomeration of catastrophes, and he raised his paradoxes to such a pitch that all his gruesome stories and hypersymbolic plays were deafening rather than breathtaking. He was not enough of a thinker to put forward original and startling ideas; nor was he enough of an artist to find a perfect medium of expression for the torments of his own mind and the virulence of his true or imaginary passions. He wrote hastily, without any sense of proportion; a literary exhibitionist, he coquetted with sufferings or intellectual anxieties. Most of his heroes are merely names; they are clothes-horses for concepts. Although he talks about the irrational, only a few of his tales can still move us by the intensity of their intellectualized emotions.

There is something *pseudo* about Andreyev. Like the eighteenth-century pseudo-classics, he was a pseudo-symbolist. He used all the paraphernalia and outward techniques of symbolism in a chill way, sometimes insisting upon them to the point of dullness. This accounts not only for the artificiality of his style but also for its instability. After 1908 he began to write plays constructed as realistic dramas and attempted to subdue and restrain his tragic effects and his love for monstrosity. These plays of 1908–14 — *The Days of Our Life* (1908), *Black Masks* (1908), *Anfissa* (1909), *Gaudeamus* (1910), *Catherine Ivanovna* (1912), *Professor Storytzyn* (1913), *He Who Gets Slapped* (1914), and his satirical drama, *The Sabine Women* (1912) — oscillate between melodrama and allegory. Most of them deal with the triviality and tedium of life and depict Russian intellectuals; they show a strong Chekhovian influence. Although done with an excellent understanding of stage techniques, which made them a part of Russian repertoires and accounted for their transitory success in the West, they indicated a decline in Andreyev's creative power. Between 1912 and his death he wrote only pale imitations of his early works.

Professor Alexander Kaun, the American biographer and admirer of Andreyev, has stated that Andreyev was an incarnation of the twentieth-century Russian intellectual, tormented by an inner quest. Some critics saw in him a follower of Dostoevsky's religious search; they linked him with all the novelists and poets, from Tiutchev to Sologub, who had ever talked about chaos, evil, sex, and death. Modern literary historians do not deny Andreyev's connection with some of the basic trends in Russian literature, but are inclined to grant him the rank of an able vulgarizer: he made available for the average reader, in concise and ready form, the philosophical and religious unrest of his times and the symbolistic tendencies of contemporary art. There is little use denying his talent, his dialectical forcefulness, his sense of the nocturnal side of man and the universe. Some of his stories, such as 'Seven Who Were Hanged,' 'The Governor-General,' and 'Lazarus,' still survive — but merely as the rubble of an ambitious edifice that time has not spared.

9

BLOK AND THE SYMBOLISTS

I   As an aftermath of 1905, the fashion of the day was clearly anti-realistic. Gorky's star was declining, while Andreyev's was still shining brightly. The Decadents, who had been sneered at a decade before, were now acclaimed as masters by a large audience. Ethics were replaced by aesthetics, mysticism was triumphantly opposed to 'earthy materialism'; symbolism, exoticism, and individualism were prevailing in literature and the arts. Schoolboys learned by heart the formula of Sologub: 'Two eternal truths, two ways of knowledge are given to man: one is lyrical — it denies and destroys this world; the other is ironical — it accepts the world to the end.' Bookshop windows displayed, instead of the dull green wrappers of the *Znanye* publications, the futuristic jackets of the widely read literary almanac of the younger generation, the bright yellow covers of *Apollo,* the Symbolist monthly, and an assortment of books by foreign and native poets and novelists brought out by such publishing houses as The Griffon and The Scorpion.

The most striking evidence of the Symbolists' triumph was furnished by the theater. Since the success of Chekhov's plays the Moscow Art Theater had been turning away from realistic staging and attempting new forms. Teamwork, ensemble acting under a single leadership, still remained its main purpose; but it strove for a unity of style rather than fidelity to life. Each production was designed to present a general concept, a mood, a symbol. During this period, in the presentation of such plays as Maeterlinck's *The Blue Bird,* Andreyev's *The Life of Man,* Hamsun's *At the Gates of the Kingdom,* Hauptmann's *The Sunken Bell,* and *Hamlet* (the last staged by Gordon Craig), lavish sets were abandoned for a stylized system of allegoric symbols and forms. Moscow Art Theater

184

Workshops, called studios, were busied with various anti-realistic experiments and with training many talented actors and directors, some of whom, such as Vakhtangov, subsequently emerged as leading figures. Vera Kommissarzhevskaya (1864–1910), the leading actress of the time, whose deep and ringing voice and high-strung personality moved audiences in plays by Ibsen, Chekhov, and Maeterlinck, fell under the spell of the Symbolists. After having been the leading lady of the Alexandrinsky Theater, she found her own theatrical venture with Vsevolod Meyerhold (at one time an actor with the Moscow Art Theater) as stage director, and experimented with new plays and new methods of acting.

After Kommissarzhevskaya's premature death while on tour in Central Asia, Meyerhold (1874–1941) went on with his brilliant and checkered career of 'quest and innovation.' At first he was attracted by stylization and conventionalism. His aim was to reveal 'the inner mysteries of life' and to bring symbolic messages to the audience. In the plays of Maeterlinck he tried to 'dematerialize' the stage and to break down the barriers between the actor and the public. He produced them close to the footlights, against sets of decorative screens, with actors whose plastic movements and 'metallic' diction forbade any 'imitation of reality.' Later (in 1910) he turned the Alexandrinsky Theater into a showcase of stage effects, resorting by turns to the primitively grotesque, to Punch-and-Judy devices, to the techniques of the *commedia dell'arte,* or to sumptuous, fantastic pageantry. He presented Molière's *Don Juan* with all the house lights on, lavish and fanciful sets, and a succession of shrewd stunts, including blackamoors who drew the curtains and tended the actors.

Other stage directors concentrated on psychological interpretation and theories of the stage. Alexander Tairov's (1885–1950) Kamerny Theater, founded in 1914, produced symbolic plays by the French poet Claudel and stirred public opinion by daring and highly Modernistic performances. Nicholas Evreinov (1879–1955), whose plays and whose main work, *The Theatralization of Life,* were well known among the Modernists, worked out a doctrine of the monodrama, which considered the principal actor, the protagonist, as Ego, and the spectator as his double or Alter-Ego. Evreinov insisted that the stage instinct was deeply rooted in human nature: life was a continuous performance, and the stage simply symbolized and expressed man's theatricality. Theories, however, were not limited to literary manifestations: they were followed by theatrical ventures of greater or lesser scope in which professionals and amateurs tested new ideas. Each of these ventures found support among various literary groups and rallied round them poets, novelists, and essayists. All the Symbolist leaders were associated with the theatrical movement. Sologub wrote plays for the 'theater of single will,' while

Viacheslav Ivanov promoted the 'theater of congregate action,' which was to convey religious feeling and create the emotion of communion and the sense of myth. Blok spent considerable time helping to stage his own poetic dramas — *The Stranger, The Little Show-Booth,* and *The Rose and the Cross.* Briussov was a member of the repertoire committees, advising both Kommissarzhevskaya and Meyerhold. Experiments in the anti-realistic spirit were conducted at the St. Petersburg Musical Drama, which had introduced brilliant innovations in the operatic art, in the House of Intermedies, and in the widely popular theater-cabarets of grotesquerie and satire: The Crooked Mirror, Nikita Baliev's Chauve Souris, and many others. The same trends prevailed in the productions of the Russian ballet abroad: Diaghilev had skillfully utilized all the achievements of the Russian theatrical directors and added to them quite a few inventions of his own.

In music Symbolism was represented by Scriabin, and his *Prometheus* and *The Poem of Ecstasy* were hailed as works of mystical illumination. An array of composers, from Medtner to Glière and Gnessin, were putting lyrics of the Symbolist poets to music. In art such masters as Vrubel, Roerich, and Vasnetzov were expressing the same moods and concepts as those put forth by the Symbolists in letters.

The 'new' art was in keeping with the general atmosphere of the times and answered the need for escape, excitement, or sophistication.

But while the general public felt the impact of Symbolism and acclaimed, without much discrimination, Decadents, aesthetes, mystics, and freaks, Russian Symbolism was undergoing an intricate change. It had departed from aestheticism as well as from the religious revival. Its mysticism was becoming more and more tinged by concern with social and cultural problems. In Russia more than anywhere else Charles Péguy's observation that *la mystique conduit à la politique* proved to be true. In 1905 the Symbolists and mystics met with the radicals and socialists at the crossroads of revolution — and this meeting left deep marks. The events of 1905 also inaugurated a new phase. Former aesthetes and idealists could not merely wave aside the complex social and political reality; they were confronted with large issues of tremendous impact. The generation of Symbolists that came to the fore after 1905 was aware of this, and they differed from their elders. A new direction was given to the whole movement, and new leaders — Ivanov, Bely, and Blok — emerged as its spokesmen.

Of the three men who personified this change Viacheslav Ivanov (1866–1949) was the most intellectual and esoteric. Born into the family of a civil servant, he studied in Moscow, then in Berlin under the famous historian Theodore Mommsen; he traveled extensively in Europe and the Near East and was erudite in the humanities. When, in 1903, he published *Pilot Stars,* his first collection of poems, the literati were somewhat puzzled: they hardly expected lyrics from this professor of thirty-seven who looked like a Biblical prophet and seemed to know Latin and Greek better than Russian. Yet this scholar, whose philological and philosophical treatises could be understood only by qualified readers, soon assumed a leading position among the Modernists. After 1905, under the influence of his doctrine, a whole current of mystical symbolism became associated with his name. Poets, scholars, artists met regularly in Ivanov's St. Petersburg apartment, called The Tower. His Wednesdays were literary reunions, religious forums, and sessions of an exclusive club the members of which belonged to the intellectual and artistic elite of Russia. The host officiated like a high priest and was listened to as an oracle. By 1911 he was unanimously acclaimed the King of Poets and was spoken of as Viacheslav the Great.

It is almost impossible to dissociate Ivanov's poetry from his philosophic writings, particularly from his *Hellenic Religion of the Suffering God.* Parting company with the doctrines of *The Birth of Tragedy* by Nietzsche, with whom he had so many points in common, Ivanov stressed the tragic fate of Dionysus. He interpreted the dismemberment and resurrection of God as 'the keys to the mysteries of life.' They represented supreme realities, eternal absolutes, which Greek mythology revealed under the guise of poetic symbols. Ivanov was not satisfied with the statement of Briussov: 'In secret dreams I created a world of ideal nature, next to which all these steppes, rocks, and waters are mere dust.' For Ivanov steppes, rocks, and waters reveal the splendor of the Lord's creation. The whole universe is a system of signs pointing to hidden truth. Ivanov's own fairly complicated mythology establishes a scale of concepts: Female and Male, I and Thou, Unity and Multiplicity, Nature and Man, and, finally, Dionysus and Apollo correspond respectively to the Earth and the Sun. Apollo symbolizes the power of contemplative vision in memory, as well as the principle of individualization, while Dionysus embodies the orgiastic exaltation of being. Dionysus is the tragic aspect of reality; he symbolizes pain, sacrifice, and horror, the sense of the tragic — oblivion — as opposed to memory. But he is also Resurrection, and therefore the religion of Dionysus is basically the religion of Christ.

From these premises Ivanov concluded that true culture was essentially religious; it had to include the sense of the tragic as well as the hope of resurrection, the ecstasy of ruin and the joy of renewal. Taking up Solovyov's idea of solidarity and community, he insisted on the collective and universal character of culture and identified the social with the religious. Art, too, was for him of a religious nature. It created myths with deep universal meanings, and the poet was bound to be the bearer of a spiritual message; he voiced the collective soul of the people, and in his theurgic activity was, like the priest, a bridge between Man and Divinity. The highest artistic achievements were collective — the epic, tragedy, popular songs, and mystery plays — and derived from the same source as that of myth and religion. This represented a complete break with the aesthetes and Parnassians, who spoke of 'purposeless beauty.'

Ivanov, like Solovyov, defined his own era as one of change and upheaval. Cultures had to die before new life could rise from the tomb, and he hailed the work of destruction in the cycle of eternal renewal. In his widely known poem, 'The Nomads of Beauty,' he acclaimed the barbarian invasion that brings new blood, and compared poets with the Nomads:

> Hurl from your flooding numbers
> Your hordes in hurricanes,
> Where the low valley slumbers
> And slaves are proud of chains.
> Trample their paradises,
> Attila! Waste anew!
> And where your bright star raises,
> The steppe will bud for you.[1]

It is noteworthy that this Symbolist, whose philosophy had a strong anti-bourgeois tendency, was reasserting the favorite Russian concept: the responsibility of the artist. In the years of reaction, when any social message was rejected as obsolete, the Symbolists were demanding a religious message. The theory of art for art's sake, of art as play, entertainment, or escape, did not seem to hold any attraction for the Russians. It could seduce them for a short while, like some challenging paradox, but they always came back — often by devious paths — to the idea of instructive, useful literature, to art as value, force, and significance.

The poetry of this scholar and master of versification offered a curious mixture of erudition and subtlety and, at times, of spiritual elation. His best collections of poems, *Eros* (1907) and *Cor Ardens* (1911), were ponderous, solemn, full of symbols, quotations, mythological names, and scholarly allusions. He used Church Slavonic expressions and terms from the Greek Orthodox liturgy side by side with neologisms of Latin and foreign origin, and achieved surprising linguistic effects. Anticipating Ezra Pound and T. S. Eliot, he delighted in intellectual acrostics, but the fabric of his long-winded or obscure ballads remained impeccably classical. As the Master, the High Priest of Apollo, he could not afford the

[1] Translated by C. M. Bowra in *The Book of Russian Verse*, Macmillan, London, 1943 (by permission of the translator).

liberty of a loose line or a defective rhyme. His stanzas either have the sculpturesque solidity of Grecian statues or resemble the chants of ancient religions, old rituals, and magic incantations. Critics compared the richness of their texture with the lavishly brocaded robes of the Byzantine clergy. This majestic poetry, constructed on several planes and reminding one of Derzhavin's sonorous declamatory style, never reached a large audience. Even among the elite, Ivanov was much more admired and talked about than read. A few initiates studied and commented on every line he wrote, as if each one were a kind of divine revelation.

In 1911 Ivanov moved to Moscow. Although nothing had changed in his style and general ideas, his new poems and articles revealed more than ever his Populist and Slavophile bent. This poet, who had been a staunch Westernizer and a representative of Greco-Roman and Christian traditions, who had transplanted into Russian thought many achievements of European art and philosophy, was now particularly concerned with the destiny of Russia and all Slav peoples. He talked of their special cultural and religious mission and made surprising remarks about their Scythian nature, which rejected the middle-class ways of the West. These messianic and nationalistic notes indicated the changes within the Symbolist movement, of which he was the official leader.

After 1917 Ivanov published *Winter Sonnets* (1920) and a remarkable *Correspondence from Two Corners* (1921). He was staying at that time at the Writer's House in Moscow with the essayist and philosopher Michael Gershenzon, and they wrote letters to each other on the problem of culture. Gershenzon championed freedom from tradition, while Ivanov affirmed the continuity of cultural heritage throughout political and social upheavals.

Ivanov left Russia in 1924 and settled as an *émigré* in Italy. As a professor of classical literature and philosophy in several universities he became converted to Roman Catholicism and contributed to Russian publications only occasionally. During World War II he is said to have written an epic poem on Russia's national saint, Saint George the Conqueror, but this, as well as his other later works, remains in manuscript. He died in Rome in 1949, at the age of 84.

II   The influence of Ivanov, deep but limited in range and of short duration, was felt more in the field of general ideas than in literary forms. Andrei Bely, on the contrary, introduced during his erratic career several stylistic innovations that have left a strong impress on Russian prose and poetry.

Boris Bugaev (1880–1934), who wrote under the pen name of Andrei Bely (White), was the son of a Moscow professor of mathematics known for his erudition and absent-mindedness. In his early youth the poet was attracted by natural sciences but later shifted to literature; the influence of Darwin and John Stuart Mill was replaced by that of Solovyov and the German Romantics. Bely studied science as well as philology in Russia and abroad, and was widely read and traveled. At the age of 20 he joined the Symbolists and soon rose to a leading position among them: between 1903 and 1917 his poems and his highly experimental prose never failed to provoke a stir. Most of his poetic works (*Gold in Azure,* 1904, *The Cup of Blizzards,* 1908, *Ashes* and *The Urn,* 1909, and others) were constructed as musical compositions. Not only did he use musical terms for titles and call entire collections 'symphonies,' but he excelled in multiform auditory effects. He displayed a staggering virtuosity in new inflections and tonalities, in slowing down and accelerating his meters, in alternating consonances and assonances. This remarkably gifted poet knew well what he was doing: his treatises on Russian verse (particularly his *Glossolalia*) and his essays are of distinct literary merit.

A great many of his poems seem strained or obscure, and critics qualified them as both impressionistic and artificial. Most of them, however, possess an elusive, almost ambiguous quality that well reflected the instability of character and the inner dynamism of their author. Nervous, impassioned, ready to become excited over any kind of new intellectual or verbal extravagancy, Andrei Bely was a man of many contradictions. He went through frequent changes of attitudes and opinions and often made and broke literary and philosophical allegiances. He was attracted by 'pluralism' and affirmed his right to change: 'All masks are merely aspects of but one face.' An enthusiastic disciple of Solovyov, a follower of Merezhkovsky, both friend and foe of Blok, Populist, revolutionary, and patron of the Futurists, Bely became in 1913 a devout pupil of Rudolf Steiner and was one of Russia's leading anthroposophists. Toward the end of his life he proclaimed himself a Marxist — and his Marxism, combining as it did mysticism and dialectical materialism, was indeed of a very peculiar brand.

His searchings and questings were genuine enough, but at the same time there was something deceptive and ambiguous about this craftsman-mystic. He could be sly and devastating in ridiculing his friends and preceptors and highly ironical even about his own mysticism. In private conversations (as the present writer well remembers), which usually turned into extended monologues, Andrei Bely would tear to shreds Merezhkovsky, Hippius, Sologub, and many other contemporaries who were his intimates. Yet these diatribes would be immediately followed by protestations of love and tenderness.

The duality so manifest in his elongated face, with the high forehead of a thinker, the pale-gray eyes of a visionary, and the heavy-set, curving mouth of a sardonic sensualist, prevailed in his general outlook as well — particularly before 1917, when the central theme of his philosophy was the distinction between being and consciousness. The force of life (he held) is chaotic and irrational, like a lava flow; the efforts of reason to find a safety valve or to seal up the mouth of the volcano with science, culture, progress are all feeble and useless. Revelation of the fiery substance of the universe comes amid calamities, amid storms and shipwrecks; it is also manifest amid the bustle and jumble of phenomena; passions and delirium, the fantasies of myth, and the whirlwind of music can also disclose the glow of truth. He attacked those Russian intellectuals, such as Merezhkovsky or Viacheslav Ivanov, who had erred through indulging in cerebral mysticism and rational symbolism — the two cardinal sins of pseudo-mystics. From then on the ironic twist becomes predominant in his work. At the peak of the Symbolists' victory, in 1908, he published realistic poems in a satirical vein, dealing with a provincial railroad station, a trivial love affair between a divinity student and a minister's daughter, and various scenes of coarse and stupid existence. With malicious pleasure and a Gogolian grin he depicted this very world of muddled reality, of material contingencies, from which he was trying to liberate himself through symbolic images of Love and Sun, through mystical contemplation of the Godhead and eternity. *Ashes,* a collection of poems on political and social subjects, disclosed his kinship with Nekrassov. Bely, the Symbolist and avowed Westernizer, attempted to merge his mysticism with Populism. He now insisted (and quite rightly) that Russian Symbolists were much more the heirs of Dostoevsky, Gogol, and Chekhov than followers of Nietzsche, Ibsen, and Hamsun. He also stressed their connection with the poetic heritage of Boratynsky, Fet, and Tiutchev. Russia and her problems became one of his main themes. In several poems (subsequently collected under the titles *Stanzas on Russia* and *In the Fields,* 1904) Bely questioned himself about the right path for this starving people enslaved in the vast freedom of its plains. Why had 'iron fate cursed this fatal, icy land'? — 'O, Mother Russia, O angry motherland — who has played such a jest upon thee?'

In his novel *The Silver Dove* (1909), Bely analyzed the 'national' traits the mild liberals had failed to comprehend amid the whirlwind of the Days of Freedom. He also attempted to deal with the problem of the two cultures, the Eastern and the Western, and with the gap separating them. Darialsky, a poet, the hero of the novel, who had been engrossed in the culture of ancient Greece, turns for illumination to the people. He finds dark mysticism in a crude sect of the Dissenters, whose religion is a strange mixture of eroticism, asceticism, the fire cult, and sadistic practices. Their orgiastic rites remind him of the Eleusinian mysteries, and he abandons his gentle financée Katia for the pockmarked Matriona, the goddess of the sect, and perishes miserably, the victim of superstition and ignorance. The primitive Doves — the sectarians — are the Orient, the blind force that has not yet found its path; they manifest their chaotic, maddening energy in wild outbursts and murder. The cerebral Darialsky, the bearer of the chill reason of the West, is as erring as the Old Believers (or Dissenters) who kill him. A meeting of the two principles is possible only on a higher plane of the metaphysical. The novel as a whole is unsatisfactory, but it does contain some startling descriptions and has a definitely Gogolian mixture of fantasy and observation.

Bely's next transition was from a mystical to a political interpretation of the problem of Russia. He came to the conclusion that autocracy was fettering the national energy and preventing the people from fulfilling their mission. In his work the Symbolist current that had its origin in Western influences flows into the Populist stream; mystical aspirations merge with national emotions and radical dreams. Bely regretted that the Revolution of 1905 did not fulfil its promise, but expected a new upheaval that would finally release the latent possibilities of the nation. This special brand of mystical and revolutionary Populism found its expression in *Petersburg* (1911–13), one of the most arresting Russian novels of the twentieth century. The plot is presented as a jumble of mistakes, love, betrayal, accidents, and *quid pro quos* — a true picture of the confusion and hodgepodge of reality, of the muddled world of phenomena. Apollon Ableukhov, an old bureaucratic dignitary, becomes suspicious that his son Nicholas, who had joined the revolutionaries, wants to murder him — and his apprehensions turn into certitude when a bomb masked as a can of sardines explodes in his empty study. Nicholas is unable to prove his innocence; he is too deeply involved with Lippanchenko, the agent-provocateur who is driving him to parricide; with Dudkin, the alcoholic terrorist, who finally kills the traitor; and with Sophie, the wife of his friend Likhutin.

Although father and son stand at opposite poles, both are wrong. The old dignitary hopes to tame the wilderness of Russian immensity through strict regulations; the geometrical lines of the capital's avenues are superimposed upon the fantastic disorder of the Russian anarchical torrent. Nicholas hopes to pacify the chaos through intellectual schemes; he studies Kant and believes in the organized action of the revolutionary party. Both father and son are proponents of Mongolism, since they personify a spiritual void, a destructive nihilism. They are not alive, they are ghosts in a ghost-like city. The messy drama of vanity, murder, revolution, reaction, and farcical situations is played out in the eerie atmosphere of a cold, foggy winter, of inexorably straight avenues, on the banks of frozen canals, where Gogol's petty officials lose their souls, and Pushkin's Bronze Horseman terrifies his victims.

Bely reverted repeatedly to the theme of St. Petersburg — one of the most tragic and fascinatingly peculiar themes in nineteenth-century Russian literature — but for him the unreality of this seat of autocracy and European rationalization, the flimsiness of this spectral capital of water and granite, reflected the shipwreck of a culture. St. Petersburg's culture had exhausted itself, had fallen apart, had been reduced to 'mist, moss, mess.' Its strength was illusory, its hold on the country shadowy; it would dissipate in a swirl when the tempest dispelled the fog that had come from the Baltic. The Russia of the Ableukhovs — father and son — of grimacing, criminal Lippanchenkos, of empty-headed Likhutins, of pseudo-spiritual Dudkins, this Russia of hobgoblins and charlatans was bound to collapse. St. Petersburg was rotten and condemned. It was the kingdom of the Dragon, the symbol of darkness and non-existence. Christ was fighting the Dragon — and the West must help Russia in her struggle against the Orient of the Dragon.

Bely talks about Christ and the Dragon in almost the same terms he used in his attacks against the 'Asiatic spirit' in Russian life; but, of course, the Mongolism Bely wanted to see uprooted from his native country was not only the 'yellow peril' of Solovyov but also the embodiment of soulless materialism.

By 1917–19 Bely's Populism definitely assumed the form of a religious and revolutionary messianism. He saw future dawns in the catastrophic years of Russia's civil war. In the poem 'Christ Is Risen' he affirmed that Russia's sufferings were a Golgotha and so necessary for the salvation of mankind. Russia, in fact, was being crucified for the sake of all men — and she would bring atonement and liberation: the newly crucified Christ would be resurrected in Russia. Thus the messianic faith of the Slavophiles, the revolutionary pathos of the Populists (Bely was a close friend of the Social Revolutionaries), and the Christian-mystical flight of Symbolism were all blended in this vision of Russia announcing the new Gospel amid storm and blood.

Bely's importance lies not in his ideas, which were eclectic and derived from various sources — from Solovyov and the Populists to Nietzsche and Steiner — but in the contribution he made to Russian prose. His *Petersburg* and his autobiographical novels (*Kotik Letayev* and *Kotik Letayev's Crime*, 1915–1922) are specimens of Russian surrealism and also of style and pattern as represented in English by James Joyce. Independently of Joyce, however, and on a different psychological and formal level, Bely arrived at a polyphonic prose with neologisms, world-ofnebulae coinages, the interior monologue (or stream of consciousness), and a myth-like structure of plots. A clever juggler, he submitted the word, which became in his hands a sonorous and plastic instrument, to all conceivable experiments. It is dynamic and a symbol of gesture; it emerges onomatopoetically out of word roots without regard to grammatical rules, and is thus the agent of a stylistic revolution. Bely's rhythmic prose, with its assonances and plays upon meanings, expresses the slightest and least perceptible shades of spiritual life, and at times tries to communicate states of being beyond consciousness. For instance, his *Kotik Letayev,* begun in 1915 and published in 1922, is an attempt to build up a cosmology on a system of parallels: the pre-natal impressions of a nightmare and of a symbolic world are, with the birth and growth of the child, resolved into ordinary three-dimensional manifestations that yet secrete a memory of a fourth dimension. Certain passages of his later works, such as *The Moscow Eccentric, Moscow Under the Blow,* and *Masks* (1926–32), are definitely 'beyond the mind's grasp,' and their spiral-like devices convey completely irrational, almost delirious experiences.

In his poetry, and even more so in his prose, Bely focused his attention on the word: as a sound, as an image and a symbol, it acquired an autonomy, became an entity in itself. Phonetical tricks, whimsical distortions of colloquial expressions, and fanciful amalgams gave rise to hints and allusions and pointed to hidden ideas. This was a new brand of literary nominalism, and to name meant to interpret and to create. It is obvious that such prose is hard to read. Bely's novels are heavy-set, esoteric, often irritating and puzzling — and full to the brim with verbal brilliancy and imagination. Their inventiveness is the delight and the despair of students of philology: Bely transformed verbs into nouns, prepositions into adjectives; he blended popular speech with abstract philosophical terminology, showered neologisms, and displayed a superb defiance of grammar, syntax, and all rules of language.

The composition of Bely's novels is as involved as his style. He deliberately mixes all the planes — the real, the symbolic, and the ideological — and offers a series of separate episodes, providing a clue only at the very end of the narrative; thus there finally emerges a symphony composed of these fragmentary chords. Fantasy and reality are treated in a truly Gogolian manner; details of observation are presented as stage effects, comic and tragic incidents overlap, satire always overflows into grotesquerie. The prevalent spirit of this motley and bizarre creation is the author's conviction that life is merely an appearance, that we see only masks and reflections of truth; the task of the artist is to disclose this truth in a supreme vision that is supernatural, dim, glorious, and frightening — on the frontier of senses and reason, on the border of the sublime and the ridiculous.

Although Bely did not fully realize the style he was striving for, at least he made a break with the past and an astonishing attempt at renewing the realistic and Symbolist traditions. What he wanted to accomplish is, however, greater than what he actually did accomplish. This explains the disparity between his influence and his popularity. He served up such an overloaded fare of metaphors and experiments that it was indigestible; he piled up so many verbal tricks and linguistic eccentricities that his work became heavy, pretentious, and tiresome. And, above all, his art is so cerebral, so artificial, that its effect is merely an indirect one. Bely missed by a hair being a genius, but if, as some critics maintain, his work is on the whole a failure, it is nevertheless a magnificent failure — much more significant than many dull successes. A generation is indebted to Bely, and the historian of Russian literature will discover many traces of the impression he made during the first half of the twentieth century.

Bely augmented his creative experiments with a number of critical and philological essays that marked a period of revision and innovation in the field of literary language. His works on Symbolism, on the principles of Russian prosody, on rhythmics in poetry, all laid the foundations for a special branch of formal criticism: the analysis of rhythmical structure, of the melody and euphony of verse. No less valuable are his treatises on Gogol and Lermontov, and his revaluations of Batiushkov and Zhukovsky as reformers of Russian versification.

This romantic writer, for whom symbols were an all-embracing system of images and ideas, attained a curious merging of the old and the new. His was a supreme effort to unite Symbolism and Populism by reviving the religious messianism of Russian letters. The echoes of Gogol and Dostoevsky are distinct in Bely's compositions, in his complex plots teeming with criminals and frantic heroes. But his novels have the 'poetization' of the language that Dostoevsky ignored yet Gogol knew too well: they are symphonies with that atonality which is so typical of modern music.

During the last ten years of his life Bely was simply tolerated in Soviet Russia, mainly because of his revolutionary sympathies. In his memoirs (*At the Watershed of Centuries,* 1930, and others), which offer valuable though highly subjective material for the history of Russian Symbolism, he attempted to show that the Symbolists were moving toward a reunion with the socialists. The polemics resulting from his assertions could not give him much satisfaction, since they were conducted on a low level of political opportunism. Influential Soviet critics did not hide their feelings about Bely — 'that anachronistic relic of the past.' His 'formalism' was invariably condemned as hostile to the spirit of socialism. Those very writers who had borrowed not a few whimsies from Bely's bag of tricks repaid him by being nasty. Fortunately for Bely, he was so absorbed in his work that he could not be hurt by human pettiness. Yet, shortly before his death, he often felt bitter and unhappy and sometimes repeated his own prophetic verse:

> He believed in the shimmering sheen of gold,
> Yet was slain by the golden darts of the Sun;
> In his thought he measured centuries
> Yet had no time to live his own life.

III   Russian Symbolism still awaits its historian: this rich and complex movement, with all its ramifications, is not as yet thoroughly explored. But one thing we know with certainty is that its whole course has been encompassed by and summarized in the work of Alexander Blok (1880–1921), the greatest Russian poet of the twentieth century. His name must be added to the list of five luminaries of Russian poetry: Pushkin, Lermontov, Nekrassov, Fet, and Tiutchev. As time goes by Blok grows in stature and acquires a prophetic significance. He was not simply a man who wrote beautiful verse; he was the embodiment of Russian culture. If Pushkin inaugurated an entire period of Russian civilization and indicated its further development, Blok — heir to the legacy of Pushkin — marked the last flowering and the end of that period. He expressed a world that came to completion and destruction during his lifetime — and he accepted its collapse in the name of the future. He tried — in his own words — to 'hearken to the music of the revolution,' which was drowning out the music of culture. This attempt compelled him to deny and reject what he cherished and to welcome a new era of strangers and Scythians. Therein lay his tragedy: he could not reconcile the two truths, could not accept one to the exclusion of the other — and he remained torn by his inner struggle, at the watershed of two eras, turning backward and looking forward, like double-faced Janus. This tragic duality caused the cleavage in his poetry as well as in his life.

Alexander Blok's father, a professor of law, an excellent scholar and musician, was moody and ironical, cruel and rebellious — Dostoevsky wanted to write a novel about him. He was incessantly quarreling with his wife, the idealistic and highly cultured daughter of the botanist Beketov, rector of the University of St. Petersburg. The parents separated when Alexander was three years old. The child was brought up for the most part at Shakhmatovo, the Moscow estate of his maternal grandparents. It was a typical gentlefolk's nest, an aristocratic manor enveloped in an atmosphere of artistic and intellectual refinement.

Blok began writing poems at the age of five, and the Russian and European classics were familiar to him from early childhood. Protected from material cares, sheltered from ugliness and coarseness, he grew up among flowers, books, and music, surrounded by men and women whose chief interests were literature, science, and art. His development was organic — what others had to study came to him as easily as breathing; he naturally belonged to the top group of Russian educated society.

At the age of eighteen this tall, athletic, handsome, gray-eyed youth of restrained manners conveyed the impression of strength, purity, and depth. In 1898 he met 15-year-old Liubov Mendeleyeva, daughter of the famous chemist, on whose large estate amateur theatricals were organized each summer. She played Ophelia, and he fell in love with her. This love coincided with another event — his acquaintance with the work of Solovyov — and Blok's feelings for the blue-eyed, ravishingly beautiful girl blended with those about Solovyov's mystical search for Eternal Womanhood.

Literary symbolism, religious aspirations, and youthful passion created in Blok a peculiar state of mind that lasted several years and resulted in two cycles of poems (*Ante Lucem* and *Verses about the Lady Beautiful*). All his friends (among whom were Andrei Bely and a few young men who later became minor Symbolists) were completely under the spell of Solovyov. They shared his mystical expectancy and his feeling of the imminent end of history (which they awaited in comfortable surroundings). Above all they accepted enthusiastically his concept of Sophia, the Eternal Wisdom, which was also Eternal Love. And was not Liubov Mendeleyeva the embodiment of this idea, and did not Blok's love for her bear all the signs of platonic and mystical passion? In their imagination she was the Belle Dame to whom poems were offered up like incense. Her gestures and words were watched and interpreted as mystical revelations. Blok's stanzas, translucent in their symbolic imagery, sang of the delicate tints of the dawn, the azure of the sky; in fragrant meadows the Lover awaited the descent of Light, which was the Glory of the World and the Beloved.

The mystical sweetness of these lyrics (which were slightly reminiscent of certain pieces of the Pre-Raphaelites) had, however, an emotional quality that Blok's friends failed to understand but that captivated the readers of the poems. Blok used all the Symbolistic terminology and imagery, of which he had an exceptional grasp, but his *Verses about the Lady Beautiful* were different from the erudite chants of Ivanov, the exuberant songs of Balmont, the gelid odes of Briussov, and the ambiguous lines of Hippius. They had a genuine emotional force, their spiritual flights were presented as spontaneous revelations of earthly love — and this bestowed upon them a unique tone. The poems in which his friends saw 'heavenly accents' and allusions to 'the illuminating essence of all things under the coarse bark of matter' had been inspired by incidents of real life. The seven hundred pieces of these chivalric ballads,[2] which sounded like a litany and in which the poet's 'tireless ear was attuned to the distant call of another soul, the flutter of angelic wings,' were a lyrical diary, an intimate story of Blok's personal experience. The *Canzoniere* of Petrarch offer the closest literary parallel to this highly subjective and enchantingly musical poetry.

Blok and Liubov were married in 1903, and those who met them at that time always spoke of the harmonious light this couple irradiated: they seemed the embodiment of happiness, beauty, and triumphant youth. Blok himself said then that he had found 'the fixed fount,' 'a firm ground of mystical faith which spreads its blessings over life.'

In 1904, when *Verses about the Lady Beautiful* was published, Blok became a welcome guest in the salons of St. Petersburg literati. Merezhkovsky and his wife, Hippius, saw in him the prince of a religious revival; a veritable cult of admirers rallied round the minstrel of the Belle Dame. Most of them failed to perceive in the behavior of their idol the ominous signs of an approaching crisis. But for those who had more insight Blok's frigidity, the stony gaze of his gray eyes, his abrupt silences in response to outbursts at mystical eloquence, his cryptic and often caustic remarks appeared suspicious. He suffered from fits of depression, and often felt a satanic urge to be ironical and destructive.

His peace of mind had been disrupted by an unconscious restlessness. 'I am longing for something clear, calm, and white,' he wrote to his mother at the time. In vain did Merezhkovsky try to chain him to his logical formulas and to interest him in various religious theories. Blok, in whom the symptoms of an inner discord were growing daily, followed his own painful path. The Russian troubadour was through. The mystical mist that had beautified all contours and hidden reality under a haze of pink and gold was being swept away by the contact with the reality of life during the stormy pre-Revolutionary days. Blok was falling from his mystical heights into the vale of tears, peopled by prostitutes instead of the Lady Beautiful, and crowded with factories rather than fairy castles. It was a debacle and a new birth: he was reborn into the world of sin and pain. His faith in the supernatural was badly shaken, heaven became distant and chill, and his mystical beliefs were shattered when confronted

[2] Only 314 out of 687 were included in the first collection.

with the ugliness of man's condition. A terrifying moral problem suddenly yawned before him like a chasm.

Together with his father's spirit of rebelliousness and irony he had inherited, on his maternal side, Beketov's realistic and analytical disposition. His critical sense was as keen as his aesthetic sensitivity. He could perceive, with pitiless precision, both his inner self and the external world. Every day he was shedding his youthful illusions about love, about his own wife, his friends — and about poetry and Russian life. These illusions melted away like the sugar-candy angel on top of a Christmas tree bright with many candles.

An emotional crisis, combined with a crisis of his conscience, upset his entire way of life. He still spent Sunday evenings at Sologub's, where the Modernists read their ophidian and demoniac works; he still attended Merezhkovsky's salon (transformed into a hothouse by a profusion of lilies and roses) and listened to Hippius as she discoursed on Christ, mystical bliss, and asceticism, smoking long, perfumed cigarettes the while; he still climbed up to The Tower, where Viacheslav Ivanov, master of ceremonies, made subtle comments on theurgical art, on Eros, Dionysus, and the religion of popular myth — but Blok's heart was with none of them: he had tired of their sterile sophistication. These intellectuals dwelt in an artificial world of their own making, and real life — the life of persecuted revolutionists, starving peasants, striking workers, and homeless tramps — had nothing to do with that world. In Blok's case the inevitable discrepancy between ideal vision and coarse reality, which leads to conflict, frustration, and rebellion — the three phases of romantic plight — had been made all the more bitter by the bankruptcy of the 1905 Revolution, which he resented as a terrible blow.

His new cycles of poems, 'Earth's Bubbles' (1905) and 'The City' (1906), dealt with grimacing hunchbacks and witches; 'nocturnal violets' blossomed but seldom in his landscapes of city tenements, factory walls, barracks, and street lamps blinking in the autumnal fog. Life appeared to him as a Punch-and-Judy show-booth, as a stupid children's play (*The Little Show-Booth*). He still longed for the Belle Dame — 'be thy name blest' — but he knew that 'she had gone off to the fields, never more to return.' 'I understood everything — and I am going away. Blessed be the dream of the past, but the soul is incurable.' The universe, said Blok, is impelled by music, passion, love, preference, strength — whereas he found around him only din, disharmony, bloodless hearts, and vile bodies. His 'prophetic boredom' and melancholy were, like Lermontov's, the result of his hypersensitivity. Yet he was too strong and too passionate not to attempt to overcome despair and grief. Thus began that period of dissipation which horrified Bely and led to his break with Blok. The poet sought an outlet in demonism and a wild expenditure of energy. Love affairs substituted for love, the Belle Dame was replaced by pretty women. In 'The Stranger' (1907), one of his most discussed poems, which critics such as Philosophov dubbed 'absolutely incomprehensible not only to laymen but to specialists,' the scene of his encounter with the Unknown Lady is laid not in meadows at dawn, but on a sultry evening, in a suburban restaurant, among roistering tosspots.

He did not separate from his wife, but they led independent lives. His next collections of poems, *The Masque of Snow* (1908) and *Faina* (1909), were dedicated to Natalia Volokhova, the actress, whose dark beauty held him captive for some time. The reading of these sensual, despairing, and melancholy stanzas at one of Ivanov's Wednesday nights provoked consternation and astonishment among those whom Blok styled 'professional mystics.'

Blok now entered a world of tempestuousness and madness. He compared himself to a winged demon, and found a grim satisfaction in frittering away his physical and spiritual powers on parties, feminine conquests, and drinking bouts with the gypsies. Sometimes he consoled himself by saying that all this excitement, all this turmoil conveyed to him a 'sense of the beyond,' that there was a kind of mystical experience in the intemperances of the flesh: wine, women, and song had always been the path to supersensual illuminations; the precipice of evil was closer to the heaven of purity than was sober triviality.

The attraction of evil and of demonism was, however, of short duration. He could not help feeling the contradiction between his true longings and the trumpery he was playing with: taverns, sprees, cruel or frivolous toyings with women. 'It becomes more and more difficult to live,' he complains in a letter. 'It is so cold. I am wasting a lot of money senselessly — and there is such a complete void all around me: as if everybody had left me and ceased to love me; perhaps they never did. I am on an island, in the midst of an empty, icy sea. My anxiety is not pointless: I see too many things clearly, soberly.'

His double vision tormented him: he perceived two aspects of truth, and they were forever irreconcilable. Dreams did not help; they made life more unbearable: 'It is windy out in the streets; prostitutes are shivering on sidewalks, people are starving, are hanged; there is reaction all over the country; life in Russia is cold, difficult, disgusting.' He sneered at his mystical friends: 'If all these chatterboxes were to lose weight and become quite thin because of their search (which is useless except for certain *refined natures*), nothing would change in Russia.' This hostile attitude toward intellectuals was becoming constantly intensified. He reproached them with their separation from the people, their lack of real experience in life, and questioned their 'vertical culture,' which now seemed to him artificial and highly perishable.

There was a fundamental difference between Blok and other Symbolist leaders: the others looked for principles and abstractions that would provide them with illumination, while he tried to find truth through intensely lived emotional experiences — and his poetry mirrored this intimate and individual process. His approach to art also was undergoing a change. In *The Rose and the Cross* (1913), a bizarre drama in the style of the troubadours, he insisted on the unity of art and the moral ideal: their separation was fatal to the artist; it degraded his work, and betrayed his love. His own existence in the meantime was a constant flight from himself, and he responded to his failure to find consolation by writing despairingly gloomy and poignant verse. His most striking poems of this period are contained in 'Harps and Violins' (1912), 'The Frightening World,' and 'Retaliation' (1909–16).

Complete negation pervades these collections. 'The worlds are flying. The years are flying. The empty universe looks at us through the night of its eyes — and the tired, hollow soul still speaks of happiness. What is happiness? A brief and tense moment, oblivion, a suspension of cares — and the heart-breaking, mysterious flight is resumed again.' It is a flight through a 'terrifying world' of boredom, triviality, and annihilation. The poet's personal life is a failure. His heart is a 'rouged corpse.' 'O yes, I was rich once, but now nothing is worth a copper coin: neither hatred, nor love, nor gossip, nor gold—not even my moral grief.' There is nothing to adore and to hope for, everything is shattered, and he is lost upon paths of demonism and revelry, even as he had previously been lost on the Path of Light. Duality prevails: 'This world is too narrow for my heart.' He is weary of passion: 'The same caresses and entreaties, the boring quiver of eager lips, and of too familiar shoulders.' 'Well, kiss my dying lips, undo your woeful zone.' 'The soul did not escape the invisible decay.' 'He who has once tasted the air of freedom can no longer breathe here below.' As the poet Khodassevich put it, Blok suffered from insomnia of the heart.

After the deaths of his young child and his father in 1909, Blok went abroad, but his protracted travels did little to change his mood. He found in Europe the same feeling of instability, the same failure of the intellectuals, and the triumph of that very bourgeoisie and that same middle class which he hated with the double hatred of a romantic and a Russian radical. 'Men disgust me; life is horrible,' he wrote from France. 'European life is as revolting as that in Russia; in general, the life of all men the world over is a monstrous, dirty puddle.'

But paralleling these statements there is an effort to find a way of salvation and a growing interest in problems of culture, art, and Russian history. With the same emotional intensity that made him suffer because of the discrepancy between dreams and reality, Blok feels the dichotomy between his sense of justice and his search for truth, and the unjust social and political conditions in Russia. When, in 1908, he delivered a public lecture on the intelligentsia, his audience was shocked by the violence of his diatribe: he accused the intellectuals of not understanding their own country and of having lost all ties with the people. Scion of the culture created by aristocrats and intellectuals, he questioned that culture's validity and predicted its imminent collapse. Gogol, said Blok, talked of Russian taciturnity and slumber; they had come to an end, however, and the Gogolian troika — symbol of Russia — was rushing onward like the wind and the intellectuals ought to throw themselves under the hoofs of the steeds. Sacrifice and self-annihilation were the only things left to them: 'They are regarding us from the brink of the blue precipice of the future and are luring us thither.' Thenceforth the theme of Russia became the prevalent one in his poetry and determined its further development. He turned to his country with the passion and exasperation a lover feels toward a perfidious yet irresistible woman. In his allegoric drama, *The Song of Fate* (1909), Faina, an enigmatic, passionate, and dissolute woman who disappears in a blizzard, symbolizes Russia, while Herman, the lover whom she at first rejects, represents the intellectuals.

It was soon like a new infatuation: he fled 'into the fields, the endless plain, to the people, to Russia.' He tenderly devoted his lyrics to 'our roads and our fogs and the whispers of our oats.' The poverty and humility of the countryside moved him to tears: 'O my starving land, what are you telling my heart? — O my wife, why are you weeping so bitterly?' 'O Russia, beggarly Russia, your gray huts, your soughing songs are for me like the first tears of love.' His feelings for her are as dualistic as Lermontov's 'strange love'; Blok talks of his 'beloved fatal country.'

His best and most popular stanzas compare Russia to women: to a wench whose eyes shine from under her shawl; to a treacherous mistress whose traits do not alter despite all her adventures; to a mother who cries over her children. But gradually new notes steal into the music he hears amid Russian scenes. He calls the era of reaction the 'years of sloth'; he sees oppression hovering like a hawk over the villages, and finally raises the question of Russia's destiny. What is the meaning of her history, what is the significance of her fate? 'I do not see thy face behind the snow, the woods, the steppes, behind thy incomprehensible width and breadth.'

History provides him an answer. In his lyrics 'On the Battle of Kuli-

kovo Field' (where the Russians fought the Tartar invaders) he exclaims: 'Eternal combat! We dreamed only of calm and peace amid
dust and blood! The mare of the steppes runs and crushes the grass!'
'Our road is the road of the steppe and of shoreless grief — thy grief O
Russia! — yet I fear not the darkness beyond the border.' The road of
struggle and suffering leads, despite oppression and misery, to wild freedom.

Blok has the premonition of an approaching catastrophe, but his
hope in Russia's glorious future remains unshaken. Through fiery puri-
fication Russia will come to a new birth. 'Russia is not yet a genius,' he
writes in his notes. 'The future is only fermenting within her. But she
stands in the very center of events, on that narrow strip where the breath
of the spirit is blowing.'

Resuming the tradition of Slavophile and messianic dreams, he now
follows in the wake of the odes of Khomiakov and Tiutchev. 'There is
art and death in Europe. Russia is life. I am neither with those who are
for old Russia nor with the partisans of Europeanization (the Socialists,
the Constitutional Democrats, Vengerov, to give examples), but for
some new Russia — or for no Russia at all: either she will no longer exist
or she will follow a road entirely different from that of Europe.' Yet instead of repeating the idyllic stuff of the old-fashioned nationalists, he
foresees clearly the industrial development of the country. In 1913 he
wrote 'The New America,' an extraordinary poem in which he predicted
the industrial transformation of Russia.

In 1912–14, in addition to his heightened interest in politics, he held
a strong conviction of the doom of aristocratic culture; he was awaiting
the cataclysm that was to destroy it: 'In our hearts the seismograph's arm
has already moved.' The publication of 'Retaliation,' an autobiographical
narrative poem with realistic descriptions of social conditions and of
the revolutionary movement, completed his break with Ivanov, whom he
attacked for his 'inane wordiness.' At the same time Blok was writing
splendid love lyrics dedicated to Liubov Delmas, the leading actress of
the Musical Drama Theater, with whom he was then in love ('Carmen'
and parts of 'Harps and Violins'). He welcomed the Revolution of 1917
as the fulfilment of a dream, as the beautiful and tragic birth of a new
world, and pleaded with the intellectuals to hearken to its music. 'I hate
the bourgeois, the devil, and the liberals.' His enthusiasm was not affected
by the events: 'Why is it so gloomy outside?' he asked — and answered:
'Because it is so bright within.' He was well aware of the destructive, fiery
elements of the upheaval, but insisted that the task of the intelligentsia
was to channel this fire, to transform the wild rebellion of the Razins and
Pugachevs 'into a musical wave.'

His 'Scythians' (1918) expressed the opinions of a considerable number of radicals, for the most part extreme Socialist Revolutionaries, whose spokesman was the critic Ivanov-Razumnik. Revolution was for them an expression of genuine national traits. 'Yes,' said Blok in this poem, 'we are Scythians; we are Asiatics with slanting and eager eyes. We have the strength of those who bent low the necks of wild horses and tamed rebellious women captives.' The Russians are capable of understanding and appreciating the West, which they had shielded from the Mongols in the past; they can understand the keen Gallic spirit and the somber Teutonic genius; they are ready to co-operate for the good of the world and humanity, but woe to the West if it refuses to respond to the Russian call and attend 'the feast of work and peace.' For then the hordes of Scythians and Asiatics would sweep together as one avalanche upon the doomed lands of Europe, and would devastate the old and dying world of Western civilization.

This ode, which reverted to Dostoevsky's concept of the scope and universality of the Russians, also deals with Solovyov's prediction of the 'yellow peril'; in Blok's vision, however, the union of Russia and Asia would occur only if Europe refused to collaborate with the Scythians.

An even greater stir was aroused by Blok's *The Twelve* (1918). The protagonists of this poem are Red soldiers who plunder and murder; they go marching through a St. Petersburg blizzard, bandits and dreamers inspired by the hatred of the bourgeois world and by a confused yearning for a better life. Christ himself appears at the end of the poem as their invisible leader. Thus the twelve bandits become the twelve apostles, and out of the blood and filth of Terror and Anarchy emerges the image of a new Gospel that justifies all the cruelty and destructiveness of Bolshevism.

The Twelve sounded like a dirge for the old Russia — and like an Easter Mass announcing the Resurrection; death and the hope for a new life were blended in it. There was a background of atonement to this panorama of ruin, bloodshed, and conflagration, as if these constituted the price Russians had to pay for all the sins they had committed. The realistically drawn figures of the poem were symbolic: the frightened bourgeois with the old cur shivering at his feet personified the past; the lady in furs cursing the Revolution and the long-haired writer whining over the end of Russia represented the intellectuals; the uncouth, ignorant soldiers were the people — blind in their violence yet marching toward a luminous goal. The image of Christ was not accidental: Populism and a religious interpretation of the Revolution were combined in this final vision of the Crucified.

The impression produced by *The Twelve* was overwhelming. The poem provoked endless discussions. Gorky saw it as a satire; Gumilev found Christ an 'artificial addition' to a dynamic piece of sharp realism; the descriptions of the capital, of the Red soldiers, of Katya, the mistress of one of them, were acclaimed as great poetic achievements even by those who rejected the idea of the poem. Blok wrote in his diary: 'Did I make a song of praise? I simply registered a fact: if you stare into the swirling blizzard on *this road* you will see Jesus Christ. But sometimes I myself deeply hate this feminine ghost . . . The Bolsheviks are right in being afraid of *The Twelve.*'

The majority of the intellectuals considered the poem a blasphemy, an offense against the humanistic tradition, and a blind acceptance of the Communist regime. The rumor spread that Blok had sold out to the Communists. Old friends refused to shake hands with him. More than thirty years after the publication of *The Twelve* Bunin attacked it in his memoirs and dubbed it ridiculous, naïve, and unpoetic.

Blok suffered from the hostility shown to him on all sides, but he admitted to a friend: 'I love *The Twelve*. I fought against what I wrote, yet I felt it as a supreme truth.' Were not the intellectuals again shying away from reality? Was it not their task to assume direction during the holocaust? Instead of helping the people they were afraid of the blood and horrors of the catastrophe; they were betraying their own country — and if Blok now hated all those who, like Merezhkovsky and Hippius, were setting the pack on him, his reasons were more ideological than personal. His tragedy lay in the fact that while he was accused of having betrayed the intellectuals and, in his turn, charging them with having betrayed the people, the Revolution had deceived and cheated him. In vain did he try to convince himself that it did not matter that the Revolution 'cruelly cheats and easily maims the worthy ones in its whirlpool, but brings the unworthy ones to the shore,' because 'this neither changes the direction of the stream nor its thunderous roar, which proclaims great things.'

Every month, confronting him with privations, executions, outbursts of hatred and violence, with terror, civil war, and failures, brought him new disappointments, made him sad and weary. The dream of revolution failed him as his other dreams had. The only thing he still continued to believe in was the presentiment of an enormous change. 'Don't you know,' he wrote Hippius, 'that there will be no Russia — in the same way that Rome ceased to exist not in the fifth century but in the first year of the first century? In the same way as there will be no Germany, England, France? That the world is already rebuilt? That the old world has already melted away?'

In 1919–20 he worked for Gorky's *International Literature,* made translations, wrote *Rameses,* a historical drama, delivered his lecture on the 'Crisis in Humanism,' in which he denounced the death of the old ideologies. From time to time he made brief appearances at public meetings: staring over the heads of the audience he would read his poems, stonily aloof to both catcalls and applause. He did not conceal his critical attitude toward the government and its policy, and was arrested as politically suspect, but was released almost immediately. In February 1921, at Pushkin's festival, Blok made a remarkably bold speech on 'secret freedom.' 'Calm and freedom are necessary for the release of harmony. Bureaucrats attempt to take them away and to force poetry into artificial channels . . . they are worse than philistines.'

In revolutionary Petrograd, city of starvation, typhus, and fear, where the relics of Imperial Russia looked like ghosts in a graveyard, Blok also seemed a ghost from a forlorn past. He was broken, dispirited, and ill. 'There are no sounds! All sounds have ceased,' he told Chukovsky. 'There is nothing to breathe with, either. It is impossible to write under such oppression.' He was too weak, too exhausted physically to leave the capital or to emigrate; his friends (including Gorky) tried to obtain a governmental permit for him to go abroad, but bureaucratic red tape delayed the issuance of a passport — and when things were cleared up, it was already too late. The last entries in his diary speak again of his 'love-hatred of Russia. At this moment, I have neither soul nor body; I am ill as I have never been before. Vile, rotten Mother Russia has devoured me, has gobbled me up as a sow gobbles one of its suckling pigs.'

This was written in May 1921. In June he was suffering from scurvy and asthmatic attacks, and lapsed into a state of severe mental depression; in July he broke down completely and went out of his mind; delirious and in excruciating pain, he died on 20 August (New Style) 1921.

IV   'What is a poet? A man who writes verse? Of course not. A poet is the bringer of rhythm. And it is the waves of rhythm that direct the universe and the human spirit.' Blok argues against Faust, who believed that 'at the beginning there was the Deed.' 'At the beginning,' Blok contends, 'was Music. Music is the essence of the world. The world grows in resilient rhythms.' The poet is bound to clash with the multitude, the mob. Their clash is inevitable, and so is the destruction of the poet. He perishes — but this is only the breaking up of the instrument; the sounds continue to ring. In the history of mankind there are non-musical epochs, when the bark of matter is thick and heavy, and music is exiled to the nether regions. Then man is alienated, divorced from music. Revolutions, cataclysms change this situation and bring forth the spirit of music from prison and out into the open.

This philosophy determined the character of Blok's work. The precision of Pushkin's sensuous perception, the harmony between his eye and his ear explain in part the plastic quality of his imagery as well as the fullness and vitality of the older poet's work. Blok's hearing, however, was more perceptive than his sight. He was guided by sound and grasped its slightest nuances — and he renders in the changing tonalities of his lilting melodious verse a wide range of phenomena, from the forest's murmur to the storm's roaring. Most of his similes and symbols are of an auditory nature. It is also typical of him to speak of 'elemental' sounds: 'the wild howl of violins,' 'the tune of the wind,' 'the harps and strings of the blizzard.' The dynamic substance of the world is revealed to him in the polyphonic peals of thunder, in the surge of the surf.

Two other elements molded his style more specifically: the refined and highly literary tradition of the Symbolists, and the low trend of popular poetry. He borrowed from the Symbolists all the technical devices of musicality and often lapsed into that 'eloquence' which he at last came to reject and despise. His less successful poems are pale and wordy; they are no better than the verses of the average twentieth-century Symbolist poet. But when he abandons the nebulous eloquence of the Symbolists, the mellowness and passionate anxiety of his poems exhibit high individuality. Blok's lines are immediately recognizable by the flow of his euphonic rhythms, by his antithetic metaphors ('hot snowy sob,' 're-sounding silence'), by his change of inflections, and by the emotional intensity, often poignancy, of his expressions. 'A poem is a canopy stretched on the sharp points of several words. Those words shine like stars,' he wrote, and this explains the parallel structure of his poems.

A poem by Blok is seldom a mere description, a narrative, or a statement: it is either an inner monologue or a conversational address, and this gives it its dramatic quality. Even in his odes, such as 'The Scythians,' which reminds one of Pushkin's 'To the Calumniators of Russia,' Blok exhorts or threatens; the figure of speech and the exclamatory turn are everywhere. This strongly inflected and accented poetry (often with an uneven number of syllables in each line) incorporates not only the classic meters of which Blok was fond, but also the melody or the texture of the old drawing-room ballad, of folklore poetry, and of the gypsy song. His predecessors (whom he loved and sometimes imitated) were Fet, Polonsky, and Apollon Grigoriev. The lilting rhythms of the gypsy song, with its uneven beat and abrupt alternation of fire and melancholy, suited Blok perfectly; many of his best lyrics are a curious transposition of gypsy tunes into the moods, forms, and vocabularies of modern Symbolism.

The folklore ballad and the rollicking, racy quatrains of the streets, factories, and villages were also molded into refined lines, particularly in *The Twelve,* in which the popular and literary currents meet and merge into musical unity. This is not the urbanism of Briussov (whom, by the way, Blok imitated in a few pieces) but a deliberate attempt to achieve the reunion of two currents: that of the intelligentsia and that of the people — or, as Blok would say, of culture and of nation. This poet of the cleft spirit, who had passed from demonism to spirituality and had arrived through the squandering of his passions at the adoration of Beauty and the Motherland, is the personification and the culmination of Russian romanticism; in his sufferings, wanderings and contradictions he is a descendant of Lermontov. But like all Russian romantics — including Gogol and Dostoevsky — Blok was not satisfied with a truth that is above and beyond men. He looked for moral and social values he could assert in his life and in his poetry. Thus, in his own evolution, he repeated not only the development of Symbolism but of Russian literature in the nineteenth century.

His attempts to gain a firm ground failed completely, and the same fate he saw for poets as the bearers of the spirit of music befell him. Many of Russia's great poets met with tragic ends, as in the cases of Pushkin and Lermontov; tragic conflicts underly the lives of Nekrassov and Grigoriev, while not a few minor poets had fates as dire as that of Polezhaev, whose body was gnawed by rats. But Blok's whole life was tragic; he had resolved none of his contradictions — and had tasted defeat as a man, as a citizen, and as an artist. His personal life had been a tormented and checkered one, and he was constantly aware of the emotional schism within himself. Always a maximalist, he could never accept the middle way, the mean that mediocrity calls golden, and he oscillated between extremes: demonism and mystical purity, blissful reverie and the crushing burden of earthiness and the flesh. His internal striving for harmony always clashed with external reality, with a world that is prey to discord — and he found himself isolated and lonely.

In addition to this emotional rift there was also a tragic conflict in his conscience: he realized the discrepancy between the vertical culture of educated society and the condition of the lower classes. The feeling of guilt within him was as acute as it was in Nekrassov, the poet who is most akin to Blok in spirit; and, like Nekrassov, he found a way of partial atonement in his love of Russia, in the Populist religious cult of the Motherland, of which he talks in erotic terms. His dream of sacrifice for and devotion to the people was destroyed when the Revolution, which he had tried to accept despite its fury, deceived his passionate expectations. One could regard the two defeats of Blok — the personal and the socio-political — as one great emotional frustration of unrequited love:

a Freudian interpretation could easily define the patriotism of this un-happy lover as substitution and sublimation.

And, finally, as a poet he aspired to something he could not wholly achieve, and this was his ultimate disappointment.

At one time he had been fascinated by the arts and had compared their hypnotic attraction to that exerted by a 'bottomless pit.' Then he had asked himself what endured in the world of art, and what would be left for a man who wanted to live by art alone, and gave the answer: 'Three strokes in a drawing by Michael Angelo, a line of Aeschylus — that is all — and a universal void, and a rope around one's neck.' He said he loved only art, death, and children, but he also stated that 'if the circle of existence is straight, that of art is even more so.'

It is amazing to what an extent this poet, whose work is a lyrical confession, was concerned with the civic duty of the artist. 'Let them say to thee "Poet, forget, return to clever coziness!" No, better to perish out in the fierce frost! There is neither coziness nor rest.' To the artist's customary preoccupation with form and content he added his own anxiety about the proper significance of poetry. In 1910 he defined himself as a 'social animal' who had a 'passion for service,' and this explains the apparent paradox: a lyricist, a lover of gypsy songs, a religious symbolist, and a highly subjective poet of passions and sorrow, Blok was at the same time a civic bard, a great national poet. Yet here again he could not attain a harmonious solution. He knew that the artist inevitably clashes with his environment, and he hesitated between the affirmation of the poet's supreme freedom and the imposition of the message he *ought* to bring to his contemporaries. In 1921, in his last poem, he turned to Pushkin and asked his help in the 'unequal struggle.' This was the struggle for the artist's freedom against the external pressure during the years of the all-absorbing Revolution, which demanded made-to-order ideas and images.

Blok's work expressed the aspirations of the old intelligentsia as well as the tragedy of his own generation. He gave clear utterance to that dim foreboding of the end which was diffused through Russian literature before World War I. The way he addressed his Muse was perfectly appropriate: 'Your mysterious refrains bear the tidings of fateful destruction.' His poetry proclaimed in prophetic lines the collapse of the world to which he belonged. He tried to transmit his message to the new world that was being born amid the chaos of an implacable upheaval, and he also attempted to discern and to welcome the future. Thus he stands at the crossroads of two epochs — and therein lies his exceptional importance for Russian literature and culture: the last poet of Imperial Russia is the first poet of its triumphant Revolution.

Blok's formal, emotional, and ideological influence was very great. His way of writing molded dozens of poets. None of his contemporaries escaped his imprint, and long after his death the echo of his poems was still resounding not only in Soviet poetry but also in the works of Russian *émigrés* scattered the world over. Blok created an important school, and many minor streams were fed from the wellspring he revealed.

His fortunes in Soviet Russia were complex and contradictory. The official line recommended acceptance of him — but not without caution and many reservations. He was recognized as one of the greatest Russian poets, and the study of his work was included in high-school curriculums; textbooks referred to him as a great master and one of the outstanding figures in national letters. This point, however, has been questioned in the course of some literary discussions. Readers have often been warned by Communist critics not only against the 'religious deviations' of *The Twelve,* or the 'Populist flavor' of 'The Scythians,' but also against the mystical and romantic trends of Blok's poetry. Anatol Lunacharsky called him the 'last poet of the nobility.' Gorbachev wrote in *Capitalism and Russian Literature:* 'Blok's work is reactionary, formally and ideologically; the proletarian literary tradition has no use for it.' During World War II Blok was hailed for his patriotic stanzas, particularly 'On the Battle of Kulikovo Field,' but as soon as the war was over, and particularly between 1946 and 1950, Soviet criticism displayed a certain hostility toward 'Blok's formalistic tendency' and his 'too subjective lyrics.' On the other hand, his anti-European stand, his 'Scythian' national pride, and his prophetic 'The New America' were quoted with definite approval. The fluctuations of the party line did not, however, affect Blok's popularity with readers: his collected works, as well as selections from his poems, find a large and ready sale.

There is no evidence that interest in Blok has ever dwindled. What Eugene Zamiatin said the day of Blok's death is as true today as it was in 1921: 'Blok will live as long as dreamers exist — and their tribe is immortal.'

10

I   IN ALEXANDER BLOK Symbolism reached its highest point; his poetry, however, also signalized the decline of the school of which he was such a major representative.

The Symbolist movement, which had begun in the 'nineties as a minor altar for aesthetes, and had progressed from victory to victory by introducing important stylistic innovations, renounced its exclusiveness when it found wide acceptance at the beginning of the twentieth century. Between 1900 and 1914 it absorbed and encompassed all the traditional currents of Russian thought: the religious quest, social and moral awareness, revolutionary dreams, messianic hopes, and an inclination for Western culture. As a matter of fact, it included by this time too many heterogeneous elements and could not preserve its unity. Its growing popularity, particularly after the Revolution of 1905, also proved a liability: the hundreds of minor writers and intellectual snobs who had swelled its ranks contributed to the vulgarization and disintegration of the school. On the eve of World War I everybody was striving to write in the 'new style' and the erstwhile rebels saw themselves treated as fashionable academicians. Symbolism was comfortably established and universally recognized as a successful literary movement, and it fatally began to drift toward smugness and stagnation. An uprising against its tenets seemed inevitable. At the same time the intelligentsia that had produced it was being gradually replaced by new social forces.

The banner of anti-Symbolism was raised by those who had been trained and whose styles had been formed in Symbolist circles. Their rebellion, therefore, was interpreted at the start as more heresy than desertion. Soon, however, the threat of a true dissension became shockingly obvious. The anti-Symbolist reaction, which had begun by posing purely stylistic problems, ended by attacking the basic principles of the school.

When Michael Kuzmin (1875–1935) published *Songs of Alexandria* [1] in 1906, with its strong homosexual overtones, and, in 1907, his exquisitely erotic *Seasons of Love,* he appeared to be a Decadent bent on the stylization of the early Byzantine and late eighteenth-century periods. His nymphs and adolescents behaved like the French marquises and *petits maîtres* of *le siècle galant;* similar attitudes were also adopted by the depraved boys and perverse maidens of his novels: *Wings* (1906) and *Travelers by Land and Sea* (1915), in which the vices of the St. Petersburg bohemia were described with amazing fidelity to amorous details. All these works, although precious in mood, were written in an excellent and direct style. Kuzmin's simplicity was, however, anything but casual; it stemmed from a very deliberate literary attitude. In a manifesto published in 1910 he had launched the new slogan of Beautiful Clarity, and his appeal to young writers proclaimed a challenge to Symbolism: 'Love the word as Flaubert did, be economic in devices and sober, precise in the use of your idiom: thus will you discover the secret of something marvelous — the beautiful clarity.' In the poem, 'Gay Metier,' he exhorted his followers to become 'cunning builders who create exact and compact form.' While hailing Epicurus in philosophy, he opposed Mozart to Beethoven in art. His own verse — precise and light — was miles away from the consecrated patterns of Symbolism: it was emphatically colloquial and aimed at rendering 'the spirit of trifles.' One of his most quoted poems, describing a picnic, deals with a bottle of Chablis in an ice bucket, the fragrant smell of toast, the color of ripe cherries, the pleasure of swimming, and concludes with: 'Yes, I am faithful to thy flavor, O blithe earth!'

In the era of political reaction Kuzmin's 'mellowed honey' sensuality had the acrid reek of decay and perversion. This aesthete and scholar, who admired rare books and handsome adolescents and showed an unusual musical gift (as a pupil of Rimsky-Korsakov he composed operettas and songs), could easily be regarded as a typical embodiment of a declining cultural cycle. What increased his significance was his refusal to accept the esoteric and the vague in poetry, and the earthy quality of his work, which presaged an imminent change. The mood of Symbolism — the blending of mystical contemplation, transcendental flights, and prophetic expectations — was definitely gone.

In 1910–14 the educated strata were rapidly getting over the effects of the stormy years. Economic stability had given the bourgeoisie a sense of security, industrial production was rising, the Russians were rapidly

[1] To be compared with Pierre Louy's *Chansons de Bilitis.*

catching up with the West in technical matters, the growing urban population had reached 30 million by 1914 (17.5 per cent of the total population of 175 million). The material welfare of the bourgeoisie and of the middle class had brought about a more realistic attitude and this general trend was soon reflected in literature. Readers had become tired of climbing Golgothas of mystical sufferings and of seeking for hidden meaning in each rhymed line. They wanted a direct contact with the outward world. 'We do not want to officiate, we wish to touch and to name,' the anti-Symbolist poets declared. The search for concreteness instead of abstractions became the order of the day: the purpose of poetry, the new rebels claimed, was to describe things and not their essence, the particular and not the universal.

This psychological change determined a new aesthetics: instead of following the Symbolist slogan formulated by the French — *pas la couleur rien que la nuance* — anti-Symbolists took to using plain colors and praising definite lines and plastic qualities. The pictorial won over the musical in poetry; clear-cut images drove out hints and allusions. Words were measured and counted, and genres were re-established. 'Art is solidity, firmness,' stated the Acmeists, the most important anti-Symbolist group of St. Petersburg. 'We are fighting for this world, for our earth; we want to admire a rose because it is beautiful, and not because it is a symbol of mystical purity.'

Some critics called this movement the triumph of expression over melody, and others saw in it the victory of 'Gallic spirit over Teutonic nebulousness and Gothic confusion.' It is true that most of the Acmeists were Westernizers: their advent coincided with an intensification of Western influence in Russia. The Symbolists, as well as the Slavophiles, had studied German philosophy avidly — from Hegel and Schelling down to Nietzsche — and German and Scandinavian writers from Novalis, Hoffman, and Hoelderlin to Ibsen, Hamsun, and Strindberg. The Acmeists, like the early Decadents of the 'nineties, were great admirers of France; they turned, however, from Verlaine and Mallarmé to the Parnassians and the poets of La Pléiade — Ronsard, Villon, Marot. The image of Rome and Italy was also haunting them; as a matter of fact, the love of Italy, which was fairly strong among the Russian writers of the nineteenth century (Gogol, Herzen, the Patrician poets) was revived in the twentieth century by the Acmeists and their friends, in a sort of neoclassical renaissance.

The first manifesto of the new group appeared in 1912 in a 'little magazine,' *The Hyporborean.* A year later Gumilev, the leader of the movement, pointed out in his challenging article, 'Acmeism and the Heritage of Symbolism' (*Apollo,* January 1912): 'Acme, in Greek, means the point of the highest achievement, the time of blossoming'; he also used the term 'Adamism,' defining it as 'a virile, firm, and clear outlook on life,' which demands 'a strict balance of forces' and 'an exact notion of the relation between the subject and the object. If the unknown is not cognizable, it is futile to make guesses; poetry can do much better with man and his body, his joys, and his sorrows. Shakespeare knew the inner life of man; Rabelais, the flesh and its delights; Villon, God and vice, while Gautier gave this world the cloak of faultless form.' For Gautier had formulated the supreme rule to be followed: 'The more dispassionate the material — whether verse, marble, or metal — the more beautiful will the work come out.'

The Acmeist group, founded by Gumilev in 1912, and succeeded by his Guild of Poets, included a great many people of diverse literary aspirations. They had no other unity save that of negation: they all rejected what they considered the aberrations of Symbolism, but they differed vastly in their personalities, the character of their work, and their contributions to literature. The leader of Acmeism, Nicholas Gumilev (1886–1921), was the son of a naval physician; he studied under Annensky in the *gymnasia* of Czarskoe Selo, at the University of St. Petersburg, and at the Sorbonne. In 1910 he married Anna Gorenko, who became famous under the pen name of Anna Akhmatova; they separated during World War I and were divorced in 1918. Gumilev traveled widely in Africa, the Near East, and Europe. In 1914 he volunteered for the army, went to the front as an officer, and was awarded the Cross of St. George for bravery. After the Revolution he boasted of his monarchical sympathies, became involved in the Tagantsev affair, an anti-Soviet conspiracy, and was executed by a Communist firing squad in August 1921.

In his short and adventurous life Gumilev displayed the same zest for action, the same romantic sense of heroic effort that he had glorified in his virile and dynamic poems. From his first book, *The Path of the Conquistadors* (1905), through subsequent collections (*Romantic Flowers*, 1908, *Pearls*, 1910, *Alien Skies*, 1911, *The Quiver*, 1916, *The Campfire*, 1918), to his last volumes of verse (*The Tent*, 1920, *The Pillar of Fire*, 1921, and *To the Blue Star*, published posthumously), he maintained an amazing consistency of direction. A disciple of the Symbolists, and particularly of Briussov, who taught him the clangorous sonority of full rhymes and the mastery of his chill poetics, Gumilev became scornful of the lyrical softness, vagueness, and femininity of the Decadents and mystics. 'Thought is movement,' he has stated, 'and poets should use verbs and not adjectives.' He gave the expressive line priority over the musical one and wanted to 'restore the forthright, direct, full, and exact meaning of words.' 'To name means to create, and poets must find virgin appellations.' This statement was directed against Mallarmé's dictum that the artist ought to suggest while the reader ought to guess, since 'to name means to destroy two-thirds of the enjoyment.' Gumilev rejected the obscurity and the morbid 'mystery' of the Symbolists. His poetic credo called for clarity, concreteness, and plasticity. Descriptive and realistic imagery regains its place in his work; it goes hand in hand with a somewhat Nietzschean streak of 'virile individualism' and attachment to earthy sensations.

This poet, who celebrated the fullness of being, struggle, motion, fulfilment, loved the poetic forte. Most of his poems are in a major key, and he uses striking and often brutal images and resounding rhymes. The richness of his vocabulary and the abundance of his metaphors are, however, toned down by the severity of his highly polished rhythms. 'Be calm, my Muse: like bronze thy voice shall ring — that is the only way to sing.'

Heroism and exoticism colored most of Gumilev's poems during the first stage of his development. He admired pioneers, conquistadors, gallant soldiers, and bold mariners. His heroes are the adventurers, the lusty captains of the seven seas — the names of Columbus, Vasco de Gama, La Pérouse, and Cortez often appear in his poems. These men knew that 'a blind nothing is better than a golden yesterday'; they rejected the fusty routine of security, and each spring the Muse of Distant Travels pushed them toward new endeavors.

Gumilev's collections of African verse, in which some Soviet critics found a 'reflection of colonial imperialism,' revealed the same romantic predilection for the heroic — but this time with an exotic background of fierce combats, savage natives, and East African landscapes (these are to be found for the most part in *Quiver*). In the forest and deserts of the Dark Continent he found not only proud fighters who die superbly, such as his Dahomean warlord, but also a violence of colors, a power, and a spontaneous and magnificent outburst of the life instinct. He confided to his friends what a genuine relief all this was after the sophistications of a Viacheslav Ivanov and the twilight of St. Petersburg.

It is quite possible that Gumilev's idealization of strength, combativeness, and virility was a means of overcoming his own sensitivity and shyness: the intrepid conquistador was not the real Gumilev, but his romantic superego, what he wished and attempted to be. Moreover, there was often a mixture of genuine feelings and of braggadocio in Gumilev's gestures, and even in his literary activity. This poet who introduced Kiplingesque overtones into his work was basically a product of those very aesthetic, Symbolist, and individualistic milieus against which he fought so successfully in his poems and articles. Although heroic and soldierly motifs never disappeared from his poetry, he struck new chords about 1915, when Acmeism was at its apogee. Next to stressing man's stoic acceptance of his fate, Gumilev glorified romantic visions of love and hidden religious aspirations. He addressed to his beloved lyrical songs of a troubadour and assured her that 'the flutter of her eyelashes was more delectable than an angel's trumpetings.' At the same time he revealed a somewhat mystical bent, spoke of the Sun of the Spirit, and indulged in surrealistic dreams in which all the limitations of time and space were abolished and psychic experience foretold his own death in a prophetic illumination ('The Last Trolley,' one of his most impressive poems of those years). Toward the end of his life the romantic and idealistic trends of this anti-Symbolist became extremely obvious; he spoke of the fourth dimension and predicted the expansion of man's perception: 'Under the scalpel of nature and art our spirit screams, our flesh is racked in giving birth to the organ of a sixth sense.' Yet even the most daring poems of this new trend of his were firm in structure, verbally precise, and perfectly intelligible: Gumilev remained faithful to the Acmeist aesthetics. Although the last book Gumilev read in prison was the *Iliad,* he was scarcely a lover of the classics, preferring Renaissance and romantic writers; one of his best translations is that of Coleridge's *The Rime of the Ancient Mariner.*

The semi-epical form of Gumilev's ballads, the descriptive quality of his poems (including brilliant pictures of European lands and towns), and the severely beautiful mold of his verse had a strong influence on his contemporaries. He was respected as a Poet Warrior who lived his poetry and applied his code of military honor and the Nietzschean Superman morality to daily routine, and was greatly admired as a master of prosody — an assured and impeccable craftsman. This rare combination of personal and professional attributes made him an ideal person for literary leadership. He was not the genius some *émigré* critics, deeply impressed by his tragic fate, had attempted to prove him, but he was an excellent poet and he occupied an important place in pre-Revolutionary letters. He enjoyed his position and was quite conscious of his role of having initiated a vast poetic movement; he opposed the accepted canons of Symbolism not only with new themes and moods, but also with a new, vigorous, and expressive style. The concreteness of his approach, his masculine 'anti-eloquent' attitude, his technical mastery all had a stimulating effect. The Guild of Poets became, under his leadership, a training school for dozens of prominent literati, and many contemporaries learned a great deal from Gumilev.

Although his name is omitted from Communist textbooks and his works are seldom quoted by Soviet critics without a conformist addition of derogatory qualifications, the truth is that the impact of this 'Decadent counter-revolutionary' is evident in many Soviet poets, from Tikhonov to Bagritsky. The praise of heroism and vitality that has become almost a commonplace in post-Revolutionary letters can be traced directly to Gumilev's poetic tradition. The Acmeists and their leader fought against Symbolism in order to prepare for the advent of a more concrete, sober, and strong poetry inspired by this earth and not by any illuminations from beyond. In this they are predecessors of trends that Soviet critics have erroneously declared to be the exclusive features of Communist art. It is somewhat paradoxical, however, that a monarchist executed as a counter-revolutionary plotter should be one of the formal teachers of proletarian poetry. No wonder Moscow critics obstinately refuse to admit any such degrading lineage, and interpret Acmeism as 'a new phase of Symbolism,' claiming that the mysticism and exoticism of the latter are fully maintained in the poetry of Akhmatova and Gumilev, and that Gumilev also expresses his hatred of the proletarian Revolution. 'Acmeism is the fullest and most consistent expression of Imperialism in Russian literature' — this statement and others like it have become clichés of Soviet criticism.

Ii   Ossip Mandelstamm (1891–1942), another spokesman of Acmeism, represented a different bent: he was an outright classicist and, more specifically, hailed Greek poetry as a supreme model.

In many ways Mandelstamm was the opposite of Gumilev: this shy and awkward man, with a poor physique and ridiculous manners that often provoked amusement and condescension, was a typical introvert. He studied literature and philosophy in St. Petersburg and Germany and devoted himself to writing. His father, a middle-class business man, considered this sheer nonsense and cut off his son's allowance. Mandelstamm was penniless all his life, and survived by luck, accident, or miracle. Helpless and impractical, he was a victim of unfavorable circumstances and had a genius for getting into scrapes. In the early 'thirties he was deported, presumably because of an epigram on Stalin; he was allowed to return to Moscow, but had the misfortune to fall into the category of the politically suspect and was banished again. He died during World War II, probably in 1942; there are indications that he succumbed to the hardships of exile.

Mandelstamm's early poetic training was thoroughly Symbolistic, but he soon rebelled against his masters and joined the Acmeists. He used severe classical meters and chose words in the manner of a master builder selecting his stones: in fact, the title of his first book of poems (1913) was *Stone*. The Symbolistic strain, however, was fairly strong in the metaphors and almost surrealistic imagery of his later works — particularly in *Tristia* (1922) and in his remarkable books of prose, *The Noise of Time* (1925) and *The Egyptian Stamp* (1928), as well as in *Poems of Armenia* (1931).

The measured pace of Mandelstamm's poems, their firm structural lines and sonorous vocabulary conveyed the impression of majesty and gravity. Most of his verse belongs to the declamatory tradition of Derzhavin or Tiutchev: he used Church Slavonic archaisms next to expressions of common speech; as a matter of fact, one of his stylistic achievements lies precisely in a skillful 'poetization' of colloquialisms, which appear invigorated and sublimated in a perfect framework of classical purity. It is revealing that in his articles on Acmeism Mandelstamm speaks of Bach in almost the same way as Kuzmin spoke of Mozart: some of Mandelstamm's poems have the breadth and solemnity of Bach's oratorios, and while some of Blok's poems remind one of strings, the poems of Mandelstamm sound more like pieces for the organ.

He has left a series of poems that at first glance could be mistaken for realistic portraiture. His pictorial evocations of St. Petersburg, of Dickens' England, or of a cinema have a delightful exactitude of details, but he was writing for the most part on art and culture and not about external reality. He could produce an excellent parody, permeated with subtle humor, or draw a fine sketch, yet behind both there was always the vision of a dreamer. He dreamed of beautiful forms and of that world of Russian culture to which he, a typical Westernizer, was bound body and soul. It was amazing how this man, brought up in a provincial Jewish environment, could feel so strongly and render so perfectly the spirit of Greek Orthodox liturgy, the religious fervor of old Russian icon-painting, or the magnificence of Imperial St. Petersburg. Gogol and Dostoevsky feared the threat and unreality of Peter's capital and talked of its foggy mysteries; this vision, enhanced by the Symbolists (particularly by Andrei Bely), was too vague and unsubstantial for those of Mandelstamm's generation: they admired this city of emperors and cathedrals, they loved its proud palaces and vast granite quays, and they celebrated this lavish and haughty seat of the Empire. In Mandelstamm's poems it emerged triumphant and majestic.

After the Revolution he became aware that his beloved and familiar world was collapsing, that the City of the Great Czar was bound to become the City of Lenin — and he bade farewell to his dear Petropolis in odes that struck poignant, almost tragic, notes ('Twilight of Liberty' and 'The Death of Petropolis'). But even in these melancholy pieces the emotion is restrained and subordinated to the mastery of expression. The same is true of all the stanzas revealing his own state of mind. Understatement of emotions, the search for harmonious proportions, the solemnity of tone, and a verbal fastidiousness bring about a certain air of coldness and detachment in Mandelstamm's work. Soviet critics labeled this 'social aloofness,' while Mandelstamm himself has stated: 'I am nobody's contemporary.'

Yet his poetry is far from being passionless or abstract: in reality it belongs completely to the period in which it originated. Mandelstamm had a keen sense of history, he heard the tread of events. 'My century, my beast,' he apostrophizes in one of his late poems, 'who will look into thy pupils, who will cement with his own blood the disjointed vertebrae of two centuries?' He could not do it because he belonged so completely to the old world, at the same time reflecting the attitudes and dreams of those who, like him, had intuitively felt a strange kinship between Imperial Russia and the mellowness of Athens and Rome on the verge of their downfall. His was a last song of a luxurious, sophisticated, and doomed civilization. Mandelstamm is one of the best pre-Revolutionary poets and, as time goes by, his masterful and beautiful work grows in importance.

III   When Gumilev married Anna Gorenko (b. 1888), a girl of noble Ukrainian descent, he looked down upon the 'poetic exercises' of his young wife. But after the publication of *The Rosary* in 1912, her popularity under her pen name of Anna Akhmatova soon outshone his own. For a decade Akhmatova, a friend of Blok's, remained one of the most widely read and truly beloved Russian poets. A generation of intellectuals memorized her lines, and quoted them in their letters and diaries. She served as their sounding board: they found their own pains and laments and aspirations in her short poems.

After her separation from Gumilev, Akhmatova became one of the most admired, courted, and discussed women of St. Petersburg. Her name was associated with many real and imaginary love affairs, and she married three times after the tragic death of her first husband. Her literary career also underwent many changes. Despite the tremendous vogue of her slender and scarce books of poetry (*Evening,* 1910, *The Rosary,* 1912, *The White Flock,* 1917, *The Buckthorn,* 1921, *Anno Domini,* 1922) she maintained a silence of eighteen years, from 1923 to 1940, when *A Selection from Six Books* was published in Moscow. During World War II she wrote new poems, among which were a few patriotic verses, and this comeback was welcomed in the literary circles of Moscow and Leningrad. Her resurgent influence was promptly quashed in 1946, however, when the central committee of the Communist party passed a resolution in which Akhmatova's poems were labeled decadent, pessimistic, mystical, and therefore harmful to Soviet youth. Andrei Zhdanov stated in his report that Akhmatova represented 'eroticism, mysticism, and political indifference, while her interests were divided between the drawing room, the bedroom, and the chapel'; her work was intended for 'the upper ten thousand' and reflected the theory of art for art's sake. This meant ostracism: Akhmatova was expelled from the Union of Soviet Writers and officially became anathema to her colleagues. She was again sentenced to silence, and between 1946 and 1950 her name in the Soviet press was almost synonymous with evil. Her situation must have been almost unbearable. In 1950 she was permitted to publish a few poems in a popular weekly, but after Stalin's death the ban was lifted, and her verse reappeared in leading Soviet periodicals. Between 1954 and 1962 collections of her poems were published in the USSR.

The official condemnation of Akhmatova cannot alter the fact that she is probably the outstanding woman poet in modern Russian literature — with Carolina Pavlova (1810–94),[2] Marina Tsvetayeva (1892–1941), and, to a much lesser degree, Myrrha Lokhvitzkaya (1869–1905) and Zinaide Hippius as her closest rivals. During the anti-Symbolist movement Akhmatova's epigrammatic poems, which stressed intonation and expressiveness rather than lulling musicality, were enthusiastically received by the public because of their originality of form and freshness of meter. At the same time the emotional forcefulness of their subject matter was no less striking. Her volumes seemed chapters of a lyrical diary devoted to love, song, and prayer; they sounded like the confession of a passionate nun who had fled the convent and opened her heart to earthly love, yet still wore a hair shirt; Blok styled her a Christian gypsy.

To the protagonist of an Akhmatova poem love comes as a revelation and a tragedy; it drains her energy like a malaise and sears like flame; in her calvary of passion rare moments of felicity alternate with long spells of bitterness: the woman always suffers through indifference or betrayal. When she yearns for tenderness, she meets the hungry look of lust and, after the intoxication of the senses, she is left to solitude and misery. She attempts to stifle her disappointment in dissipation, in facile intrigues and the game of pretense. After all these illusions, complications, and sufferings, after this frenzy of the senses and these vagaries of the heart, she seeks consolation in nature and prayer; she enjoys the simple life, solitary walks on the shores of a secluded lake or in the fields of a forlorn countryside.

In this mixture of passion and ascetic aspirations, of God and sin, the St. Petersburg lady is akin to Catherine in Ostrovsky's *The Thunderstorm:* in fact her feelings and lamentations are those of a woman of the

[2] See *The Epic of Russian Literature*, p. 129.

people. The high priestess of Acmeism and the refined poetess of the old intelligentsia wrote village ballads identifying herself with a lass whose peasant husband 'lashed her with a doubled belt.' Akhmatova's melancholy landscapes, her love for hamlets where peace, humility, and poverty veil the passions are conveyed in truly Russian accents. The same can be said of the remarkable lyrics she wrote after the Revolution. Gumilev's widow was neither a monarchist nor a radical; nevertheless, her religious interpretation of events coincided with that of the Populists and the Symbolists. She saw a divine significance in privations and misfortunes, and from the depths of her sufferings welcomed the dawn of the morrow.

Her patriotic feeling surmounted all temptation, and she refused to leave her native land and to emigrate. The spirit of her poetry was not, however, in tune with the dominant tones of Soviet Russia, and she 'sealed' her lips:

> No one will now listen to songs;
> The world has ceased to be wonderful.
> This is my last song.
> Do not break my heart,
> Do not sound any more.

The main virtue of this poetry of sin and atonement, of carnal passion and spiritual fervor, lies in its reserve. In 1848 Turgenev wrote about Rachel, the famous French tragedienne: 'She is emotional and restrained; a calm, a reserve completely envelop her outbursts of passion and bestow upon them a purity of line, an ideal and real beauty which is the only and true beauty of art. The greatest grief is always calm.' This restraint and control mold Akhmatova's style. Like Chekhov, she conveys emotions through understatement and a careful selection of significant details; the inner world is always presented through external signs. To indicate the growing indifference of a lover she says: 'He touched my knees with fingers which almost did not tremble.' Mundane trifles hint at feelings and convey only indirectly the idea of their intensity: at the last meeting the woman puts the left glove on her right hand; there are so many stairs to descend — 'yet before there were just three.'

Akhmatova's style is decidedly colloquial, her phrasing neat and brief, her poetic speech articulate, sharp, and expressive. It may be said that her poetry has only a narrow range and that her voice lacks power — yet it possesses an enchanting timbre and a penetrating intimacy of rendition. These lyrics have a moving, poignant quality, charged with emotional overtones, and it is little wonder that thousands of readers, regardless of official pronunciamentos, still respond to her lines.

IV   Despite all the differences in temperament and poetic personality, the leaders of Acmeism represented a generation of post-Symbolists. Theirs was the last fruitful poetic movement in the tradition of patrician and intellectual culture: in fact, theirs was the privilege of uttering the last songs of Imperial Russia. The impact of the Acmeist school was widely felt, and a galaxy of minor poets joined its ranks. Their contribution helped to broaden and on occasion to deepen the influence of Acmeism — without, however, adding to it anything particularly new or important.

Among the many young men and women who gave their support to the Acmeists, the most talented were George Ivanov (b. 1894), who made a good start with *Heather,* his first volume of poems, and eventually became an *émigré;* Boris Sadovskoy (b. 1884), who devoted his poems (*Samovar,* 1914) and short stories to stylized depictions of the Russian way of life; Vladimir Narbut (b. 1888) and Michael Zenkevich (b. 1888), both of whom stressed the descriptive, almost pictorial, tendencies of the school; some of their sketches possess a Flemish fidelity and are amazingly graphic and vivid.

Of somewhat greater importance was Serghei Gorodetsky (b. 1884), who in 1912 was considered one of the founders of Acmeism. In 1920 he joined the Communist party and, after Gumilev's execution, vilified his former friend; he also denied any connection with the 'bourgeois school of Acmeism.' His early poems aimed at the 'poetization and ornamentation of life'; later ones went on to folklore and imitations of the Russian Style, resorting to obvious patterns and frequently falling into the cheap and the blatant. There was, however, some savage force in his stanzas, which sounded like the pagan incantations of the ancient Slavs. (*Yar,* 1907, *Collected Poems,* 1909). He also evinced a Populist bent and was leader of a group of peasant poets, of whom Essenin and Kluyev were the most representative.

Despite their battles Symbolism and Acmeism had common roots. A much more vigorous opposition was presented by those who called themselves the Futurists.

From 1908 to 1912 dozens of circles and groups mushroomed in Moscow and St. Petersburg, as well as in the big provincial cities, including Odessa, Kiev, Kazan, and Nizhni Novgorod. The air was filled with aesthetic and philosophic controversy. Young men from the Ukraine or the Urals flocked to the capital with the same lust for glory and success with which heroes of Balzac came to Paris in hopes of conquering it. These beginning poets fell an easy prey to the extreme ideas and formulas for a radical reformation of the arts; having but scant respect for the past, they were anxious to overthrow the idols. Some of them had a healthy 'Scythian' confidence in their forces; there was a strong tang of the soil about these anarchically inclined painters and poets who, by 1910, had dubbed themselves Futurists.

Despite the quarrels and the formation of splinter groups — Ego-Futurists, Cubists, Cubo-Futurists, and many others — they were all members of the same family. Their theories, particularly in art, were indubitably of Western origin. Alexandra Exter, Michael Larionov, Nathalie Goncharova had all declared war on 'perspective painting' — that outmoded legacy of the Renaissance — and championed French post-Impressionism, from primitivism to early Picasso. The Jack of Diamonds group of Kulbin and Kandinsky, and the Ass's Tail coterie of Tatlin, Malevich, and Larionov had organized rival exhibitions and public debates, and vied for notice by their vociferous discussions and eccentric manners. The poets, however, outdid the painters in extravagance: Mayakovsky, one of the leaders of Futurism, appeared on the rostrum in a bright orange jacket and without a necktie but sporting a silk top hat. (Later he dumfounded Moscow pedestrians by strolling about·in a yellow-striped blazer.) The first meeting of these creators of language in Moscow (1913) ended in a free-for-all. *The Moribund Moon,* the first anthology by the Men-to-Be, published in the same year, provoked quite a stir because of all the abuse, billingsgate, and unprintable words it contained.

In Europe, and particularly in Italy, the cradle of Western Futurism, the new movement launched an attack against bondage to the past, against provincialism and nineteenth-century backwardness. It expressed, after a fashion, the moods of the bourgeois of Milan, Turin, and Rome, who dreamed of a colonial and highly industrial empire. In the arts the Futurists wanted to create a new style of speed and dynamism, of machine-like techniques and modern urbanism. They claimed, not without reason, that the technological and industrial revolution of the twentieth century had by-passed the arts. The emphasis on the struggle against conservative traditionalism, against mausoleum-museums and the grip of the dead over the living, was perfectly justified in Italy, but it made less sense in Russia, particularly in the field of graphic and plastic arts. The Russians had no petrified, centuries-old forms of literature, painting, and sculpture, and their Academy of Fine Arts counted barely one hundred and fifty years of existence. Consequently, 'A Slap in the Public's Face' (1912), the manifesto of the Futurists, had a somewhat preposterous sound: 'The past is narrow; Pushkin and the Academy are less comprehensible than Hieroglyphic; we must jettison Pushkin, Dostoevsky, Tolstoy, and all the others from the ship of modernity.' As a matter of·fact, the wrath of the Futurists was directed against 'all the others' much more than against the classics. What they are really after was a scrap with their contemporaries. In the 'Growling Parnassus' manifesto they abused Gorky, Briussov, Sologub, Gumilev, and Bunin, thus evincing their animosity toward all trends — realism and Symbolism as well as Acmeism.

The general public paid heed only to the antics of the Futurists who strutted about with painted faces and in motley attire, challenged their audiences with swearing and abuse, broke up 'respectable' literary meetings with catcalls, and, in general, behaved like hooligans. Mayakovsky, the two Ukrainians, David and Vladimir Burliuk, as well as some members of the Jack of Diamonds and the Ass's Tail groups were masters of sensationalism and showmanship: all means were good to 'shock the bourgeois,' to attract attention, and to arouse indignation.

The youthful exuberance of the Futurists, their publicity stunts and hoaxes, could not, however, hide a serious purpose. They were reflecting a literary and cultural crisis and announcing a new era — and this despite a lack of unity among the motley groups and circles within the movement.

At its right wing was Igor Severianin, the pen name of Lotarev (1887–1942). This half-educated and gifted youth from a small provincial town had no idea about French symbolists and Parisian painters: his masters were Fofanov and Lokhvitskaya. It was from them he had learned easy, melodious rhythms; but what he wanted to celebrate was 'modern Things' — the telephone, airplanes, and motorcars — in a new language. The Futurists had proclaimed their detestation of all conventional forms of speech and promised 'to enlarge the dictionary with arbitrary and derivative words.' Taking their slogan of 'The Word as Innovation,' Severianin created hundreds of neologisms; most of his coinages, however, were foreign words that he Russified in a haphazard fashion. He was also eager to render 'the refinements of urban civilization': in his dark and dank basement room adjoining a laundry in a St. Petersburg slum he wrote of 'pineapples in champagne,' of gorgeous women who drove about in 'electric landaulets,' and called himself 'a precious weaver of daydreams.' He also produced poems on 'lilac ice cream' and on 'imaginary queens' who 'fed on pomegranates,' and gave themselves 'tempestuously' to young pages.

Although everybody derided him for styling himself a genius who 'filmed omni-earthly, enthroned urbi-cordially,' just before World War I his poems suddenly attained a wide popularity on the periphery of the intelligentsia and the middle class.

His poetry was an ersatz for all those who were ready to dupe themselves by buying cheap toilet water instead of an expensive perfume —

because they could not afford the latter. Despite all the gaudy and ma-caronic elements of his poems, however, Severianin was not devoid of talent and his efforts to 'renovate' and 'enrich' the language were genuine enough. Yet he was shallow, had no taste, often lapsed into vulgarity and cheap preciousness; his attempts to 'beautify' landscapes and objects had an artificial and a rather ludicrous ring. He was, on the whole, a poet for the half-educated and the unsophisticated. After a few years of glamorous success, he disappeared from the literary scene; in 1919 he emigrated to Estonia, where he lived in retirement and obscurity until his death during World War II.

The 'true' Futurists regarded Severianin as mild and superficial, almost as a traitor to the cause. Their aims were more radical and am-bitious; they wanted to blast all existing forms of expression and to create a new idiom. Where others were introducing reforms they were striving for a revolution.

The most intransigent (and perhaps the most original) among them was Victor Khlebnikov (1885–1922), who adopted the first name of Velemir — an ancient Slavonic appellation. Born at Khan Quarters on the Volga River, and interested from childhood in the dialects of the various tribes of his native region, he was as much philologist as poet. His first poem was simply a list of the derivatives from a single word. He went on to uncover the roots of words, to invent new terms and turns of speech, in which he made use not only of Russian but of the languages of all the nationalities in the Empire. With Scythian daring this genuine Slavophile, who was greatly attracted by Slav mythology and folklore, disregarded grammatical rules and the usages of written idiom. The poems he jotted down on hundreds of small squares of paper were for the most part unintelligible to the uninitiate; to the general public the name of Khlebnikov was synonymous with gibberish. His friends, however — including Mayakovsky and most of the Futurists — fell under his spell, and people like Andrei Bely and the whole clique of young philologists, such as Jacobson, Eichenbaum, Zhirmunsky, Shklovsky, and others, ap-preciated this obscure, shy, stammering but extremely gifted man. His savage onslaught on syntax and grammar had a truly rebellious and an-archical tone; his poems (and exceedingly interesting prose tales) were often 'beyond all comprehension' and represented experiments rather than final achievements. Though Khlebnikov did not leave anything that could survive as an accomplishment, his role is undeniable.

Khlebnikov is typical of a period when poets and scholars were seek-ing to break away from traditional images and forms. Thus Victor Shklovsky, in a speech at the Stray Dog (a Bohemian club), defined Fu-turism as an attempt 'to sharpen the perception' by making words sound strangely different and by offering a 'difficult style' that stimulates the mind and the senses, instead of polished surfaces that are too smooth to incite imagination.

Khlebnikov's disciples — Vadim Shershenevich (b. 1893), Alexander Kruchenykh (b. 1886), and Vassily Kamensky (b. 1884) — were associated with a group of painters, including Nicholas Kulbin, a professor of the Military Medical Academy and known as the Mad Doctor, and David Burliuk (b. 1882). They carried on the 'creation of a new language,' on occasion amusing themselves by phonetically reproducing a series of meaningless, incomprehensible sounds the significance of which was as obscure to them as to their occasional readers. Shershenevich preached 'the free creation of words,' very much as French Dadaists proclaimed, in 1919, 'mots en liberté'; other Futurists advocated that 'beauty of speed is the beauty of form.' The only follower of Khlebnikov who met with complete success, however, was Mayakovsky: he surpassed the esoteric experiments of his own group and produced poems that were not only stylistically original and challenging but thoroughly intelligible. The theories, broadsides, and trial balloons of Futurism converged in Mayakovsky and found adequate expression in his *A Cloud in Trousers* and *The Spine Flute* — the two best specimens of his pre-Revolutionary verse.[3]

But aside from its tricks and artifices, Futurism did exert a vivifying influence. It represented a real yearning after life, after a flesh-and-blood art that would dispose of both pallid aestheticism and desiccated academism. It also reflected the spirit of rebellion and a strong national trend. This last statement may appear controversial — particularly if we stress the European influences in left-wing painting, the Westernization of idiom, as in the case of Igor Severianin, and the close relationship between Russian Futurism and similar movements in France and Italy. Taken within the general framework of European arts and letters before World War I, Russian Futurism is but a national brand of an international movement. Yet its special characteristics sprang forth when Marinetti, the leader of Italian Futurists, visited Russia in 1914. The Russians spoke to him of the renewal of language, the problem they were most interested in — but the Italian dismissed such discussions as secondary and kept repeating his slogans: 'War is the hygiene of the world; all the past is a cemetery; the only beauty is that of speed — long live heroes and warriors, down with women and femininity.' He orated enthusiastically not only of machines and automobiles, but also of super-capitalism as the expression of urbanism, and of authoritarian Rome as the epitome of virility. The Russian Futurists, however, hated war, disliked capitalism, and did

[3] Mayakovsky's poetry is analyzed in my book on Soviet literature (1963).

not care for any kind of autocracy — especially their native variety. They were rebellious and anarchically inclined, they believed in revolution and proudly admired the genius of the Russian people. Little wonder, then, that they were terribly disappointed in Marinetti: after his departure Khlebnikov and Benedict Lifshitz stressed in a manifesto the psychological as well as the ideological differences between 'the turbulent Futurism of Asiatic Scythians and effete, bourgeois, and predatory Europe.' This rift was extremely significant: it was the last time before the Revolution that the paths of Russian and Western literary schools crossed, becoming widely divergent thereafter. A few years later Marinetti headed the Fascist Academy of Mussolini, while Mayakovsky became the official poet of the Soviets.

At any rate, Futurism was highly significant for its times: in a rough, often formless manner it represented a rebellion against the culture of the Empire. It had no central theme, it was not articulate and could scarcely find its own words: it was merely shouting in an instinctive outburst. But it did proclaim a crisis and strove for revolutionary changes; it also indicated that behind the decorous façade of Russian arts and literature great destructive forces were gathering in a blind revolt. Mayakovsky was premature by a few months when he wrote: 'The year 1916 advances in the thorny crown of revolutions.'

Communist critics do not accept such an interpretation of Futurism. In 1946 A. Zhdanov formulated the official view on the entire movement: 'Symbolism, Acmeism, and Futurism reflected the ideological disintegration, the panicky fear of the imminent revolution, which had gripped the ruling classes and the bourgeois intelligentsia. All these schools, despite their differing colorations, were connected with the ideology of the bourgeoisie and the nobility . . . Gorky has called the decade of 1907–1917 "the most shameful and impudent decade in Russian literature." '

v   The struggle against Symbolism in poetry had all the connotations of an outright rebellion. In prose the situation seemed more complex and less drastic. On the one hand, Andrei Bely (who flirted with the Futurists), Sologub (a Decadent), and, to a lesser extent, Andreyev represented, each in his own way, a renewal of the novel and the short story. Symbolism was also exceedingly successful in the theater, and there was a steady flow of translations of Symbolist playwrights from various European languages. Yet the achievements of the Symbolists in prose were almost insignificant by comparison with the changes they brought about in poetry.

Symbolism, however, had never replaced the realistic tradition; it influenced the latter by infiltration and corrosive action. The impetus the realistic school had received from Chekhovian Impressionism, which had dominated the short-story genre in Russian letters, and from Gorky's social romanticism, was strongly felt in current writing. Next to the 'veterans of realism,' such as Korolenko, there were Kuprin, Bunin, the followers of Gorky (the *Znanye* group), and a number of writers of the younger generation. Among these were Boris Zaitzev (b. 1881), a disciple of Chekhov, who wrote delicately shaded tales full of 'moods,' descriptions of nature, and vague religious feelings, and Ivan Shmelev (1875–1950), whose stories dealing with the lower middle class and particularly his novel about a waiter, *The Man from a Restaurant* (1912), had almost Dostoevskian overtones in their pathos and compassion for the downtrodden. Zaitzev's chief works — *The Golden Pattern* (1925), a novel on Moscow intelligentsia, *A House in Passy* (1935), a description of Russian *émigrés* in Paris, and *Gleb's Journey* (1939), an autobiographical narrative — have the smooth lyrical quality of pale watercolors, but they are marred by monotony and lack of strength. In this Zaitsev is very different from Shmelev, whose rhetorical forcefulness and almost pathological sensitivity found their expression in loud and impressive descriptions of civil war and Red terror (*The Sun of the Dead,* 1923) or in romantic revivals of the past (*Inexhaustible Cup,* 1925, *The Moscow Nanny,* 1941). Both writers emigrated after 1917 and were staunch enemies of Communism.

But the most important renewal of realistic forms was brought about by a group that was closer to Andrei Bely than to Bunin or Kuprin. It attempted to blend tradition and novelty and held a prominent position on the eve of World War I and the October Revolution. The traditional elements in the works of Remizov, Zamiatin, Sergheiev-Tsensky, Alexis N. Tolstoy, Prishvin, Chapygin, Shishkov, and a number of lesser writers were to be found in their treatment of concrete actuality as a protest against the abstractions and psychological amorphousness of the Symbolists. The Neo-Realists, as they may be called, depicted Russian provincial life, portrayed characters from among the people, stressed the national traits of their heroes, and dwelt on the minutiæ of everyday existence.

Alexis N. Tolstoy was thirty-one in 1913, when he launched his colorful tales about the cantankerous landowners of the forest region beyond the Volga, describing their feats and feasts, their eccentricities and turbulent way of life, in stories and novelettes that had a refreshing touch of the fantastic and the grotesque (*The Lame Gentleman, Across the Volga, The Adventures of Rasteghin*). In 1911 Eugene Zamiatin stirred up a critical tempest with his *Tale of a District,* which depicted the rough life in the extreme north of Russia through an arrangement of a system of sharp images and bizarre visions. His second novel, *At the World's End*, dealt with weird happenings in a military garrison located in a god-forsaken town in Eastern Siberia, on the shores of the Pacific. Michael Prishvin excelled in ethnographic descriptions of Russian's northern wilderness (*Where Birds Are Fearless,* 1907) and of hunting adventures (*Stories,* 1914). A regional spirit ran through the *Siberian Legends* (1913) of Viacheslav Shishkov and the short stories of Alexis Chapygin, who had an extensive knowledge of the steppes around the Caspian Sea. Another literary figure of significance was Serghei Sergheiev-Tsensky, who had begun as a follower of Symbolism but, by 1912, had progressed from a rhetorical, allusive style, full of philosophical hints, to a sober manner of vigorous character-drawing and excellent depictions of nature (*The Peacock, Helen Recumbent, Transfigurations*).

A number of minor writers became adherents of the new school; between 1912 and 1917 the young Neo-Realists were gaining recognition as one of the most thriving literary movements. Of course they employed many devices of the Symbolists, and particularly those introduced by Andrei Bely, under whose influence they had all fallen to some degree. They adopted his rhythmic prose; they followed his linguistic innovations; they merged the descriptive and the imaginative, the realistic and the fantastic; they stressed the ironical, the grotesque, the lyrical, and the subjective at the cost of straight narrative. The emphasis on the national and the popular in language and subject matter was a common trait of the Neo-Realists — and this despite the fact that all of them had received a Westernized education and were well acquainted with European culture. The irony of fate made Remizov an *émigré;* Zamiatin lived abroad for many years and died in Paris; Alexis N. Tolstoy spent considerable time in France and Germany.

Alexis Remizov (1877–1957) was undoubtedly the main leader of Neo-Realism. The son of a Moscow merchant, he was reared in a strict religious atmosphere and in his adolescence made many pilgrimages to monasteries and saintly shrines. Later, as a student at the University of Moscow, he joined Socialist circles, was arrested and subsequently exiled. In 1904 he settled in St. Petersburg, devoted himself to writing, and published several novels — *The Pond* (1907), *The Story of Ivan Stratilatov* (1908), *Sisters in the Cross* (1910), *The Fifth Pestilence* (a volume of short stories, 1912), and such folklore dramas and mystery plays as *Czar Maximilian, The Tragedy of Judas,* and others. In 1921 he left Russia and, after a sojourn in Berlin, made Paris his home. Despite difficult conditions and poor health he wrote many novels, short stories, legends, and apocryphal tales, as well as autobiographical sketches that elude definite classification. His most significant works written in exile were *Flaming Russia,* an excellent chronicle of the revolutionary upheaval of 1918–20, *Noises of the Town, Three Sickles,* and *Moscow Legends* (all published in 1921); *Russia in Charts,* an evocation of Moscow, and *On a Field Azure,* the life story of a Russian girl — presumably his own wife — who had joined the Socialist Revolutionaries (both brought out in 1922); *Parables of Nikola* (the Slavic St. Nicholas), 1924, *Zga — Tales of Wonder* (1925), and a good many pieces that were published only in excerpts. He never achieved wide popularity, and the average *émigré* reader regarded him as an eccentric and a literary freak, but true lovers of the Russian language and of literature admired him as a first-rate writer and the uncrowned head of an integral artistic movement.

In his formative years Remizov had been closely associated with the Symbolists, with whom he maintained personal ties of friendship and gratitude, but he gradually developed his own original manner. Although he always utilized certain of the Symbolists techniques — such as lyricism, rhythmic structure of sentences, systems of allusive images, and so on — the tone of his work was determined, in time, chiefly by two basic tendencies: his search for a 'national style' based on folklore tradition and philological studies, and his interest in religious and moral problems. The source of his inspiration lies in the popular speech and the oral and written tradition of Kiev and Moscow, which had not been vitiated by Latin or French influences.

His knowledge of the living idiom was enhanced by historical research: a diligent and indefatigable reader and an interpreter of ancient texts and forgotten documents, he absorbed the Christian as well as the pagan traditions of the Russian language. To restore the freshness and vividness of the popular tongue and to liberate it from the trammels of bookishness and preciosity were among Remizov's aims, and no other Russian writer of the twentieth century proved to be a more national stylist than this 'magus of the word.' The verbal craft, the turn of a sentence, the effects a grouping of words can produce interested him beyond all else, and he evolved an amazing skill in and an extraordinary power over his medium.

His works present a maze of involved patterns, linguistic sleights, verbal and onomatopoeic play, and grammatical tours de force. His shifts from the lyrical to the colloquial and from the pathetic to the comic, the luxuriance of his vocabulary, the flexibility of his syntax, the bold twist of his sentences, the complex, tortuous, circuitous, or fragmentary structure of his tales — all the formal richness of this ornamental prose together with a weird sense of humor and the charm of a storyteller assures Remizov of a unique place in Russian letters.

Remizov's work (by contrast with Bely's mental acrobatics) is firmly rooted in folklore, from which he borrows not only his themes but his artistic devices. At the same time, like Bely, he imposes style upon reality. Art is for him a world of play and fantasy; the purpose of writing is not the representation of life but a transformation and 'theatricalization' thereof. Only through an act of imagination do we acquire a deep sense of things and events and characters — the fairy tale, the grotesque, the dream, the whimsical flight are inseparable from the true creative effort. All the techniques of poetry are therefore justified in prose writing. Hence Remizov's devices and artifices for producing a mingling of the real and the fantastic, his detailed descriptions of trivia, of insignificant occurrences followed by explosive displacement of the three-dimensional images. Devils, spooks, hobgoblins, and diverse animals, whether existing or mythical, abound in his stories; sometimes he merely tells his own dreams, which resemble the illuminations of medieval manuscripts or the woodcuts of the sixteenth century chapbooks: this universe of uncanny creatures and odd visions is depicted with the precision of a monastic miniaturist, who draws every line or curve with utmost meticulousness.[4]

The peculiarities of Remizov's art naturally limit the number of his readers to those who can truly relish each phrase of the great craftsman. More respected than loved by the public at large, Remizov is often considered as a writer's writer and, as a matter of fact, he has exerted a profound influence on many of his contemporaries, among them such prominent Soviet novelists as Alexis N. Tolstoy, Michael Prishvin, Eugene Zamiatin, Viacheslav Shishkov, and a score or so of lesser storytellers.

Gogol and Dostoevsky were, of course, two of Remizov's masters. From Gogol he derived his banter (which often borders on mockery) and his fondness for contortions and grimaces. Critics maintain that Remizov is constantly sneering and scoffing; like a jester, he is forever inventing new quips and gibes, ridiculing his own heroes, and playing cat-and-mouse with his readers. He resembles a malicious sorcerer who delights in wonderful feats, yet can also cast weird spells and metamorphose men into beasts.

This love of grotesque and chuckling playfulness was evidenced even in his personal life: for many years he maintained in his study a bizarre collection of talismans, charms, phantasmal toys, and symbolic objects.

---

[4] It would be interesting to compare Remizov's poetic works and drawings with those of William Blake.

He founded and was the Grand Master of the Order of Simians, a fantastic society into which he lured the most prominent writers and artists of Russia through a magnificent ritual, gorgeous regalia, and grandiloquent titles. Whoever had the privilege of meeting this withered little man who was almost a hunchback, and of listening to his insidious remarks made in a strange hollow voice of rich inflections, will long remember his weird and none too kindly humor.

Yet at the same time this grinning gnome who loved practical jokes and invented incredible stories about his friends always evinced a deep and sympathetic understanding of human grief and suffering. Like Dostoevsky, he explored with almost sadistic and masochistic curiosity the dark recesses of man's soul, and was always highly sensitive to pain. In the world he described — and it was usually the inane and senseless world of provincial monotony, of ugliness and monstrosity — the men and women are racked by poverty, injustice, and evil. 'The Devil has spread himself all over the world like the shadow of a clock-tower, and God has forsaken His creatures' — this is Remizov's main theme, and he stresses again and again that man has been betrayed by the Almighty and cast into the abyss of loneliness, pain, and death. It was, therefore, quite natural for the French Existentialists to discover after World War II that Remizov was a kindred spirit.

There is, not infrequently, in the characters of Remizov a resemblance to Akaky Akakyevich, the poor and humble clerk of Gogol's *Overcoat:* Remizov is concerned with the fate of the little man, of the underdog, of defenseless 'orphans of the earth' who are exposed to cruelty and frustration, and a profound sense of pity, a warm humanity which he loves to mask under various stylistic or symbolic disguises, forms the backdrop of all his work.

Dostoevsky's *Man from the Underground* also makes his reappearance in the stories of Remizov, who always portrays unhappy creatures who fear and tremble and are trampled down by the ruthless 'masters of life.' Why is man sentenced to pain and misery? And who has dared to claim that suffering has a purifying, sublimating effect? Here is one author who does not believe in it: 'No, suffering and oppression gnaw at the heart; they distort and humiliate.' And there is no justification for all the crosses on which living creatures are nailed during their brief passage through this earthly vale. The traditional theme of the 'simple heart' who merits admittance into the kingdom of God, of the average man crushed by evil forces, runs through all of this strange writer's work; it is complemented by the recurrent images of a mild and melancholy Christ and of kind old Nikola the Miracle Worker — the favorite saint ᶠ the Russians. The religious strains in Remizov's writings are entirely humanized: his Christianity is but a major aspect of his keen feeling for the brotherhood of man.

The greatest impact of Remizov's works, however, lies not so much in the idea they convey as in the manner in which they are expressed. This highly subjective prose, which avoids conventional portraiture of characters but mingles realistic exposition with the author's lyrical or moral comments, dicta, and personal recollections, is undoubtedly a 'slanted and stylized' prose. This was Remizov's main contribution — and most Soviet writers of the 'twenties, from Pilniak to Vsevolod Ivanov, learned their craft from him and from Bely.

Another, and by no means the least important, contribution of Remizov was his innovation of language. This he accomplished not by the invention of neologisms as the Futurists did, but by restoring the lost unity between the written literature of the intellectuals and the pure linguistic sources of the people. In this field his efforts were both national and democratic.

This Neo-Realist and friend of the Symbolists, whose progression was in the same direction as that of Blok and Bely, attempted to merge technical refinements that had originated in the West with the national trend represented by the Populists and the Writers of the Soil; he advanced the revival of an art based on folklore and the colloquial language of the masses. The fact that such a tendency could assert itself on the very eve of the Revolution constituted a decisive factor in the further development of Russian prose during the Soviet era.

Notes

THERE ARE several anthologies of Russian prose, among them Bernard G. Guerney's *A Treasury of Russian Literature* (Vanguard Press, New York, 1943) and *The Portable Russian Reader* (Viking Press, New York, 1947); *A Treasury of Russian Life and Humor* by John Cournos (Coward-McCann, New York, 1943); *A Treasury of Great Russian Stories* by Avrahm Yarmolinsky (Macmillan, New York, 1944); *Best Russian Short Stories* by Thomas Seltzer (Modern Library, New York, 1923).

The following collections of Russian poetry may be found useful: *An Anthology of Russian Verse* by Avrahm Yarmolinsky (Doubleday, New York, 1962); *The Penguin Book of Russian Verse* by Dimitri Obolensky (1962); *A Book of Russian Verse* by C. M. Bowra (Macmillan, London, 1943); *A Treasury of Russian Verse* by Babette Deutsch and Avrahm Yarmolinsky (Macmillan, New York, 1949); *Poems from the Russian* by Frances Cornford and Esther Polianovsky-Salaman (Faber & Faber, London, 1943).

For paperback editions see Vintage Books by Knopf, and various new translations and reprints published by the New American Library, Bantam Books, Dell Laurel Editions, Grove Press, and others.

CHAPTER 1: THE POPULIST MOVEMENT

The best descriptions of the period are in the *Memoirs of a Revolutionist* by P. Kropotkin (Houghton Mifflin, Boston, 1930), in *Underground Russia* by S. Kravchinsky (Stepniak) (Scribner's, New York, 1885, translated from the Italian), and in the *Memoirs of a Revolutionist* by Vera Figner (International Publishers, New York, 1927). The writings of Bakunin, Lavrov, and Mikhailovsky are not available in English. Excerpts from Leontiev's works can be found in *Leontiev* by N. Berdiaev (Bles, London, 1940).

CHAPTER 2: USPENSKY, GARSHIN, AND SALTYKOV

There are two translations of Saltykov's *The Golovlev Family* (see Slonim, *The Epic of Russian Literature,* p. 357) and there is a tale by the same author in *The Best Russian Short Stories* edited by T. Seltzer (Modern Library, New York, 1923). His *Fables* have been translated by Vera Volkhovsky (Chatto and Windus, London, 1931); and his *Death of Pazukhin* has been translated by Julian Leigh (Brentano's, New York, 1924). There is but one collection of Garshin's stories, *The Signal* translated by R. Smith (Duckworth, London, 1915), and none of those by Uspensky.

CHAPTER 3: NOVELISTS OF THE SOIL AND PATRICIAN POETS

Melnikov-Pechersky is not available in English. Mamin's stories are in his *Verochka's Tales* (Dutton, New York, 1922). Leskov's short stories are found in most anthologies; see also *The Cathedral Folk* translated by I. Hapgood (Knopf, New York, 1924); *The Tales of Leskov* (Routledge, London, 1944); *The Sentry* and other stories translated by A. Chamot (Knopf, New York, 1923); *The Steel Flea* (Harper's, New York, 1943); *The Amazon* and other stories (Allen & Unwin, London, 1949); *The Enchanted Wanderer* (McBride, New York, 1924) or *The Enchanted Pilgrim* (Hutchinson, London, 1946) both translated by D. Magarshak.

CHAPTER 4: CHEKHOV

Chekhov's works have been translated by Constance Garnett and published in 13 volumes by Macmillan (London, New York, 1916–22); see also the Modern Library edition of Chekhov's stories (New York, 1932). The best translation of Chekhov's plays is by Stark Young; see his analysis of other versions in *The Sea Gull* (Scribner's, New York, 1939). See also *Five of Chekhov's Famous Plays* translated by Marian Fell (Scribner's, New York, 1939). Omnibus editions: *The Works of*

Anton Chekhov (Black, New York, 1929); *The Portable Chekhov* (Viking Press, New York, 1947). There are numerous collections of Chekhov's stories by various translators. Bibliography: *Chekhov in English* by Anna Heifetz (New York Public Library, 1949).

CHAPTER 5: THE MODERNIST MOVEMENT

Korolenko's tales are available in two collections: *Makar's Dream* translated by M. Fell and *Birds of Heaven* translated by C. Manning (Duffield, New York, 1916 and 1919); also *In a Strange Land* translated by G. Zilboorg (Richards, New York, 1925); *Blind Musician* (Little Brown, Boston, 1890). The poetic works of Decadents and Symbolists are found in the Bowra, Yarmolinsky, and Reavey and Slonim anthologies. Some of Sologub's prose has been translated: *Little Demon* translated by J. Cournos and R. Aldington (Knopf, New York, 1916), *The Created Legend* translated by J. Cournos (Stokes, New York, 1916), *The Sweet-Scented Name and Other Stories* translated by S. Graham (Putnam, New York, 1915), *The Old House* (Secker, London, 1915), translated by J. Cournos.

CHAPTER 6: MYSTICS, PHILOSOPHERS, AND MARXISTS

Several of Solovyov's writings are available in English: *War, Progress, and the End of History* (Stoughton, London, 1915), the same work under the title *War and Christianity* (Putnam, New York, 1915); *The Justification of the Good* (Constable, London, 1918); *The Meaning of Love* (Bles, London, 1945); *Plato* (Nott, London, 1935); *Russia and the Universal Church* (Bles, London, 1948); *Lectures on Godmanhood* (International University Press, New York, 1944). *Solovyov Anthology* edited by S. Frank (Scribner's, New York, 1950) has a bibliography of the English translations.

Merezhkovsky's trilogy (*The Death of the Gods, The Romance of Leonardo da Vinci, Peter and Alexis*) has been translated by B. Guerney and published by Modern Library, New York, 1928–31. See also *Tolstoy as Man and Artist, with an Essay on Dostoevsky* (Putnam, New York, 1902); *December the 14th* translated by N. Duddington (Cape, London, 1923); *Jesus Manifest* and *Jesus Unknown* (Scribner's, New York, 1936 and 1937); *Akhnaton* (Dutton, New York, 1927); *Life of Napoleon* translated by O. Zvegintsev (Dutton, New York, 1929); *The Secret of the West,* translated by J. Cournos (Putnam, New York, 1931). There are three books by Shestov that have appeared in English: *Penultimate Words and Other Essays* (Luce, Boston, 1916); *All Things Are Possible* (McBride, New York, 1920); *In Job's Balance* (Dent, London, 1932).

Berdiaev's *Christianity and Class War, The End of Our Time,* and *Essays* were published by Sheed & Ward, London, in 1933 and 1934; *The Meaning of History, Spirit and Reality, The Origin of Russian Communism,* and *Towards a New Epoch* by Bles, London, 1930, 1931, 1938, and 1949; *Freedom and Spirit* and *Slavery and Freedom* by Scribner's, New York, 1935 and 1944; *The Russian Idea* and *Dream and Reality* by Macmillan, New York, 1945 and 1950.

Lenin's collected works have been brought out by International Publishers, New York, 1927; see also *Selected Works* in 12 volumes (Lawrence, London, 1936–9). Consult Plekhanov's *Fundamental Problems of Marxism* (Lawrence, London, 1929), *Essays in History of Materialism* (Lane, London, 1934), and *Art and Society* (Critics Group, New York, 1937). Works of Populist sociologists and critics are not available in English. Victor Chernov's *The Great Revolution* was published by Yale University Press, New Haven, in 1942.

CHAPTER 7: GORKY

Among the various collections of Gorky's tales the best is *Gorky's Best Short Stories,* edited by A. Yarmolinsky and M. Budberg (Grayson, New York, 1939); see also *The Story of a Novel and Other Stories* translated by M. Zakrevsky (Dial Press, New York, 1928) and *Chelkash and Other Stories* (Knopf, New York, 1929). The following novels by Gorky are available in English: *Three of Them* translated by A. Linden (Allen & Unwin, London, 1905); *Foma Gordeyev* translated by H. Bernstein (Bee De Publishers, New York, 1928); *Mother* translated by I. Schneider (Citadel Press, New York, 1947); *The Confession* translated by R. Strunsky (Stokes, New York, 1916). The three autobiographical novels—*Childhood, In the World,* and *My Universities*—have been published in one volume, *Autobiography of Maxim Gorky* translated by I. Schneider (Citadel Press, New York, 1949); this is the only unabridged version. *The Artamonov Business,* translated by A. Brown (Pantheon, New York, 1948), has appeared also under the title *Decadence,* translated by V. Dewey (McBride, New York, 1927). *The Life of Klim Samgin* was published by Appleton-Century, New York, 1930–38, in four volumes: *The Bystander* translated by B. Guerney; *The Magnet, Other Fires,* and *The Specter* translated by A. Bakshy. The latter also translated *Seven Plays by Gorky* (Yale University Press, New Haven, 1937). *Reminiscences* were translated by C. Mansfield, L. Woolf, and S. Koteliansky (Hogarth Press, London, 1949). See also Gorky's early novel *Orphan Paul* (Gaer, New York, 1945); consult his *Days with Lenin* (International Publishers, New York, 1932), and *Literature and Life* (Hutchinson, London, 1946).

Chapter 8: 1905 and Its Aftermath

Artzybashev's *Sanin,* translated by P. Pinkerton, has been published in various editions (Huebsch, New York, 1915, 1922; Viking Press, New York, 1926; Modern Library, New York, 1931). By the same author: *Tales of the Revolution* translated by P. Pinkerton (Huebsch, New York, 1917); *Breaking Point* (Secker, London, 1925); *War* translated by T. Seltzer (Knopf, New York, 1916); *The Savage* translated by G. Cannan (Boni & Liveright, New York, 1924).

Andreyev's plays, translated by H. Bernstein, T. Seltzer, G. Zilboorg, C. Mader, and F. Scott, were published by Scribner's and Brentano's, New York, between 1915 and 1923. For Andreyev's tales see H. Bernstein's translations: *The Seven Who Were Hanged, Satan's Diary* (both Boni & Liveright, New York, 1918 and 1920), *The Crushed Flower* (Knopf, New York, 1916); also *The Little Angel* translated by W. Lowe (Knopf, New York, 1916). Andreyev's novel *Sashka Jiguleff* has been translated by L. Hicks (McBride, New York, 1925).

Knopf published the following collections of Bunin's stories translated by B. Guerney: *The Dreams of Chang,* 1923, *The Gentleman from San Francisco,* 1934, *The Elaghin Affair,* 1935. Also from Knopf the I. Hapgood translation of *The Village,* 1923; see *Fifteen Tales* by the same translator (Secker, London, 1924). *Mitya's Love* was retranslated from the French in 1926. See *The Well of Days* translated by G. Struve and H. Miles (Knopf, New York, 1934); *Dark Avenues* translated by R. Hare (Lehman, London, 1949); *Memoirs and Portraits* translated by V. Trail (Doubleday, New York, 1951).

For Kuprin's works see *The Duel* (Macmillan, New York, 1916); *Slav Soul* translated by S. Graham (Putnam, New York, 1916); *The River of Life* translated by S. Koteliansky and J. M. Murry (Luce, Boston, 1916); *The Bracelet of Garnets* translated by L. Pasvolsky (Scribner's, New York, 1917), also translated by B. Guerney in his *Treasury; Gambrinus* and *Sulamith* translated by B. Guerney (Adelphi, New York, 1925 and 1926); *Sasha* translated by D. Ashley (McKay, Philadelphia, 1928); *Yama, the Pit* (translated and published by B. Guerney, New York, 1929).

Chapter 9: Blok and the Symbolists

Poems by Ivanov, Bely, and Blok appear in the Bowra, Yarmolinsky, and Reavy and Slonim anthologies, and also in the Frances Cornford selection (see Slonim, *The Epic of Russian Literature,* p. 347). *The Twelve* by Blok has been translated by C. Bechhofer (Chatto & Windus, London, 1920) and by B. Deutsch and A. Yarmolinsky (Rudge, New

York, 1931). *St. Petersburg* by A. Bely was published by the Grove Press, New York, in 1959.

CHAPTER 10: AFTER THE SYMBOLISTS

Zaitsev's *Anna* has been translated by N. Duddington (Holt, New York, 1937); Chmelev's *The Sun of the Dead* has been translated by J. Hogarth, 1927, *Inexhaustible Cup* by T. Dechtereva, 1928, and *The Story of a Love* by N. Tsitovich, 1931, all three published by Dutton, New York.

Only a few works by Remizov are available in English: *The Clock* translated by J. Cournos (Chatto & Windus, London, 1924); *The Fifth Pestilence* translated by A. Brown (Wishart, London, 1927); *On a Field Azure* translated by B. Scott (Drummond, London, 1946).

Index

Galaxy Books

LITERATURE: Criticism